Bharat
The Cultural Heritage

by

Ragini Jaiswal

Double9 BOOKS

Bharat The Cultural Heritage

by Ragini Jaiswal

ISBN: 978-93-67140-40-6

Published by

DOUBLE 9 BOOKS
2/13-B, Ansari Road
Daryaganj, New Delhi – 110002
info@double9books.com
www.double9books.com
Tel. 011-40042856

ABOUT THE AUTHOR

I am Ragini jaiswal and this book is written by me, Bharat the cultural heritage I'm very happy that I got a opportunity to write on bharaat. I am writer who loves to write about cultures and traditions of different countries. When I was 10 years old I used to wonder why this books are invented but I got the answer. I think life should be full of achievement and proud moments because we don't know how much you and me will live so why to be normal just do it, do it for you, do it for your parents just do it. I know we have the capacity to do everything just we have find it

So this was something that I think you can also relate

Well thank you for choosing the book. I dedicate this book at first to my brother and my parents and my supporters.

Thanks everyone and myself also for gaining the confidence to write something on my own country 🕮

At the end I would conclude my words by saying that if you are dreaming make sure you dream big ♥

CONTENTS

ACKNOWLEDGEMENT

It is pleasure to be able to complete this compilation work. containing various aspects of Indian culture and heritage. This material is prepared with an objective to familiarize the students of M.A History, DDCE Utkal University on the various aspcets of Indian cultueal history.

This work would not have been possible without the support of the Directorate of Distance and Continuing Education, Utkal University. I would especially like to thank Prof. Susmita Prasad Pani, the Director, DDCE, Utkal University. As my teacher and mentor, he has taught me more than I could ever give him credit for here. He has shown me, by his example, what a good teacher (and person) should be.

The compiler owes many thanks to all the reputed scholars on Indian culture and heritage whose work is being used here for the sake of making the students understand the subject. I have copied, collected, and made use of the scholarly works of great scholars whose work has been mentioned in the further reading section of each chapter.

The compiler of the present material claims no authority and originality on any topic of the materials cum textbook. As already been mentioned above the work is a compilation of already existing works of great scholars among whom name of a few have been mentioned at the end of each chapter. Besides the SLM of IGNOU and other Distance Education Institutions have been also consulted and used for preparation of this material for that I duly acknowledge those textbooks.

Would be grateful by receiving suggestions and comments to improve this material cum textbook, from the students, teachers and also the practicing professionals.

UNIT-I

CHAPTER-1
INDIAN CULTURE

CHARACTERISTICS OF INDIAN CULTURE, SIGNIFICANCE OF GEOGRAPHY ON INDIAN CULTURE

Structure

1.1.0. Objective

1.1.1. Introduction

1.1.2. Concept of Culture

1.1.3. Culture and Heritage

1.1.4. General Characteristics of Culture

1.1.5. Importance of Culture in Human life

1.1.6. Indian Culture

1.1.7. Characteristics of Indian culture

- 1.1.7.1. A Cosmic Vision
- 1.1.7.2. Sense of Harmony
- 1.1.7.3. Tolerance
- 1.1.7.4. Continuity and Stability.
- 1.1.7.5. Adaptability
- 1.1.7.6. Receptivity :
- 1.1.7.7. Spirituality.
- 1.1.7.8. Religious Dominance
- 1.1.7.9. Thoughts about Karma and Reincarnation.
- 1.1.7.10. Emphasis on Duty
- 1.1.7.11. The Ideal of Joint Family

1.1.7.12. Caste System.

1.1.7.13. Unity in Diversity.

1.1.7.14. Four Duties.

1.1.8. Indian Culture during the Contemporary Period

1.1.9. Unity and Diversity

1.1.9.1. The factors of unity in diversity

1.1.9.1.1. Geographical and Demographic Factors

1.1.9.1.2. Religious Factors

1.1.9.1.3. Cultural Factors

1.1.9.1.4. Political Factors

1.1.9.1.5. Linguistic Factors

1.1.9.2. Elements of Unity in India

1.1.10. Aspects of Indian culture

1.1.11. Significance of Geography on Indian Culture

1.1.12. Summary

1.1.13. Exercise

1.1.14. Further Reading

1.1.0. Objectives

In this lesson, students investigate various facets of Indian culture. Throughout the chapter, emphasis will be on the concept and importance of Indian culture through various ages of India. After studying this lesson you will be able to:

- *understand the concept and meaning of culture;*
- *establish the relationship between culture and civilization;*
- *establish the link between culture and heritage;*
- *discuss the role and impact of culture in human life.*
- *describe the distinctive features of Indian culture;*
- *identify the central points and uniqueness of Indian culture;*
- *explain the points of diversity and underlying unity in it; and*
- *trace the influence and significance of geographical features on Indian culture.*

1.1.1. Introduction

Culture refers to the patterns of thought and behaviour of people. It includes values, beliefs, rules of conduct, and patterns of social, political and economic organisation. These are passed on from one generation to the next by formal as well as informal processes. Culture consists of the ways in which we think and act as members of a society. Thus, all the achievements of group life are collectively called culture. In popular parlance, the material aspects of culture, such as scientific and technological achievements are seen as distinct from culture which is left with the non-material, higher achievements of group life (art, music, literature, philosophy, religion and science). Culture is the product of such an organization and expresses itself through language and art, philosophy and religion. It also expresses itself through social habits, customs, economic organisations and political institutions.

Culture has two types: (i) material, and (ii) non-material. The first includes technologies, instruments, material goods, consumer goods, household design and architecture, modes of production, trade, commerce, welfare and other social activities. The latter includes norms, values, beliefs, myths, legends, literature, ritual, art forms and other intellectual-literary activities. The material and non-material aspects of any culture are usually interdependent on each other. Sometimes, however, material culture may change quickly but the non-material may take longer time to change. According to Indologists, Indian culture stands not only for a traditional social code but also for a spiritual foundation of life.

Indian culture is an invaluable possession of our society. Indian culture is the oldest of all the cultures of the world. Inspite of facing many ups and downs Indian culture is shinning with all it's glory and splendor. Culture is the soul of nation. On the basis of culture, we can experience the prosperity of its past and present. Culture is collection of values of human life, which establishes it specifically and ideally separate from other groups.

1.1.2. Concept of Culture

The English word 'Culture' is derived from the Latin term 'cult or cultus' meaning tilling, or cultivating or refining and worship. In sum it means cultivating and refining a thing to such an extent that its end product evokes our admiration and respect. This is practically the same as Sanskriti of the Sanskrit language.

Culture is a way of life. The food you eat, the clothes you wear, the language you speak in and the God you worship all are aspects of culture.

In very simple terms, we can say that culture is the embodiment of the way in which we think and do things. It is also the things that we have inherited as members of society. All the achievements of human beings as members of social groups can be called culture. Art, music, literature, architecture, sculpture, philosophy, religion and science can be seen as aspects of culture. However, culture also includes the customs, traditions, festivals, ways of living and one's outlook on various issues of life.

Culture thus refers to a human-made environment which includes all the material and nonmaterial products of group life that are transmitted from one generation to the next. There is a general agreement among social scientists that culture consists of explicit and implicit patterns of behaviour acquired by human beings. These may be transmitted through symbols, constituting the distinctive achievements of human groups, including their embodiment as artefacts. The essential core of culture thus lies in those finer ideas which are transmitted within a group-both historically derived as well as selected with their attached value. More recently, culture denotes historically transmitted patterns of meanings embodied in symbols, by means of which people communicate, perpetuate and develop their knowledge about and express their attitudes toward life.

Culture is the expression of our nature in our modes of living and thinking. It may be seen in our literature, in religious practices, in recreation and enjoyment. Culture has two distinctive components, namely, material and non-material. Material culture consists of objects that are related to the material aspect of our life such as our dress, food, and household goods. Non-material culture refers to ideas, ideals, thoughts and belief.

Culture varies from place to place and country to country. Its development is based on the historical process operating in a local, regional or national context. For example, we differ in our ways of greeting others, our clothing, food habits, social and religious customs and practices from the West. In other words, the people of any country are characterised by their distinctive cultural traditions.

1.1.3. Culture and Heritage

Cultural development is a historical process. Our ancestors learnt many things from their predecessors. With the passage of time they also added to it from their own experience and gave up those which they did not consider useful. We in turn have learnt many things from our ancestors. As time goes we continue to add new thoughts, new ideas to those already existent and sometimes we give up some which we don't consider useful any more. This is how culture is transmitted and carried forward from generation to next generation. The culture we inherit from our predecessors is called our cultural heritage.

This heritage exists at various levels. Humanity as a whole has inherited a culture which may be called human heritage. A nation also inherits a culture which may be termed as national cultural heritage. Cultural heritage includes all those aspects or values of culture transmitted to human beings by their ancestors from generation to generation. They are cherished, protected and maintained by them with unbroken continuity and they feel proud of it. A few examples would be helpful in clarifying the concept of heritage. The Taj Mahal, Jain caves at Khandagiri and Udayagiri, Bhubaneswar, Sun Temple Konarak, Jagannath Temple, Puri, Lingaraja Temple, Bhubaneswar, Red Fort of Agra, Delhi's Qutub Minar, Mysore Palace, Jain Temple of Dilwara (Rajasthan) Nizamuddin Aulia's Dargah, Golden Temple of Amritsar, Gurudwara Sisganj of Delhi, Sanchi Stupa, Christian Church in Goa, India Gate etc., are all important places of our heritage and are to be protected by all means.

Besides the architectural creations, monuments, material artefacts, the intellectual achievements, philosophy, treasures of knowledge, scientific inventions and discoveries are also the part of heritage. In Indian context the contributions of Baudhayana, Aryabhatta, Bhaskaracharya in the field of Mathematics, Astronomy and Astrology; Varahmihir in the field of Physics; Nagarjuna in the field of Chemistry, Susruta and Charak in the field of Medicines and Patanjali in the field of Yoga are profound treasures of Indian Cultural heritage. Culture is liable to change, but our heritage does not. We individuals, belonging to a culture or a particular group, may acquire or borrow certain cultural traits of other communities/cultures, but our belongingness to Indian cultural heritage will remain unchanged. Our Indian cultural heritage will bind us together e.g. Indian literature and scriptures namely Vedas, Upanishads Gita and Yoga System etc. have contributed a lot by way of providing right knowledge, right action, behavior and practices as complementary to the development of civilization.

1.1.4. General Characteristics of Culture

Now let us discuss some general characteristics of culture, which are common to different cultures throughout the world.

Culture is learned and acquired **:** Culture is acquired in the sense that there are certain behaviours which are acquired through heredity. Individuals inherit certain qualities from their parents but socio-cultural patterns are not inherited. These are learnt from family members, from the group and the society in which they live. It is thus apparent that the culture of human beings is influenced by the physical and social environment through which they operate.

Culture is shared by a group of people: A thought or action may be called culture if it is shared and believed or practiced by a group of people.

Culture is cumulative: Different knowledge embodied in culture can be passed from one generation to another generation. More and more knowledge is added in the particular culture as the time passes by. Each may work out solution to problems in life that passes from one generation to another. This cycle remains as the particular culture goes with time.

Culture changes **:** There is knowledge, thoughts or traditions that are lost as new cultural traits are added. There are possibilities of cultural changes within the particular culture as time passes.

Culture is dynamic **:** No culture remains on the permanent state. Culture is changing constantly as new ideas and new techniques are added as time passes modifying or changing the old ways. This is the characteristics of culture that stems from the culture's cumulative quality.

Culture gives us a range of permissible behaviour patterns: It involves how an activity should be conducted, how an individual should act appropriately.

Culture is diverse: It is a system that has several mutually interdependent parts. Although these parts are separate, they are interdependent with one another forming culture as whole.

1.1.5. Importance of Culture in Human life

Culture is closely linked with life. It is not an add-on, an ornament that we as human beings can use. It is not merely a touch of colour. It is what makes us human. Without culture, there would be no humans. Culture is made up of traditions, beliefs, way of life, from the most spiritual to the most material. It gives us meaning, a way of leading our lives. Human beings are creators of culture and, at the same time, culture is what makes us human. A fundamental element of culture is the issue of religious belief and its symbolic expression. We must value religious identity and be aware of current efforts to make progress in terms of interfaith dialogue, which is actually an intercultural dialogue. As the world is becoming more and more global and we coexist on a more global level we can't just think there's only one right way of living or that any one is valid. The need for coexistence makes the coexistence of cultures and beliefs necessary. In order to not make such mistakes, the best thing we can do is get to know other cultures, while also getting to know our own. How can we dialogue with other cultures, if we don't really know what our own culture is? The three eternal and universal values of Truth, Beauty and Goodness are closely linked with culture. It is culture that brings us closer to truth through philosophy and religion; it brings beauty in our lives through the Arts and makes us aesthetic beings; and it is culture that makes us ethical beings by bringing us closer to other human beings and teaching us the values of love, tolerance and peace.

1.1.6. Indian Culture

Indian culture is one of the most ancient cultures of the world. The ancient cultures of Egypt, Greece, Rome, etc. were destroyed with time and only their remnants are left. But Indian culture is alive till today. Its fundamental principles are the same, as were in the ancient time. One can see village panchayats, caste systems and joint family system. The teachings of Buddha, Mahavira, and Lord Krishna are alive till today also and are source of inspiration. The values of spirituality, praying nature, faith in karma and reincarnation, non-violence, truth, non- stealing, Chastity, Non-Acquisitiveness, etc. inspire people of this nation, today also. Material development and materials come under civilization while Art of Living, customs, traditions come under culture. Material development is possible to a limit. This is the reason, that the civilizations got destroyed while Indian culture is present till today because the basis of development was spirituality and not materialism. Thus, Indian culture can be called an ancient culture, whose past is alive even in the present. The reminiscent of the stone-age found in Pallavaram, Chingalpet, Vellore, Tinnivalli near Madras, in the valley of river Sohan, in Pindhighev area in West Punjab, in Rehand area of Mirzapur in Uttar Pradesh, in Narmada Valley in Madhya Pradesh, in Hoshangabad and Maheshwar, make it clear that India has been the land of development and growth of human culture. On the basis of excavation done in places like Harappa and Mohanjodaro etc. we come to know the developed civilization and culture of the pre-historical era, which was flourished around 3000 B.C. Thus, Indian culture is about 5000 years old.

1.1.7. Characteristics of Indian culture

Traditional Indian culture, in its overall thrust towards the spiritual, promotes moral values and the attitudes of generosity, simplicity and frugality. Some of the striking features of Indian culture that pervade its numerous castes, tribes, ethnic groups and religious groups and sects are as follows

1.1.7.1. A Cosmic Vision

The framework of Indian culture places human beings within a conception of the universe as a divine creation. It is not anthropo-centric (human-centric) only and considers all elements of creation, both living and non-living, as manifestations of the divine. Therefore, it respects God's design and promotes the ideal of co-existence. This vision thus, synthesizes human beings, nature and God into one integral whole. This is reflected in the idea of *satyam-shivam-sundaram*.

1.1.7.2. Sense of Harmony

Indian philosophy and culture tries to achieve an innate harmony and order and this is extended to the entire cosmos. Indian culture assumes that natural cosmic order inherent in nature is the foundation of moral and social order. Inner harmony is supposed to be the foundation of outer harmony. External order and beauty will naturally follow from inner harmony. Indian culture balances and seeks to synthesize the material and the spiritual, as aptly illustrated by the concept of *purushartha*.

1.1.7.3. Tolerance

An important characteristic of Indian culture is tolerance. In India, tolerance and liberalism is found for all religions, castes, communities, etc. Many foreign cultures invaded India and Indian society gave every culture the opportunity of prospering. Indian society accepted and respected Shaka, Huna, Shithiyan, Muslim, Christian, Sikh, Jain, Buddhist cultures. The feeling of tolerance towards all religions is a wonderful characteristic of Indian society. Rigveda says-"Truth is one, even then the Scholars describe it in various forms. In Gita, Lord Krishna says, "Those praying others are actually praying me." This thought is the extreme of tolerance. There is a peaceful coexistence of various religions in India and all have been effecting each other – although this tradition has been badly affected by activities of converting religion by some religious organisations. All the religions existing in India are respected equally. Indian culture accepts the manifoldness of reality and assimilates plurality of viewpoints, behaviours, customs and institutions. It does not try to suppress diversity in favour of uniformity. The motto of Indian culture is both unity in diversity as well as diversity in unity.

1.1.7.4. Continuity and Stability.

The principles of Indian culture are today also that much in practice, as they were initially. A special characteristic of Indian culture is – its continuous flow. Since, Indian culture is based on values, so it's development is continuous. Many centuries passed by, many changes occurred, many foreign invaders were faced, but the light of Indian culture today also is continuously glowing. No Scholar can end its history of like that of the cultures Egypt, Greece, Rome, Sumer, Babylon and Syria because it is yet in the phase of construction." Indian culture can be understood by looking at its present cultural standards. The light of ancient Indian culture life is yet glowing. Many invasions occurred, many rulers changed, many laws were passed but even today, the traditional institutions, religion, epics, literature, philosophy, traditions, etc. are alive. The situations and government could not remove them completely. The stability of Indian culture is unique within itself, even today. Indian culture has always favoured change within continuity. It is in favour of gradual change or reform. It does not favour abrupt or instant change. Therefore, most changes in thought have come in the form of commentaries and interpretation and not in the form of original systems of thought. In matters of behaviour also synthesis of old and new is preferred over replacement of old by the new.

1.1.7.5. Adaptability

Adaptability has a great contribution in making Indian culture immortal. Adaptability is the process of changing according to time, place and period. It's an essential element of longevity of any culture. Indian culture has a unique property of adjustment, as a result of which, it is maintained till today. Indian family, caste, religion and institutions have changed themselves with time. Due to adaptability and co-ordination of Indian culture, it's continuity, utility and activity is still present. Dr. Radha Krishnan, in his book, 'Indian culture: Some Thoughts', while describing the adaptability of Indian culture has said all people whether black or white, Hindus or Muslims, Christians or Jews are brothers and our country is the entire universe. We should have devotion for those things, which are beyond the limits of knowledge and regarding which, it's difficult to say anything. Our hope towards mankind was based on that respect and devotion, which people had towards other's views. There should be no efforts on imposing our thoughts on others.

1.1.7.6. Receptivity :

Receptivity is an important characteristic of Indian culture. Indian culture has always accepted the good of the invading cultures. Indian culture is like an ocean, in which many rivers come and meet. In the same way all castes succumbed to the Indian culture and very rapidly they dissolved in the *Hindutva* . Indian culture has always adjusted with other cultures it's ability to maintain unity amongst the diversities of all is the best. The reliability, which developed in this culture due to this receptivity, is a boon for this world and is appreciated by all. We have always adopted the properties of various cultures. *Vasudaiva Kutumbakam* is the soul of Indian culture. Indian culture has always answered and activated itself by receiving and adjusting with the elements of foreign cultures. Indian culture has received the elements of Muslim cultures and has never hesitated in accepting the useful things of foreign culture. Therefore, it's continuity, utility and activity are still there today. The adaptability and receptivity of this culture has given it the power toremain alive in all the conditions. Due to this property, Indian culture was never destroyed even after facing the foreign attacks. Actually, Indian society and culture had facilitated foreign attackers by getting them close and becoming intimate with them and not only gave but also received many things.

1.1.7.7. Spirituality.

Spirituality is the soul of Indian culture. Here the existence of soul is accepted. Therefore, the ultimate aim of man is not physical comforts but is self-realisation. Radha Kumud Mukerjee, in his book, 'Hindu Civilization', has analysed that Indian culture, which kept it's personal specialities, bound the entire nation in unity in such a way that nation and culture were considered inseparable and became unanimous. Nation became culture and culture became nation. Country took the form of Spiritual World, beyond the physical world. When Indian culture originated in the times of Rigveda, then it spread with time to Saptasindhu, Bramhavarta, Aryavarta, Jumbudweepa, Bharata Varsha or India. Because of its strength, it reached abroad beyond the borders of India and established there also.

1.1.7.8. Religious Dominance

Religion has a central place in Indian culture. Vedas, Upanishads, Purana, Mahabharata, Gita, Agama, Tripitak, Quran and Bible affect the people of Indian culture. These books have developed optimism, theism, sacrifice, penance, restraints, good conduct, truthfulness, compassion, authenticity, friendliness, forgiveness, etc. Monier Williams has rightly said, "Although in India, there are 500 and above dialects but religious language is only one and religious literature is also one, which all the followers of Hindu religion, varying in caste, language, social status and opinion, believe and pray with devotion. That language is Sanskrit and that literature is Sanskrit literature. It is the only dictionary of Veda or other knowledge. It is the only source of Hindu Religion and Philosophy, the only mirror, which correctly reflects the Hindu views, thoughts, customs and traditions. It is the source for the development of regional languages and is also the source for getting material for the publication of important religious and scientific thoughts.

1.1.7.9. Thoughts about Karma and Reincarnation.

The concept of Karma (action) and Reincarnation have special importance in Indian culture. It is believed that one gains virtue during good action and takes birth in higher order in his next birth and spends a comfortable life. The one doing bad action takes birth in lower order in his next birth and suffers pain and leads a miserable life. Upanishads say that the Principle of fruits of action is correct.

A man gets the fruits as per the action he does. Therefore, man needs to modify his actions, so as to improve the next birth also. Continuously performing good actions in all his birth, he will get salvation, i.e. will be liberated from the cycle of birth and death. This concept is not only of the Upnishads but is also the basis of the Jainism, Buddhism, etc. In this way, the concept of reincarnation is associated with the principle of action. The actual cause of reincarnation is the actions done in the previous birth.

1.1.7.10. Emphasis on Duty

As against rights, Indian culture emphasises *dharma* or moral duty. It is believed that performance of one's duty is more important than asserting one's right. It also emphasises the complementariness between one's own duty and other's rights. Thus, through the emphasis on community or family obligations, Indian culture promotes interdependence rather than Independence and autonomy of the individual.

1.1.7.11. The Ideal of Joint Family

At the level of marriage, there is a lot of plurality in India. At the level of family, however, there is striking similarity. For example, the ideal or norm of joint family is upheld by almost every Indian. Every person may not live in a joint household but the ideal of joint family is still favoured. The family is the defining feature of Indian culture. Although Indians differentiate between individual identity and family identity, the Western type of individualism is rare in Indian culture.

1.1.7.12. Caste System.

Another characteristic of Indian culture is social stratification. In every region of India, there are about 200 castes. The social structure is made of thousands of those castes and sub-castes, which decide the social status of a person on the basis of birth. According to E.A.H.Blunt, "Caste is a collection of intermarried or intra-married groups, which have a general name, whose membership is heredity and put some bans and rules on its members residing socially together. Its members, either do traditional business or claim their uniform community." Thus, Indian culture has a special system of stratification.

1.1.7.13. Unity in Diversity.

An important characteristic of Indian culture is Unity in Diversity. There is much diversity in Indian culture like in geography, in caste, in creed, in language, in religion, in politics, etc. Dr. R.K.Mukerjee writes, "India is a museum of different types, communities, customs, traditions, religions, cultures, beliefs, languages, castes and social system." But even after having so much of external diversity, none can deny the internal unity of Indian culture. Thus, in Indian culture there is Unity in Diversity. According to Pandit Nehru, "Those who see India, are deeply moved by its Unity in Diversity. No one can break this unity. This fundamental unity of India is its great fundament element."

According to Sir Herbert Rizle, "Even after the linguistic, social and geographical diversity, a special uniformity is seen from Kanyakumari to the Himalayas." Indian culture is a huge tree, the roots of which have Aryan culture. Like a new layer is formed all around the tree every year, similarly layers of many historical eras surround the tree of Indian culture, protecting it and getting life sap from it. We all live in the cooling shade of that tree. The concept of Unity and diversity will be dealt in details in separate paragraphs.

1.1.7.14. Four Duties.

By fulfilling duties, a person can follow his religion while living in physical comforts and thus can gain salvation. Fulfilling duties is a characteristic of Indian culture. In this, in a person's life, four basis are considered-*Dharma* (religion), *Arth* (money), *Kama* (lust), *Moksha* (salvation). Religion is related to the fulfillment of moral duties. Money is related to the fulfillment of all needs. Lust is associated with pleasures in life. Salvation is the last goal. All these inspire an individual to fulfill his duties and to live in a disciplined way in society. Two contradictory thoughts are seen in the history of the world-first the world and life is momentary and destructible and second is that the success of life depends on the enjoyment.

Its best example is Western school of thought. But one can see the co-ordination between the two in Indian culture. Both should be mingled to the real nature, importance and goal of human life. The expression of this coordination is the Principle of Efforts.

It is believed that the nation, which has forgotten its culture, is not an alive nation. He used to tell the importance of Indian cultural values.

People who believe in material development can be intolerant. Those who believe in development of weapons can be unrelative. Those who consider harm done to others for their own welfare as forgivable can be liberal but the exceptional of Indian culture is that though it considers material as an essential thing but has not made it the centre of faith. Though it has used the power of weapons but has considered its welfare in it. It has considered harm done to others for its own welfare as unforgivable. The ultimate goal of life here is not luxury and desires but is sacrifice-penance and self-realisation.

1.1.8. Indian Culture during the Contemporary Period

The social structural affiliation of the classical in the traditional Indian culture had been broadly linked with princes, priests, monks, *munis, sadhus,* scholars, guild masters and other prosperous groups. During the medieval period the relationship between the classical and the folk was not disturbed. In ancient India the classical tradition was linked not only to Sanskrit but there were also streams of the classical tradition associated with Pali and Tamil. Sanskrit was the bearer of the Hindu classical tradition and the Mahayana Buddhist tradition and some of the Jain science traditions as well. Pali was the vehicle of the Theravadi Buddhist tradition and Tamil was the bearer of the South Indian classical tradition.

During the modern period, the relationship between the classical represented by English and the vernacular folk traditions has broken down. Traditional equilibrium has been affected by different factors and processes of modernization. With the impact of modern social forces the relationship between the classical and the folk traditions has been disturbed. In the urban centres a new middle class has been growing and assuming the role of the bearer of the classical tradition. The middle class has a world view and outlook that is radically different from the bearers of the folk tradition. They are mostly the bearers of Western cultural values, norms, ideas, outlook and institutions, and English has become their dominant language. Throughout history, the folk and the tribal traditions have remained relatively unaffected by changes in political structures. The importance of classical traditions has been changing from time to time with changes in political power structure but the folk and the tribal traditions have remained consistently vibrant. The classical traditions in traditional India had always accepted the importance as well as given space to the folk and the tribal cultures. The bearers of modern Western classical cultural tradition, on the other hand, have on occasions shown less tolerance towards the folk and the tribal traditions. They usually brand the traditional culture as primitive, barbaric and superstitious in comparison to the modern culture. They try to modernize and westernize all the elements and streams of Indian culture. The processes of westernization, industrialisation, urbanisation, globalisation and democratisation are influencing various aspects of Indian culture today. These modernizing and secularizing forces, however, have not yet cut off contemporary Indian culture from the traditional and cultural roots of Indian culture. The traditional cultural media not only continue to survive today, but also some aspects of it have also been incorporated in novel ways into an emerging popular and, classical culture.

1.1.9. Unity in Diversity

One feature that is most often noticed about India is its unity in diversity. This overworked cliché has become a part of India's self-identity. India is a country of sub-continental proportions. From north to south, east to west, people from diverse backgrounds have mixed and cultures have intermingled over centuries. Nevertheless, there has been an underlying continuity in identity.

There are very few countries which have such an enormous cultural diversity that India has to offer. Beneath the bewildering diversity of religion, language and customs of this vast country, the underlying unity is remarkable. The idea of unity is traced back by scholars to ancient times. The underlying cultural unity was strengthened further with the administrative unity brought about during the British rule and with the construction of India as a modern independent nation after the independence. The enduring nature of Indian unity has always been fascinating. Indian unity is the product of certain historical factors that are present in various fields of Indian social life. It appears as if the inhabitants from the Himalayas in the north to Kanyakumari in the south, and Kutch in the west to Arunachal in the east are woven together into a beautiful tapestry. In the process of its evolution, Indian society has acquired a culture characterized by stable patterns of pluralism. However, the acceptance of cultural pluralism does not detract us from the idea of promoting economic, political and social integration.

European Sociology conceptualizes unity in a society in terms of linguistic nationality or in terms of political sovereignty. Thus, the primary basis of unity belongs to a nation. According to many Indian sociologists, however, unity in India and the whole of South Asia, in fact, has been civilisational, going back to ancient times and continuing to the present day. Thus, at the civilisational level there is unity in South Asia, but this South Asian civilisation is divided today into many nations like India, Pakistan, Bangladesh, Sri Lanka and Nepal.

In terms of social institutions like the family, caste and lifestyles there is a fundamental unity in the different societies and nations of South Asia. An important source of unity in traditional India was rooted in the processes of cultural communication and interaction. Sociologists have identified the role of traders, storytellers, crafts-people and artists, for example potters, musicians, dancers in traditional India, in building common cultural traditions. The institutions of pilgrimage, fairs and festivals provide yet another link for cultural unity. In addition to these agencies, the social structure and economy forged linkages of reciprocity and interaction between regions, groups and cultural traditions.

Accommodation without assimilation has been the characteristic of Indian civilisation. Accommodation is a social process by which different elements of a society are integrated without losing their separate identity. Assimilation on the other hand is a type of integration where the earlier identity of the elements is dissolved. In Indian history and culture, additions of new components have not meant the discarding of old ones. The accommodation of diversity has been the underlying ideology and numerous social and cultural factors have contributed to the enduring nature of Indian unity. Order and stability was maintained not primarily by the state but through social, cultural, moral and technological values and institutions of Indian civilization. Indian civilization gave enough freedom for the practice of any way of life although different customary ways were ranked in a hierarchy. This created inequality and integration as well.

1.1.9.1. The factors of unity in diversity

We can discuss the following five factors of unity in diversity of India:

1.1.9.1.1. Geographical and Demographic Factors

The first striking feature about India is its diversity because of India's geographical environment and huge populations. It is difficult to imagine the vast territory that stretches from north to south and east to west as one continuous territory. It is nearly fourteen times as large as Great Britain and over ten times the size of the entire British Isles. The temperature varies from extreme heat to extreme cold. The temperate, the tropical and the polar climates are found in India. In terms of physical features of the population, there is diversity in appearance and complexion, height and figure etc.

However, geography seems to have played an important role in engendering Indian unity and the sense of Indianness. Shut off from the rest of Asia by the inaccessible barriers of the mighty Himalayas and with the seas and the ocean on all other sides, India is clearly marked out to be a geographical entity. Not only are her territories thus sharply demarcated from the rest of the world, but nature has generously placed within her boundaries all resources that human beings need for developing a rich and creative life. Thus, Indian geography has facilitated unity and continuity of her history as a country. Attempts either to divide the country or to expand it beyond its natural frontiers have mostly failed.

The vastness of the land influenced the mind of Indians in two ways. The great variety in landscape, climate and conditions of life prepared in the mind a readiness to accept differences. Besides, the vast spaces offered room for slow infiltration by newcomers and allowed each locality unhampered scope of development along its own lines. The geographical unity of the country has had its effects on the economic life of the people. The size of the country and quality of the land permitted gradual increase in population and expansion of cultivation. The fact that India has continually developed and maintained an agricultural economy for almost four or five thousand years explains in part the depth and tenacity of her culture and traditions. The primacy of agricultural economy led to the development of common characteristics and a common outlook.

The geographical unity of India is easily missed in her vastness and variety. A permanent and characteristically Indian expression of unity is found in the network of shrines and sacred places spread throughout the country. The visit to holy places as an imperative religious duty has made travelling a habit for Indians. Similarly, the multitude of monuments associated with different religious communities which have adorned the land influence the geographical consciousness of a large number of people.

1.1.9.1.2. Religious Factors

India is a multi-religious country. There are seven major religious groups in India. The Hindus constitute the majority of Indian population. The Muslims constitute the second largest religious group. The Christians, the Sikhs, the Buddhists, the Jains and others the Jews, the Zoroastrians or Parsis and the Animists may not be numerically big, but their contribution to India is as significant as the other bigger groups. Religion is both a factor of unity and diversity in Indian society. All religious groups are differentiated internally. Caste or caste like status groups are found in Hinduism, Islam, Christianity and Sikhism. Within a homogeneous society, religion plays a highly integrative role but by the same token in a multi-religious society religion can become an issue of contention and lead to conflicts. Traditionally, different religious groups have lived in India in more or less peaceful coexistence.

There are two major aspects to any religion, the spiritual and the temporal. The spiritual aspect of religion is quite similar in all religions. In every religion an emphasis is placed on the moral conduct and transcendence of the selfish ego. While this aspect of religion is a matter of personal devotion, the temporal aspect of religion is always related with the group identity and solidarity is maintained by religious rituals and community's beliefs. At the temporal level, different religious groups differ from each other. In India, there has not been only a great degree of religious tolerance among the different religious communities, but some religious places have acquired a character and popularity that goes beyond a single religious community. Similarly, some religious festivals are celebrated, at least in a limited way, by many religious communities. Places like Varanasi, Ujjain, Amritsar, Mathura, Bodhgaya, Vaishno Devi, Tirupati and Ajmer Sharif are some such religious centres.

For instance, a large number of Hindus also visit Ajmer Sharif, a Muslim pilgrimage place. Also, the economy of these religious centres often involves shopkeepers and service providers from other religions. In the field of bhakti and devotion the Hindu Saints and Muslim *Sufis* had many similarities and commonalities. Some religious festivals like Diwali, Dushehera and Holi have two aspects, ritualistic and cultural. The ritualistic aspect is restricted to Hindus but the cultural aspect is more or less celebrated by all the communities. In the same way, Christmas and Id-ul-fitr are also celebrated at many places by different religious communities. Kabir, Akbar, Dara Shikoh and Mahatma Gandhi have been instrumental in developing common ethos among the different religious communities in India. Persian Sufism took a new shade of colour in India. Poets and religious teachers such as Ramanand and Kabir tried to combine the best and condemn the worst in Hinduism and Islam alike.

At the courts of Oudh and Hyderabad there grew aesthetic standards in painting, in poetry, in love and in food, which drew on the courtly traditions of Rajasthan and Persia. Muslims borrowed caste from Hindus, Hindus took *purdah* from Muslims. Religion, however, is also a factor of diversity and animosity. The country was partitioned into India and Pakistan, primarily on religious and communal lines. Even after partition the communal problem raised its head from time to time. Communalism, which breeds hatred and violence against other religions, is the result of fundamentalism. It is a product of ignorance as well as deliberate mischief by vested interests to gain political power and economic benefits by exploiting religious sentiments of the faithful people and dividing them along communal lines.

1.1.9.1. 3. Cultural Factors

The story of Indian culture is one of continuity, synthesis and enrichment. Culture is also a source of unity as well as diversity like religion. Powerful kingdoms and empires such as the Mauryas and the Guptas did not aggressively intervene in social and cultural matters; leaving much diversity intact. Although Islam was the politically dominant religion in large parts of the country for several centuries it did not absorb Hinduism, or disturb the Hindu social structure. Nor did Hinduism, which was demographically and otherwise dominant seek to eliminate the beliefs and practices, characteristic of other religions. Various beliefs and practices are pursued and maintained by Hindus, Muslims and Christians alike. Over the time Indian society has come to be divided into innumerable tribes, castes, sub-castes, clans, sects and communities each of which seek to maintain their own style of life and code of conduct.

Many sociologists have recorded in detail the immense variety in the habits, practices and customs of the people in different geographical regions. The distribution of material traits such as dress, habitation, arts and crafts, endless variety of food and their preparation, makes India a living example of regional diversity. The role played by Indian religion, philosophy, art and literature in bringing about unity is conspicuous. Social institutions like the caste system and the joint family, which are found throughout the length and breadth of the country, are typically Indian. The celebration of festivals is observed all over India in much the same manner. Likewise, similarities in art and culture engraved on the temple and palace walls all over India have generated the feeling of oneness. Inspite of their distinctiveness the coexistence of cultures is celebrated.

1.1.9.1.4. Political Factors

It is generally believed that India's continuity as a civilisation was social and cultural rather than political. Order and stability were maintained not by means of the state but through culture and society. The vastness of the country's extreme diversity of physical features, endless variety of races, castes, creeds and languages and dialects have made it difficult to establish an all- Indian empire. This also accounts for the fact that political unity is not the normal characteristic of ancient and medieval Indian history.

However, the idea of bringing the whole country under one central authority has always been on the minds of great kings and statesmen of India. It was with this purpose that the kings of ancient India proclaimed the idea of 'Chakravarti'. Kings like Chandragupta Maurya, Ashoka, Samudragupta and Harshvardhana had put this idea into practice. The socio-political contributions of some Muslim rulers such as Akbar and Jehangir were also highly commendable. Akbar's Din-e-elahi and Jehangir's emphasis on justice deserve special mention in this regard.

In a sense, India has never been a well-organised political unit under the government of a single state. Even British India was a part of India and did not comprehend the whole of it, which was split up into about 600 states, large and small but separate and independent as autonomous entities. The British tried to establish political unification under a paramount power with regard to the defence, external relations, foreign policy and certain economic matters within the whole of India. Such attempts, however, were not uncommon in earlier periods. After the independence India was united politically and administratively but it was already divided between India and Pakistan. After the independence the unity of India is expressed in the institution of the nation. It is the product of the freedom movement as well as the constitutional legacy of the British rule. There is political and administrative unity today but there are different political parties and diverse political ideologies. Therefore, politics is both a factor of unity and diversity.

1.1.9.1.5. Linguistic Factors

India is a multilingual country. Language is another source of cultural diversity as well as unity. It contributes to collective identities and even to conflicts. Eighteen languages are recognized by Indian Constitution. All major languages have regional and dialectical variations, for example, Hindi has Awadhi, Brij, Bhojpuri, Magadhi, Bundeli, Pahari, Malwi, Odia has Sambalpuri and several other dialects. The situation is further complicated since 179 languages and 544 dialects are recognised in India. These languages and dialects are divided into three linguistic families Indo-Aryan, Dravidian and Mundari. Indo-Aryan family of languages includes Sanskrit and other North Indian languages such as Hindi, Bengali, Odia, Marathi, Gujarati, Punjabi, Urdu, etc. and their dialects. The Dravidian family of languages includes Tamil, Telugu, Kannada and Malaylam. The Mundari group of languages and dialects are found among the tribal communities of India.

During the medieval period Persian, Arabic and Urdu became popular languages. Urdu developed in India with Hindi around the same period as Hindustani language. They have different script but many similarities. Arabic and Persian played the role of official and court languages replacing Sanskrit and Pali.

In the post independence period, English replaced Urdu as the official and court language. After independence, Hindi was made the national language but English remained the language of the central government and of the courts. English has also remained the language of higher education and research in India after 1835. The importance given to English in Independent

India has also had an impact on Indian languages and literature, as well as on social structure and divisions in Indian society. The social and economic distinction between an English speaking, prosperous elite and the masses who speak the Indian vernacular languages or dialects is quite pronounced.

Linguistic diversity has posed administrative and political problems. But language too has an underlying role in the unity in diversity of Indian culture. Although there is bewildering diversity in the languages and dialects of India, fundamental unity is found in the ideas and themes expressed in these languages. There is unity also at the level of grammatical structures. Sanskrit has deeply influenced most languages of India with its vocabulary. Dravidian languages also have a number of Sanskrit words today. Persian, Arabic and English words too have become part of the Indian languages and dialects today. The spirit of accommodation, which united different ethnic groups into one social system, also expresses itself in the literatures of India.

Language is also a factor of diversity and separatism. Linguistic separatism has a strong emotional appeal. Political mobilisations and conflicts have arisen between different linguistic groups. After independence linguistic problems of India were centered around three issues, the official languages issue, the demands for the linguistic reorganization of the provinces of India whose boundaries during the British rule did not conform to linguistic division; and the status of minority languages within reorganized states.

After many deliberations, Hindi was made the official language of India but English was retained at least for a transition period. Earlier, this transition period was supposed to last for fifteen years. In 1965, English was given the status of an "associate additional official language" of the union and of inter-provincial communication. The major regional languages are used in their own provinces and recognised as other "national" languages through their incorporation into the Eighth Schedule of the Constitution. Hindi is the official language of the country but the "associate additional official language" English has retained its power, status and glamour as well.

1.1.9.2. Elements of Unity in India in different period of her history.

Due to cultural and economic interaction and geographical mobility there has emerged an all-India style, a series of inter-linkages and much commonality between different regions of India. The following few paragraphs will elaborate the elements which act as binding factors inspite of numerous diversity in India.

India is characterized by numerous local level traditions or folk traditions as well as what could be deemed as the greater classical tradition. The latter would be more widely spread over the country but also confined to certain dominant sections of society.

Common to each linguistic region are specific agriculture castes which form the core of rural communities, along with their complementary artisan and service castes. These were involved in a *jajmani*-service provider relation-ship. In the urban areas there were predominantly, castes of *banias* (traders), crafts persons and castes such as *brahmans* and *kayasthas*.

Pilgrimage centres have also led to a type of unity at the all India level. Barriers of caste, class and other social taboos were almost absent at pilgrimage centres during several cultural occasions. People from different regions were able to interact at the pilgrim centres with each other leading to the establishment of cultural bonds. Trans-sectarian pilgrim sites include Kashi, Haridwar, Rameshwaram, Dwarka, Badrinath, Gaya, similarly Amritsar and Ajmer Sharif also become pilgrimage centre during medieval period.

Cultural identity is maintained by a common metaphysical base, such as the idea of ethical compensation (*Karmphal*) and the idea of transcendence. Variants of all India epics and mythology, which emphasise certain values and goals, are found in all regions. Examples are *purusharth* (achievement ideals), *rinas* (obligations), *dana* (sharing), *Samskara* (sacraments) at birth, death and marriage, *vrata* (the ritual to earn merit) and *prayaschita* (penance or expiation).

Traditional personal laws and social customs of the Hindus were applicable in different regions. The *dayabhaga* system of inheritance was popular in Bengal whereas the *mitakshara* prevailed over the rest of the country, except in Kerala and Bengal. Most Indians believe in the ideas of heaven and hell and cherish the idea of *moksha*, salvation or *nirvana* liberation from the cycle of life and death. This concept of *moksha* or *nirvana* is linked with the perception of the one ultimate *Brahma*.

In the middle ages when the world witnessed the most intensely fought religious wars in Europe and the Middle East, India stood out as a country where many religions co-existed in relative social harmony. The role of the ruler like Akbar was also very important in this context. Islam seems to have strengthened the de-ritualising and egalitarian trends in Medieval Hinduism, while Hindu philosophy seems to have strengthened the mystical spiritual strain in Muslim religious thought. For example, the *Bhakti* movement initiated by the Nayanar Saints of South India found strength in the context of Islam and Muslim dominance in North India. In the same way, the mystic and devotional aspect of Islam was strengthened in the philosophical milieu of Hinduism. Ramanand, Kabir, Nanak and Dara Shikoh played a significant role in the spread of mutual understanding among the Hindu and the Muslim masses.

A unified culture in language, music and the arts was developed during the medieval period. Hindi and Urdu are the product of this unified Hindustani culture of medieval India. Both languages have common roots, common vocabulary but these are written in different scripts – Devanagari and Persian respectively. In music and arts, the Hindus and the Muslims had come together. North Indian (Hindustani) music was nurtured at the king's courts and in the Hindu temples. Hindus sang at the Muslim courts and Muslims have sung *bhajans* at Hindu temples. Krishna, Radha and the *gopis* have provided the staple theme for many of the compositions sung by Hindu and Muslim masters alike. In architecture the process of blending Hindu and Muslim elements was perfected during the medieval period. During the rule of Akbar, a synthesis of the Turko-Persian conceptions with Indian style was attempted. In Jehangir's time the Hindu influence seems to have had increased. The tomb of Akbar at Sikandra shows, in spite of its Muslim arches and domes, the general pattern of Buddhist *viharas* or of the *rathas* of Mahablipuram. Jain influence is found on the mosque of Fathehpur Sikri and Mount Abu. The Mughal architecture acquired new qualities which neither the Persian nor the old Indian styles had ever possessed. Painting also developed a new style during this period through the blending of the Turko-Iranian with the old Indian style. Akbar founded an academy of painting at his court where Indian and Persian artists worked together. Jehangir was not only a patron of art but was himself an artist, and during his time Mughal painting reached its zenith.

During the colonial rule different factors led to significant changes in the structure of Indian society. The traditional framework of unity in Indian civilization came under tremendous stress. Modern education introduced by the colonial rulers initiated a process of cultural westernisation. The freedom movement (1857-1947) created new sources of unity in Indian society. Now, nationalism replaced religion and culture as the cementing force within Indian society. Despite the partition in 1947, the experience of freedom movement is still the foundation of Indian unity in modern India.

After the independence the nation and its different organs have become the pillars of unity in India. The constitution built on the pre- existing unity of India has strengthened it still further by emphasizing the values of equality, fraternity, secularism and justice. In contemporary India the pillars of unity include the following:

The Indian Constitution is the most fundamental source of unity in India today. Indians believe in the basic framework of the Constitution.

Indian Parliament is the national legislative organ of the Indian nation. Representatives are elected by the people and every adult citizen (above 18 years) of India has a right to vote. This represents the people's will in general.

The Government of India is formally headed by the President who rules on the advice of a council of ministers headed by the Prime Minister.

The Judiciary is the legal guardian of Indian people. The judiciary is an autonomous body at the local, regional and central levels. It works as the custodian of the Indian Constitution.

The bureaucracy, the police and other educated professionals such as engineers, scientists, doctors, academics and journalists have played an important role in governing the country, maintaining law and order and in carrying out various development projects and schemes of the government. The military services deserve special mention in view of the wars, insurgency and the inter-border tensions experienced during the last few decades, as also during national calamities like floods, earthquakes, cyclones etc.

Modern means of communication, the network of railways, surface transport, civil aviation, post offices, telegraph, telephones, print media, radio and television have played important roles in maintaining and strengthening the national ethos and creating a "we" feeling among Indians.

Industrialisation, urbanization and other economic factors have led to the creation of the capitalist and the middle classes and have also created mobility of labour and services throughout the country.

Thus, the above account on the aspect of unity in diversity speaks us that Indian has a traditional culture with cosmopolitan outlook. Since time immemorial inspite of having scores of differences the country is still united in spirit, in politics, in the mind of the inhabitants and will remain in such condition perpetually.

1.1.10. Aspects of Indian culture

Art and Architecture : Indian art is inspired by religion and centre around sacred themes. However, there is nothing ascetic or self-denying about it. The eternal diversity of life and nature and the human element are all reflected in Indian art forms. The art of architecture and sculpture was well developed during the Indus valley period. India has the largest collections of folk and tribal artifacts.

Music: The popular term for music throughout India is *Sangit,* which included dance as well as vocal instrumental music. The rhymes of the *Rigveda* and the *Samveda* are the earliest examples of words set to music. The oldest detailed exposition of Indian musical theory is found in *Natyashastra,* attributed to the sage Bharata who lived at the beginning of the Christian era. North Indian Hindustani classical music and South Indian Karnatak music are the two major forms of classical music in India. More specific schools of classical music are associated with particular *gharanas.* This is one aspect of Indian culture that has achieved worldwide recognition. Song and dance has always been a part of social gatherings and get-togethers in India. Fairs, marriages, festivals and other celebrations are not complete without them. Films, film songs and music have had an important role to play in the further popularisation of music among the masses in modern times.

Dance: Classical Indian dance is a beautiful and significant symbol of the spiritual and artistic approach of the Indian mind. Traditional Indian scriptures contain many references to *nritta* (music) and *nata* (drama). Dance and music are present at every stage of domestic life in India. One classification divides Indian dancing into three aspects-*Natya, Nritya* and *Nritta. Natya* corresponds to drama. *Nritya* is interpretative dance performed to the words sung in a musical melody. On the other hand, *nritta* signifies pure dance, where the body movements do not express any mood (*bhava*) nor convey any meaning. There is a rich variety of classical and folk dances in India. *Kuchipudi* (Andhra Pradesh), *Odissi* (Odisha), *Kathakali* (Kerala), *Mohiniattam* (Kerala), *Bharatnatyam* (Tamil Nadu), *Manipuri* (Manipur), *Kathak* (Uttar Pradesh) and *Chchau* (Orissa, West Bengal and Jharkhand) are some of the most notable dance forms in India. Besides, India has a rich tradition of folklores, legends and myths, which combine with songs and dances into composite art forms.

Theatre: While classical dance in India is linked to its 'divine origins', the origin of Indian theatre lies with the people. Bharat's *Natyashastra* is still the most complete guide to traditional Indian theatre. 'Modern Indian theatre' of recent times originated in three colonial cities— Kolkata, Mumbai and Chennai. It is strongly influenced by conventions and trends of European theatre. 'Traditional Indian theatre' includes distinct streams. This theatre remained confined to courts and temples and displayed a refined, carefully trained sensibility. In the second popular stream the spoken languages and dialects of different localities and regions were used. Theatre in India is usually staged in the post-harvest season when actors as well as spectators have free time. It is staged in open-air theatres. The narrative, often a myth already known to the audience, is enacted through dance, music, mimetic gesture and stylized choreography.

1.1.11. Significance of Geography on Indian Culture

The ancient civilization in India grew up in a sharply demarcated sub continent bounded on the north by the world's largest mountain range- the chain of the Himalayas, which , with its extensions to east and west, divides India from the rest of Asia and the world. The barrier, however, was at no time an insuperable one, and at all periods both settlers and traders have found their way over the high and desolate passes into India., while Indians have carried their commerce and culture beyond her frontiers by the same route. India's isolation has never been complete, and the effect of the mountain wall in developing her unique has often been over rated.

The importance of the mountains to India is not much in the isolation which they give her, as in the fact that they are the source of her two great rivers. The cloud drifting northwards and the westwards in the rainy seasons discharge the last of their moisture on the high peaks, whence, fed by ever-melting snow, innumerable streams flow southwards, to meet in the great river systems of the Indus and the Ganga. On their way they pass through small and fertile plateau, such as the valleys of the Kashmir and Nepal, to debouch on the great plain.

Of the two river systems, that of the Indus, now mainly in Pakistan, had the earliest civilization. And gave its name to India, as the Indian knew this river as *Sindhu*, and the Persians, who found difficulty in pronouncing as initial *s*, called it *Hindu*. From the Persia the word passed to Greece, where the whole of India became known by the name of the western river. The ancient Indians knew their subcontinent as Jambuidvipa or Bharatavarsa. With the Muslim invasion the Persian name returned in the form of Hindustan, and those of its inhabitants who followed the old religion became known as Hindu. Not only this, more than two thousand years before Christ the fertile plain of Punjab, the and of five rivers, watered by the five great tributaries of the Indus- such as the Jhelum, Chenab, Ravi, Beas and Satlaj- had a high culture, which spread as far as the sea and along the western seaboard at least as far as Gujrat. The lower Indus, in the region of Pakistan known as Sind, passes through barren desert, though this was once a well watered and fertile land.

The basin of the Indus is divided from that of the Ganga by the Thar, or desert of Rajasthan, and by low hills. The watershed, to the north-west of Delhi, has been the scene of many bitter battles since at least 1000 B.C. The western half of the Ganga plain, from the region around Delhi to Patna, and including the Doab, or the land between the Ganga and its great tributary river Yamuna, has always been the heart of India. Here , in the region once known as *Aryabarta,* the land of the Aryans, here classica culture was formed. Though generations of unscientific farming's, deforestation, and other factors have now much reduced its fertility, this was once among the most productive lands in the world, and it has supported a very large population ever since it was brought under the plough. As its mouth in Bengal the Ganga forms a large delta, which even in historical times has gained appreciably on the sea, here the Ganga joins the Brahmaputra, which flows from Tibet by way of the valley of Assam, the easternmost outpost of Hindu culture.

South of the great plain is a highland zone, rising to the chain of the Vindhyan mountains. These are by no means as impressive as the Himalayas, but have tended to form a barrier between the North and the South. The south as called as Deccan, is a dry and hilly plateau, bordered on either side by long range of hills, the western and Eastern Ghats. Of these two ranges of hills, the western is the higher, and therefore most of the rivers of the Deccan, such as the Mahanadi, the Godavari, the Krisna and the Kaveri, flow eastwards. Two large rivers only, the Narmada and the Tapti, flow westwards; near their mouths the Deccan rivers pass through plains which are smaller than that of the Ganga but almost as populous. The south-eastern part of the Peninsula forms a larger plain, the Tamil country, the culture of which was once independent, and is not yet completely unified with that of the North. The Dravidian peoples of Southern India still speak languages in no way skin to those of the North, and are of a different ethnic character. Though there has been much intermixing between Northern and Southern types. Geographically Ceylon is a continuation of India, the plain of the North resembling that of South India, and the mountains in the centre of the Island the Western Ghats.

From Kashmir in the North to Cape Comorin in the South the Sub-continent is about 2,000 miles long, and therefore its climate varies considerably. The Himalayan region has cold winters, with occasional frost and snow. In the northern plains the winter is cool, with wide variation of days and night temperature, whereas the hot seasons is almost intolerable. The temperature of the Deccan varies less with the season, though in the higher parts of the plateau nights are cool in winter. The Tamil Plains is continuously hot, but its temperature never rises to that of the northern plains in summer.

The most important features of the Indian climate is the monsoon, or the rains. Except along the west coast and in the parts of Ceylon little rains falls from October to May, when cultivation can only be carried on by carefully husbanding the water of rivers and stream, and raising a winter crop by irrigation. By the e4nd of April growth has practically ceased. The temperature of the plains rises as high as 45°C. or over, and an intensely not wind blows. Trees shed their leaves, grass is almost completely parched, and wild animals often die in large numbers for want of water. Works is reduced to a minimum, and the world seems asleep.

The, clouds appear, high in the sky, in a few days they grow more numerous and darker, rolling up in banks from the sea. At last, in June, the rains come in great down pouring torrents, with much thunder and lightning. The temperature quickly drops, and within a few days the world is green and smiling again, and the earth is covered with fresh grass. The torrential rains, which fall at intervals for a couple of months and then gradually die away, make travels and all outdoor activity difficult, and often bring epidemics in their wake, but, despite these hardships, to the Indian mind the coming of the monsoon corresponds to the coming of spring in Europe. For this reason thunder and lightning, in Europe generally looked on as inauspicious, have no terrors for the India, but are welcome signs of the goodness of heavens.

It has often said that the scales of natural phenomena in India, and her total dependence on the monsoon, have helped to form the character of her peoples. Even today major disasters, such as floods, famine and plague, are hard to check, and in old days their control was almost impossible. Many other ancient civilizations, such as those of Greeks, Romans and Chinese, had to contend with hard winters, which encouraged sturdiness and resource. India, on the other hand, was blessed by a bounteous nature, who demanded little of man in return for sustenance, but in her terrible anger could not be appeased by any human effort. Hence, it has been suggested that Indian character has tended to fatalism and quietism, accepting fortune and misfortune alike without complaint.

How far this judgment is a fair one is very dubious. Though an element of quietism certainly existed in the ancient Indian attitude to life, as it does in India today, it was never approved by moralist. The great achievements of ancient India, their immense irrigation works and splendid temples, and the long campaigns of their armies do not suggest a devitalized people. If the climate had any effect on the Indian character it was, we believe, to develop a love of ease and comfort, an addiction to the simple pleasure and luxuries so freely given by nature, a tendency to which the impulse to self-denial and asceticism on the one hand, and occasional strenuous effort on the other, were natural reactions.

Thus, although India was isolated largely by the geographical features and different climatic zone, yet her vast dimensions, variety of racial elements, wide differences of climate, great diversities of soils and different physical characteristics not only prevented her from being a stagnant pool but gave it a continental character. It enabled her to generate the forces of action and reaction which led to the development of rich civilization and culture.

1.1.12. Summary

- Culture has been derived from Latin term 'Cult' or 'Cultus' meaning tilling or refining.
- Sanskriti' is derived from Sanskrit root 'Kri' meaning to do. Culture may be defined as the way an individual and especially a group live, think, feel and organize themselves, celebrate and share life.
- Culture has different characteristics. It can be acquired, lost or shared. It is cumulative. It is dynamic, diverse and gives us a range of permissible behaviour-pattern. It can change. Culture includes both material and non-material components.
- In deeper sense it is culture that produces the kind of literature, music, dance, sculpture, architecture and various other art forms as well as the many organizations and structures that make the functioning of the society smooth and well-ordered.
- Culture provides us with ideas, ideals and values to lead a decent life.
- Self restraints in conduct, consideration for the feelings of others and for the rights of others, are the highest marks of culture.
- A cultural heritage means all the aspects or values of culture transmitted to human beings by their ancestors to the next generation.
- Architectural creations, monuments, material artifacts, the intellectual achievements, philosophy, pleasure of

knowledge, scientific inventions and discoveries are parts of heritage.

- Indian culture is characterised with the famous notion of unity in diversity and show continuity and adaptability with times.
- The geographical location and the physiographic division of India created an isolated condition for the country. The various physical features of the country and the strategic location immensely help the Indian culture.

1.1.13. Exercises

1. Discuss different aspects of Indian culture.
2. Discuss the concept of Unity and diversity in Indian Culture.
3. Explain the salient features of traditional Indian culture.
4. How will you define the concept of culture?
5. What are the general characteristics of culture?
6. What is cultural heritage?
7. What is culture? Discuss it.
8. Write a note on significance of geography on Indian culture.

1.1.14. Further readings

1. Gore, M. S., *Unity in Diversity: The Indian Experience in Nation-Building,* Rawat Publication, Jaipur, 2002.

2. Kabir, Humayun, *Our Heritage,* National Information and Publications Ltd., Mumbai, 1946.

3. Malik, S. C., *Understanding Indian Civilisation : A Framework of Enquiry,* Indian Institute of Advanced Study, Simla, 1975.

4. Mukerji, D. P., *Sociology of Indian Culture,* Rawat Publications, Jaipur, 1948/1979.

5. Pandey, Govind Chandra, *Foundations of Indian Culture,* Books and Books, New Delhi, 1984.

CHAPTER-II
SOCIETY IN INDIA THROUGH AGES

ANCIENT PERIOD- *VARNA AND JATI*, FAMILY AND MARRIAGE IN INDIA, POSITION OF WOMEN IN ANCIENT INDIA, CONTEMPORARY PERIOD; CASTE SYSTEM AND COMMUNALISM

Structure

1.2.0. Objective

In this lesson, students investigate society of India through ages. Throughout the chapter, stress will be on various aspects of Indian society from early days to present time. After completing this chapter, you will be able:

- *examine the structure of Indian society;*
- *describe the practice of untouchability which became prevalent in the Indian social system;*
- *give an account of the institution of slavery as it existed in India;*
- *understand Purushartha, Ashrama and Samskara;*

- *assess the role of family and marriage in Indian Social System;*
- *discuss issues like caste system, and various substance in it etc.;*
- *assess the position of women in the Indian social structure; and*
- *examine the different issue of Indian society in contemporary period such as caste system and communalism .*

1.2.1. Introduction

The study of Indian society necessitates that we try to understand the basic elements which provide the blueprint for thought and action. Indian society is extremely diverse in terms of societies, cultures and social behaviour. Sociologists, however, point to caste system as an organizing principle of Indian society. It is seen to be providing the basic frame around which relationships across groups are organized. Legitimacy for the caste divisions is derived from Hinduism the great religion of the Indian continent.

The Indian society has evolved through the ages and advancements have taken place in diverse fields. You have also read in earlier lessons about social reforms in the Indian society. However, in every society there are socio-cultural issues that need to be addressed and tackled. Security of people, particularly of the vulnerable sections, such as women, children and the elderly people is a major concern in the contemporary Indian society. In this lesson, we will read about the major socio-cultural issues that need our immediate attention, if we have to preserve our social and cultural values. Some of the important socio-cultural issues that need to be addressed today are casteism, and communalism etc. The issues discussed here are not comprehensive. There are many other issues faced by the nation in general and regions and communities in particular, that all of us should think about.

Sociologists, however, also point out that earlier social science understandings were derived from great Hindu texts that these act as the guiding principles for social behaviour. The contextual realities vary a great deal. In the first section we discuss the blueprint for social organization of Indian society i.e. varna system, belief system and its relevance in understanding the system and subsequently this chapter also discuss the growth of communalism in India and other contemporary issue of Indian society.

1.2.2. Varna System

In the Indian social system, Varna is only a reference category and not a functioning unit of social structure, and only refers broadly to the ascribed status of different *jatis*. It is also a classificatory device. In it, several *jatis* with similar ascribed ritual status are clustered together and are hierarchically graded. The three upper levels-the Brahman, the Kshatriya, and the Vaishya- are considered twice-born, as in addition to biological birth they are born a second time after initiation rites. The Sudra, the fourth level, includes a multiplicity of artisans and occupationally-specialized jatis who pursue clean, i.e. non-polluting occupations. Though the Varna hierarchy ends here, but there is a fifth level which accommodates those following supposedly unclean occupations that are believed to be polluting. They are *Antyaja,* i.e., outside the Varna system. They constitute what are known as the Dalit.

1.2.2.1. Origin of the Varna

There are several passages in the oldest Vedic literature dealing with the origin of the varnas. The four orders of society are believed to have originated from the selfsacrifice of *Purusha*-the creator, the primeval being. *Purusha* is said to have destroyed himelf so that an appropriate social order could emerge. The oldest is the hymn in the *purusha-sakta* of the Rig-Veda which says that the Brahmana Varna represented the mouth of the purusha,- which word may be translated as the "the Universal Man", referring perhaps to mankind as a whole, - the Rajanya (i.e. Kshatriya) his arms, the Vaisya his thighs and the Sudra his feet.

But it has been shown that there are other passages, apart from the Purusha-Sukta, in which the division of society into Varnas, though not in the rigid form of later times, is mentioned. Thus, in Rig-Veda, the three varnas, the Brahma, Kshatam, and Visah are mentioned; while in Rig-Veda, the four varnas are referred to thus: "One to high sway (i.e. Brahmana), one to exalted glory (i.e. the Kshatriya), one to pursue his gain (i.e. the Valsya) and one to his labour (i.e. the Sudra),- all to regard their different vocations, all moving creatures hath the Dawn awakened. The original parts of the Vedas do not know the system of caste. But this conclusion was prematurely arrived at without sufficiently weighing the evidence. It is true that caste system is not to be found in such a developed state; the duties assigned to the several castes are not so clearly defined as in the law books and Puranas. But nevertheless the system is already known in the earlier parts of the Vedas, or rather presupposes. The barriers only were not as insurmountable as in later times.

S.C. Dube gives the Triguna theory of the origin of the Varna system i.e. the philosophic speculation of ancient India identified three *gunas*-inherent qualities-in human beings, animate and inanimate objects, and in human actions: *sattva, rajas,* and *tamas. Sattva* consisted of noble thoughts and deeds, goodness and virtue, truth and wisdom. *Rajas*, on the other hand, were characterized by high-living and luxury, passion and some indulgence, pride, and valour. At the bottom was *tamas*, with the attributes of coarseness and dullness, overindulgence without taste, the capacity to carry out heavy work without much imagination. Those with *sattvic* qualities were classified as Brahman, those with *rajasic* as Kshatriya and Vaishya, and those with *tamsic* qualities as Sudra. Another third theory takes account of ethnic admixture, culture contact, and functional specialization. Any of these three components cannot singly explain the origin of the Varna. In the initial stage of the evolution of Hindu society-the Vedic stage-race and complexion were important factors, but in its fully evolved form it was only a make-believe phenomenon, not a biological reality.

Aryanization was the result of culture contact, but it was not a one-way process involving donor-recipient relations. The Vratya pre-Aryan traditions asserted themselves and in the process modified the Aryan scheme of social organization, rituals, beliefs, world-view, and its ethos. Groups were incorporated *en masse* into the emerging social order, adopting some new features, retaining some old characteristics, and imparting their imprint on the wider society. Reverting to the *Purusha-Sakta*, an allegorical meaning is by the whole *sakta* with reference to the *Purusha* and the creation of varnas from his limbs. The *Purusha* is described as being himself "this whole universe, whatever has been and whatever shall be" Further, we are also told that the moon sprang from his mind (*manas*), the Sun from his eyes, Indra and Agni were created out of his mouth, and air or wind from his breath. Again, from his navel arose the atmosphere (*antarikshum*), from his head the sky, from his feet the earth (*bhumi*), and from his ear the four quarters (*disah*); in this manner, the worlds were created. There is a great deal of theorizing in the Epic and the Dharma-Sastra literature on the problem of the origin and development of varnas; There were no distinct castes or classes of men in the *Krita* Yuga, according to the Mahabharata At another place, the sage Bhrigu says that only a few Brahmanas were first created by the great Brahman. But later on, the four divisions of mankind Brahmana, Kshatriya, Vaisya and Sudra developed. The complexion (*varnah*) of the Brahmanas was white (*sita*) that of Kshatriyas red (*lohitah*), that of the Viasyas yellow (*pitakah*), and that of the Sudras black (*asitah*) - thus does the rishi Bhrigu explain his theory of the origin of the varnas to Bharadwaja.

At first the whole world consisted of Brahmanas. Created equally by Brahman, men have, on account of their acts, been divided into various varnas. The theory goes on to explain how the four varnas and other castes (*jatayah*) arose out of the one original class of Dvijas (twice-born). Those who found excessive pleasure in enjoyment became possessed of the attributes of harshness and anger; endowed with courage, and unmindful of their own dharma, (*tyakta-sva-dharmah*), those Dvijas possessing the quality of redness (*raktangah*), became Kshatriyas. Those again, who, unmindful of the duties laid down for them, became endued with both the qualities of Redness and Darkness *(pitah)* and followed the occupations of cattle breeding and agriculture, became Vaisyas. Those Dvijas, again, who were given to untruth and injuring other creatures, possessed of cupidity (*lubdhah*), who indiscriminately followed all sorts of occupations for their maintenance (*sarva- karmo'pa -jivinah*), who had no purity of behaviour (*saucha-paribhrashtah*), and who thus, nursed within them the quality of Darkness (*krishnah*) Became sudras. Thus "divided by there occupations,the Dvijas, (who were, in the first instance, all Brahmanas) due to falling away from the duties of their own order, became members of the other three varnas. None of them, therefore, is prohibited from carrying out all the activities of dharmas and yajnas. Further, those who, through their ignorance, fell away from their prescribed duties and led a loose life (svachchandacharacheshtitah), endied in reducing themselves to the various lower castes (jatayah), viz. the Pisachas (feinds), the Raksasas (globilins), the Pretas (the evil-spirited), and the various mlechchha (barbarian or outcast)jatis (castes).

The theory that the four varnas proceeded from the limbs of the creator is also held by Manu-Smriti. And, in order to protect this whole universe (*sarvasya)*, differential duties and occupations have been assigned to the different varnas (prithak-karmani) by him. Manu then goes on to eulogise the Brahmana varna as the supreme creation of God. He further positively asserts that the Brahmana, Kshatriya, Vaisya and sudra are the only varnas in existence; there is no fifth varna; and with this, Yajnavalkya, Baudhayana and Vasishtha also agree.

Manu's theory of the origin of mixed castes is, in certain respects, different from that of the Mahabharata. Sons begotten by twice-born men (dvijas, i.e. Brahmanas, Kshatriyas and Vaisyas) of wives from the immediate lower class belong no doubt to the varna of their fathers respectively but they are censured on account of the fauly inherent in their mothers (*matri-dosha*). Such is the traditional (*sanatana*) law (*vidhih)* applicable to children of a wife from a varna only one degree lower than her husband's. The real mixture of varnas (varnas-samkarah) therefore arises with offsprings born of a woman two or three degrees lower. Thus the son born of a Brahmana father and a Vaisya mother would be called an Ambashtha; that born of a Brahmana father and a sudra mother would be called Nishada, and so on. The mixture of *varnas* takes place in other ways also. Of a Kshatriya father and Brahmana mother spring issues belonging to the Suta caste; children born of a Vaisya father and Kshatriya mother or a Brahmana mother belong to Magadha and Videha castes respectively; and so on And, inter- marriages between these new castes give rise to newer and newer castes, so that the process goes on multiplying. Here in this sloka, Manu has used the word *Jati* as distinct from *varna*. This sloka opens the topic concerning off springs begotten on a woman of higher *varna* by a man of lower varna. Thus, the Suta, the Magadha and the Vaideha are so named according to their "jati" (jatitah). And, in the next sloka, Manu also uses the term Varna-samkarah, mixture of varnas, in this connection. Though Manu refers to four *Varnas* only, he mentions about fifty seven *jatis*, as a result of *Varna-samkarah*.

1.2.2.2. Duties of the Varna

The division into four Varnas is here correlated to the duties of each Varna. Their origin is a symbolic representation of the rank and functions of the four *Varnas*. In the cultural body-image the head, the arms, the thighs, and the feet are ranked in descending order, so are the traditional functions.

The *Purusha-Sukta* has been interpreted as having an allegorical significance behind it from another point of view. Thus, the mouth of the *Purusha* from which the Brahmanas are created is the seat of speech; the Brahmanas therefore are created to be teachers and instructors of mankind. According to Manu, a Brahman should always and assiduously study the Veda alone and teach the Vedas. It is also the privilege of a Brahman to officiate as a priest and as a means of livelihood permitted to receive gifts from a worthy person of the three higher *varnas*. This is known as *pratigraha*. The arms are symbol of valour and strength; the Kshatriya's mission in this world is to carry weapons and protect people. Thus, defense and war, administration and government were the functions assigned to the Kshatriya. It is difficult to interpret that portion of the hymn which deals with the creation of the Vaisyas from the thighs of the Purusha. But the thigh may have been intended to represent the lower portion of the body, the portion which consumes food, and therefore the Vaisya may be said to be created to provide food to the people. Trade, commerce and agriculture were the work of the Vaishya. The creation of the Sudra from the foot symbolizes the fact that the Sudra is to be the "footman", the servant of other *varnas*. The Sudra ranked the lowest by serving others though crafts and labour.

The whole social organization is here conceived symbolically as one human being the "Body Social", we may say – with its limbs representing the social classes based on the principle of division of labour. The Mahabharata states the same thing thus: Our obeisance to That (*Purusha*) who consists of Brahmanas in the mouth, Kashtras in the arms, Vaishya in the entire regions, stomach and thighs, and Sudras in the feet.

1.2.2.3. Mobility of the Varnas

There seems to be a constant upward and downward social mobility between the different Varnas. Yajnavalkya speaks of two kinds of such mobility. When a lower Varna changed into a higher varna, it was known as *jatyutkarsa* or uplift of the caste. On the other hand, if a person belonging to a higher varna gradually descended into a lower Varna, it was known as *jatyapakarsa* or the degeneration of the caste. Provisions for both these processes of social mobility in stratification were laid by different Dharmasastras with minor distinctions about the conditions. It was particularly based upon two conditions, firstly, upon the following of the vocation of some other Varna for five to six generations and secondly, marrying into different Varnas for as much period. It may be easily guessed that in practice such mobility happened only in exception, since the process had to be covered for several generations, but it is clear that the Dharmasastras did prescribe change of Varnas by means of interaction between the Varnas both upwards and downwards. This can be through marriage and education.

While varna dharma had to be followed in normal circumstances, in abnormal circumstances the Dharmasastras prescribe what is known as *Apad* Dharma or that which is worthy of following in exceptional circumstances. Manu enumerate ten means of maintaining oneself in *apad*(distress) *viz,* learning, arts and crafts, work for wages, service i.e., carrying out another's orders, rearing cattle, sale of commodities, agriculture, contentment, alms, money-lending. Out of these some cannot be followed by Brahmin or a Kshatriya when there is no distress. The Dharmasastras maintained that Brahmins doing certain things are to be treated as Sudras. Without studying the Veda but works hard to master something else is quickly reduced to the status of a Sudra together with his family. Thus, *Apad* Dharma does not mean the license to do whatever one likes to do in the times of trouble. There are numerous cases of so many notable persons who refused to change their allotted duties even in the face of extremely adverse circumstance. Again, even when such a change was permitted, it was always looked down and never appreciated.

1.2.2.4. Ascending order of Responsibilities and Status

In the above mentioned fourfold classification of duties according to Dharmashastras, there was an ascending order of responsibilities. While Brahmin was given the highest position he was also entrusted with maximum responsibilities. The entire task of preserving Dharma was mainly the responsibility of the Brahmin. The next social status in Varna hierarchy was given to the Kshatriya as he had the responsibility of defending the nation in times of war and administering law and order in the society. He provided social justice with the help of the Brahmin scholar. The Vaishyas and Sudras had lesser responsibilities and therefore were assigned lower status. The Sudra gradually came to be so much looked down upon that he could not touch a Brahmin. The Sudra could not be initiated into the Vedic study and the only ashram out of the four that he was entitled to, was that of the householder.

The abovementioned descriptions are largely derived from what is called as the 'book view' of society that is from the great tradition or the scriptures. The ground situation or the 'field view' often does not correspond with these ideal notions and is quite flexible. The book view is also said represent the brahmanical view of society not largely adhered by the so-called 'lower castes.' In real life the operational categories are in fact not the varna but the jati or sub castes who do have their own interpretations of caste hierarchy.

1.2.3. Caste(or jati)

1.2.3.1. Definitions of Caste

Caste may be defined as a hereditary endogamous group which decides the individual's status in the social stratification and his profession. Caste is also defined as an aggregate of persons whose share of obligations and privileges is fixed by birth, sanctioned and supported by magic and or religion. Ketkar(1909) defines caste as a social group having two characteristics-memberships confirmed to those who are born of members and includes all persons so born and the members are forbidden by an inexorable social law to marry outside the group. Thus caste is a phenomena of social stratification and social restriction in Indian society, where there is no scope of inter-marriage and inter dinning between different caste.

1.2.3.2. Origin of Caste in India

According to G.S. Ghurye, caste in India is a Brahminic child of the Indo-Aryan culture, cradled in the land of the Ganges country. Abbe Dubbois first propounded the political theory of the origin of Caste in India. However, the complex social structure based upon castes appears impossible that the aim of caste system would have been to maintain the dominance of the Brahmin priests over Hindu society. The traditional theory attributes the origin of the caste system to the creator Brahma who created the four varnas. According to Hutton, the caste system originated in the religious customs and rituals of the non-Aryan group particularly the theory of Manu. The traditions of endogamy, untouchability etc. has their roots in Manu. According to Majumdar, caste system was developed to save Aryan Race and culture from intermixing with other races.

1.2.3.3. Characteristics of Caste

There are various characteristics which determine the caste of a person. These are given below:

Determination by birth : The membership of a caste is determined by birth. A person remains the member of a caste unto which they are born and this does not undergo change even if change takes place in his status, occupation, education, wealth, etc.

Rules and regulations concerning food : Each individual caste has its own laws which govern the food habits of its members. Generally, there are no restrictions against fruit, milk, butter, dry fruit, etc. but kachcha food (bread, etc.) can be accepted only from a member of one's own or of a higher caste.

Definite occupation : In the Hindu scriptures there are mention of the occupations of all varnas. According to Manu, the functions of the Brahmins, Kshatriyas, Vaishyas and the Sudras are definite. The function of the Brahmins is to study the Vedas, teach, guide and perform religious rituals, to give and receive alms. Sudras have to do menial work for all the other varnas. Having developed from the varna system, the occupations in caste system are definite.

Endogamous group : The majority of persons marry only within their own caste. Brahmins, Kshatriyas, Sudras and Vaishyas all marry within their respective castes. Westermarck has considered this to be a chief characteristic of the caste system. Hindu community does not sanctify inter-caste marriage even now.

Rules concerning status and touchability: The various castes in the Hindu social organization are divided into a hierarchy of ascent and descent one above the other. In this hierarchy the Brahmins have the highest and the untouchables the lowest place. This sense of superiority is much exaggerated and manifests in the south. The very touch and sometimes even the shadow of a member of the lower caste is enough to defile an individual of a high caste. The stringent observation of the system of untouchability has resulted in some low castes of the Hindu society being called 'untouchables' who were, consequently, forbidden to make use of places of worship,cremation grounds, educational institutions, public roads and hotels etc., and were disallowed from living in the cities.

1.2.3.4. Caste Structure and Kinship

Caste structure is intimately related to the kinship system amongst the Hindus in India. The sole reason for this relationship lies in the endogamous nature of caste system. Caste is basically a closed system of stratification, since members are recruited on the criteria of ascribed status. In other words, an individual becomes a member of a caste in which he or she is born. Thus it is an ascribed status. Even if there is social mobility in the caste system through the process of Sankritisation, urbanizations, etc it is only a positional change rather than a structural change.

A person remains the member of his/her caste irrespective of his/her individual status. Any movement in the structure occurs in the social mobility of the caste group in the local hierarchy of the society, which is only a shifting of its position from one level to another. Kinship is a method or a system by which individuals as members of society relate themselves with other individuals of that society. There are two types of kinship bonds. One is consanguinal and the other is affinal. Consanguinal ties are ties of blood such as, between mother-daughter, mother-son, father-daughter, etc. Affinal ties are ties through marriage, such as, between husband-wife, husband-wife's brother, etc.

Kinship in India is largely an analysis of the internal structure of the sub-caste. Subcaste is the largest segment of a caste and it performs nearly all the functions of caste like endogamy, social control, etc. For example, the Brahmin caste has several subcastes like endogamy, social control, etc. For example, the Brahmin caste has several sub-castes like the Gaur Brahmins, the Kanyakubjis, the Saraswat Brahmins, etc. It is these segments of the main caste of Brahmins which form the effective functioning group within which social interaction, marriage etc. takes place. However, these segments are also subdivided and have a regional connotation too, like the Sarjupari Brahmins of North India are those who originally lived beyond the river Saryu or Ghaghara.

The effective caste group is the caste population of a single village while the effective sub caste group within which marriage and kinship takes place is composed of the people belonging to the region around the village having several scores of settlements. Due to the practice of endogamy and restriction in social intercourse a person marries within the sub-caste group, or at the most caste group in India; which extends generally, beyond the village to a larger region. Kinship system found in various parts of India differs from each other in many respects. However, generally speaking, we can distinguish between the kinship system in the Northern region, the Central region and the southern region. North India is in it self a very large region, having innumerable types of kinship systems. This region includes the region between the Himalayas in the North and the Vindhyas in the South. In this region a person marries outside the village since all the members of one's caste in a village are considered to be brothers and sisters, or uncles and aunts. Marriage with a person inside the village is forbidden. In fact, an exogamous circle with a radius of four miles can be drawn round a man's village.

Hypergamy is practiced in this region according to which a man takes a wife from a clan, which is lower in status to his own clan. That is, a girl goes in marriage from a lower status group to a higher status group within a sub-caste. The effect of the hypergamy and village exogamy is that it spatially widens the range of ties. Several villages become linked to each other through affinal and matrilateral links.

The clans, lineages, and *kutumbs* are all part of the internal structure of the caste at the same time being part of the kinship organisation. These groups are all the time increasing and branching off with time. The organisation of family in the northern region is mainly patriarchal patrilineal and patrilocal. The lineage is traced through the male, i.e., patrilineal system is followed in this region. It is patriarchal because authority lies with the male head of the family and it is patrilocal because after marriage the bride is brought to reside in the father's house of the bride-groom. Generally, in most of the castes the "four-clan" rule of marriage is followed. Acording to this rule,

i) A man cannot marry in the clan to which his father (and he himself) belongs:

ii) To which his mother belongs;

iii) To which his father's mother belongs; and

iv) To which his mother's mother belongs

In the northern region, therefore, marriage with cousins, removed even by two or three degrees is viewed as an incestuous union. In most parts of the region, as mentioned earlier, village exogamy is practiced by most of the castes, especially the Brahmin, kshatriya and Vaishya castes. This rule is known in Delhi, Haryana and Punjab, as the rule of *Sassan*.

In Central India which includes Rajputana the Vindhyas, Gujrat, Maharashr and Odisha we find the general practice of caste endogamy. Hypergmy is most characteristic of the Rajputs of this region and village exogamy is also found in this region. However, in this region especially in Gujarat and Maharashtra amongst some caste communities we find cross-cousin marriages being practised. Here there is a tendency for a man to marry his mother's brother's daughter. But marriage with the father's sister's daughter is taboo. The preference for a single type of cross-cousin marriage seems to move away from the taboo of marrying cousins of any class in the northern region. Thus, in many ways this preference suggests a closer contact with the practices of the southern region.

The southern region comprises states like Karnatak, Andhra Pradesh, Tamil Nadu and Kerala where the Dravidian languages are spoken. This region is distinct from the northern and central regions of India in the sense that here we find basically preferential rules of marriage. Here a man knows whom he has to marry while in most areas in the north a man knows whom he cannot marry.

Most of the parts of the Southern region except some, like the Malabar, follow the patrilineal family system. Here also we find exogamous social groups called *gotras.* The difference between the exogamous clans in the north is that a caste in a village is held to be of one patriclan and therefore, no marriage is allowed within a village. Sometimes even a group of villages are supposed to be settled by one patrilineage and marriage between them is prohibited.

In the South, there is no identification of a *gotra* with one village or territory. More than one inter-marrying clans may live in one village territory and practice intermarriage for generations. Thus the social groups; which are formed due to this kind of marriage pattern in the South shows a centripetal tendency (of moving towards a centre) as against the centrifugal (of moving away from the centre) tendency of social groups found in north Indian villages. In the South, a caste is divided in to a number of *gotras*. The first marriage creates obligations about giving and receiving daughters.

Hence, within exogamous clans, small endogamous circles are found to meet interfamily obligations and a number of reciprocal alliances are found in South Indian villages. Apart from castes, which are patrilineal in the southern region, we also find some castes, such as the Nayars of Malabar district who follow matrilineal system of kinship. Their household is made up of a woman, her sisters and brothers, her daughters and sons and her daughter's daughters and sons. Amongst them, property passes from the mother to the daughter. But the authority even in this system lies with the brother, who manages the property and takes care of his sister's children; Husbands only visit their-wives in this system. The Nayar matrilineal house is called a *Tharavad*. Nayar is a broad category of castes of which not all of them follow the same kinship system.

The relationship between the caste structure and the kinship system is so inter-twined that we cannot understand one without understanding the details of the other. In this section we have explained the regional variations found in the relationship between the caste structure and related kinship pattern.

1.2.3.5. Sub-Caste

A sub-caste is considered a smaller unit within a caste. In the village setting usually we find that there is only one sub-caste living there. A larger number of sub-castes indicate the late arrivals to a village. Thus for all practical purposes a sub-caste represents the caste in the village. In the wider setting of a region, however, we find many sub-castes. One example from Maharastra is of Kumbhar (potters). The subcaste is the smallest endogamous groups and it has some mechanisms like *panchayats* to regulate the behaviour of members in the traditional setting. In a village, the difference between caste and sub-caste does not come to the surface but in a region, the difference is visible. In the following section we shall discuss the ideal life course prescribed for Hindus in the scriptures.

1.2.3.6. Changes in the Caste System

Studies by historians like Romila Thapar, A.R. Desai, and M.N. Srinivas have shown that Indian society was never static. The main traditional avenues of social mobility were sanskritization, migration and religious conversion. Lower castes or tribes could move upward in the caste hierarchy through acquisition of wealth and political power. They could consequently claim higher caste status along with sanskritising their way of life, by emulating the life style and customs of higher caste.

Occupational association of caste has marginally changed in rural areas. Brahmins may still work as priest but they have also taken to agriculture. Landowning dominant castes belonging to both upper and middle rung of caste hierarchy generally work as supervisory farmers. Other non-landowning lower castes, including small and marginal peasants, work as wage labourers in agriculture. Artisan castes like carpenters and iron-smith continue with their traditional occupations. However, migration to urban areas has enabled individuals from all castes including untouchables to enter into non-traditional occupations in industry, trade and commerce and services.

Inter-caste marriage is almost non-existent in rural areas. Restrictions on food, drink and smoking continue but to a lesser degree because of the presence of tea stalls in villages patronized by nearly all the castes. The hold of untouchability has lessened and distinction in dress has become more a matter of income than caste affiliation. People migrate to cities and bring back money which has changed the traditional social structure. Caste has acquired an additional role in the operation of interests groups and association in politics since the introduction of representative parliament politics.

Thus, we find that caste has undergone adaptive changes. Its traditional features, i.e., connubial (matrimonial), commensal (eating together) and ritual, still prevail in rural areas. The core characteristics of the castes, which have affected the social relations, are still operative. However, the status quo of the intermediate and low castes has changed due to their acquiring political and economic power. The hegemony of the high castes has given way to differentiation of these statuses in some regions of India so that high castes do not necessarily occupy a higher class position or power.

1.2.3.7. Factors for Casteism

Casteism is partial or one-sided loyalty in favour of a particular caste. It is a blind group loyalty towards one's own caste or sub-caste which does not care for the interest of the other castes and seeks to realize the social, economic, political and other interests of its own group. The factors of casteism are as follows:

Sense of Caste Prestige : the most prominent cause of casteism is the desire of people belonging to a particular caste to enhance the prestige of their own caste. In order to achieve this objective every caste provides its members with all the possible privileges in order to raise their social status.

Endogamy or Marriage Restrictions : Under the caste system the restrictions that apply to marriage turn every caste into a monogamous group in which each individual looks upon himself as related in some way to all the others and for this reason the solidarity within caste group increases which in its turn encourages caste.

Urbanization : With the advent of urbanization it became possible for all caste to collect in large numbers in towns and cities.

Modernization : Modernization has lead to better communication and better means of transport which help in the spread of propaganda. This improvement has led to the establishment of intimate relationships between members of a caste who were previously separated because of distance. The feeling of casteism is also easily spread through the medium of newspapers, journals and the internet.

1.2.4. The Four Stages of Life

It is the *dharma* of a Hindu to pass through four different *ashram* (stages) in their life. The first Ashram is called *brahmacharya ashram* (the educational stage) from which the fourth Varna, Sudra and women of the first three *varna* are barred. It ends at marriage. The second stage of life is called the *grihasthashram*. During this a man rears a family, earns a living and performs his daily personal and social duties. After this a man gradually enters the third stage of life called the *vanaprashthashram*. During this stage the householder relinquishes his duties in the household, and devotes his time to religious pursuits. His links with his family are weakened. During this ashram a man retires into the forest with or without his wife leaving behind the householder's cares and duties. The final phase of Hindu's life begins with the stage known as the *sanyasashram*. In this stage one attempt to totally withdraw oneself from the world and its cares by going to the forest and spending the rest of life in pursuit of *moksha*. Like the Varna system, the *varnashram* is a model that is not compulsory but recommended.

1.2.4.1. Sanskaras

Since eternity man has strived to improve his own self. This realisation, unique only to mankind, has led him to think deeper about his physical, mental and spiritual well being. Towards this end, the Vedic seers prescribed a set of observances, known as Samskaras. The nearest English word for samskara is sacrament, related to the phrase 'rite of passage'. In the Oxford English Dictionary, sacrament is defined as a "religious ceremony or act regarded as an outward and visible sign of inward or spiritual grace." In classical Sanskrit literature texts, such as Raghuvamsha, Kumarsambhava, Abhijnan-Shakuntal, Hitopadesha and Manu Smruti, samskara is used to mean: education, cultivation, training, refinement, perfection, grammatical purity, polishing, embellishment, decoration, a purificatory rite, a sacred rite, consecration, sanctification, effect of past actions (karmas), merit of karmas, etc.

Purpose of Samskaras

Cultural: The variety of rites and rituals related to the samskaras help in the formation and development of personality. In the Parashar Smruti it is said, "Just as a picture is painted with various colors, so the character of a person is formed by undergoing various samskaras." Thus, the Hindu sages realised the need of consciously guiding and molding the character of individuals, instead of letting them grow in a haphazard manner.

Spiritual: According to the seers, samskaras impart a higher sanctity to life. Impurities associated with the material body are eradicated by performing samskaras. The whole body is consecrated and made a fit dwelling place for the atma. According to the Atri Smruti a man is born a Shudra; by performing the Upanayana Samskara he becomes a Dvija (twice born); by acquiring the Vedic lore he becomes a Vipra (an inspired poet);

and by realising Brahman (God) he becomes a Brahmin. The samskaras are a form of spiritual endeavor (sadhana) - an external discipline for internal spiritual edification. Thus, the entire life of a Hindu is one grand sacrament. The Isha Upanishad reveals that the final goal of the samskaras, by observing the rites and rituals is "to transcend the bondage of samsara and cross the ocean of death." To this we can add that after transcending the cycle of births and deaths, the atma attains Paramatma - the Lord Purushottam. Although the number of samskaras prescribed by various scriptures varies, we shall consider the sixteen that are a consensus among scholars:

Pre-natal Samskaras

Garbhadan (Conception)

'Garbha' means womb. 'Dan' means donation. In this the man places his seed in a woman. The Gruhyasutras and Smrutis advocate special conditions and observances for this, to ensure healthy and intelligent progeny. Procreation of children was regarded as necessary for paying off debts to the forefathers. Another reason for having progeny is given in the Taittiriya Upanishad. When the student ends his Vedic studies, he requests permission to leave from his teacher. The teacher then blesses him with some advice which he should imbibe for life. One of the commands is: **"Prajaatantu ma vyavyachchhetseehi..."** (Shikshavalli) "Do not terminate one's lineage - let it continue (by having children)."

Pumsavana (Engendering a male issue)

Pumsavana and Simantonayana (the third samskara) are only performed during the woman's first issue. Pumsavana is performed in the third or fourth month of pregnancy when the moon is in a male constellation, particularly the Tishyanakshatra. This symbolises a male child. Therefore the term pumsavana literally means 'male procreation'. Sushrut, the ancient rishi of Ayurveda, has described the procedure in his Sushruta Samhita: "Having pounded milk with any of these herbs - Sulakshmana, Batasurga, Sahadevi and Vishwadeva - one should instil three or four drops of juice in the right nostril of the pregnant woman. She should not spit out the juice."

Simantonayana (Hair-parting)

In Gujarati this is known as Khodo bharavo. In this, the husband parts the wife's hair. The religious significance of this samskara is to bring prosperity to the mother and long life to the unborn child. It also wards off evil influence. The physiological significance is interesting and advanced. Sushrut believed that the foetus's mind formed in the fifth month of pregnancy. Hence the mother is required to take the utmost care for delivering a healthy child. Stipulating the details, Sushrut enjoined the pregnant mother to avoid exertion of all kinds: refrain from sleeping during the day and keeping awake at night, and also avoid fear, purgatives, phlebotomy (blood letting by slicing veins) and postponing natural excretions.

Besides samskaras which affect the physical health of the foetus, ancient scriptures contain examples of learning samskaras imprinted on it. From the Mahabharat, we know that Arjun's son, Abhimanyu, learnt the secrets of battle strategy while in his mother's, Subhadra's, womb. The child-devotee Prahlad of the Shrimad Bhagvatam, learnt about the glory of Lord Narayan while in his mother's, Kayadhu's, womb. Just as a foetus can grasp good spiritual samskaras from the external world, the opposite is also true. It can definitely be affected by certain undesirable habits of the mother. Today we know that smoking, alcohol, certain medications and drugs have a detrimental effect on the foetus. The Varaha Smruti prohibits eating meat during pregnancy. Therefore, the Smrutis enjoined the husband to take every possible care to preserve the physical, mental and spiritual health of his pregnant wife. The Kalavidhan prohibits him from going abroad or to war, from building a new house and bathing in the sea.

Childhood Samskaras

Jatakarma (Birth rituals)

These rituals are performed at the birth of the child. It is believed that the moon has a special effect on the newly born. In addition, the constellation of the planets - nakshatras - also determine the degree of auspiciousness. If birth occurs during an inauspicious arrangement, the jatakarmas are performed to ward off their detrimental effects on the child. The father would also request the Brahmanishtha Satpurush for blessings.

Namkaran (Name-giving)

Based on the arrangement of the constellations at birth, the child is named on a day fixed by caste tradition. In the Hindu Dharma, the child is frequently named after an avatar, deity, sacred place or river, saint, etc., as a constant reminder of the sacred values for which that name represents. In the Swaminarayan Sampraday, the devotees approach Pramukh Swami Maharaj or the other senior sadhus to name their children.

Nishkrama (First outing)

In the third month the child is allowed agni (fire) and chandra (moon) darshan. In the fourth month he is taken out of the house for the first time, by the father or maternal uncle, to the mandir for the Lord's darshan **(7) Annaprashan (First feeding)** Feeding the child with solid food is the next important samskara. For a son this is done in even months - the 6th,

8th, 10th or 12th months. For a daughter this is done in odd months - 5th, 7th or 9th months. The food offered is cooked rice with ghee. Some sutras advocate honey to be mixed with this. By advocating this samskara, the wise sages accomplished two important considerations. First, the child is weaned away from the mother at a proper time. Second, it warns the mother to stop breast feeding the child. For, an uninformed mother, many out of love, continue breast feeding the child, without realising that she was not doing much good to herself or the child.

Chudakarma (Chaul) (Shaving of head)

This samskara involves shaving the head (of a son) in the 1st, 2nd, 3rd or 5th year, or when initiating him with the janoi (Upanayan). According to Sushrut, the significance of this, together with nail cutting, is to give delight, lightness, prosperity, courage and happiness (Chikitsasthan). Charak also voiced a similar opinion. In the Swaminarayan Sampraday, the son is first taken to Pramukh Swami Maharaj, or senior sadhus, who clip a tuft of hair. The remaining hair is shaved off shortly afterwards. A tuft of hair (shikha, chotli) is left in place at the top of the head for longevity. Sushrut points out its significance, "Inside the head, near the top, is the joint of a shira (artery) and a sandhi (critical juncture). There, in the eddy of hairs, is a vital spot called the adhipati (overlord). Any injury to this part causes sudden death" (Sharirsthan Ch. VI, 83). In the course of time, the shikha was regarded as a symbol of the Hindu Dharma and its removal came to be regarded as a grave sin (Laghu Harita IV).

Karnavedh (Piercing the earlobes)

The child's ear lobes are pierced either on the 12th or 16th day; or 6th, 7th or 8th month; or 1st, 3rd, 5th, 7th or 9th year. Sushrut reasoned, "The ears of a child should be pierced for protection (from diseases such as hydrocoele and hernia) and decoration (Sharirasthan, Chikitsasthan. One sutra says that a goldsmith should pierce the ears while Sushrut advocates a surgeon. For a boy, the right earlobe is pierced first and for a girl, the left. For boys today, this samskara is only prevalent in some states of India. In girls, this samskara has lost its religious

Educational Samskaras

Vidyarambh (Learning the alphabet)

This samskara is also known as Akshararambha, Aksharlekhan, Aksharavikaran and Aksharavishkaran. It is performed at the age of five and is necessary before commencing Vedic study -Vedarambh. After bathing, the child sits facing west, while the acharya (teacher) sits facing east. Saffron and rice are scattered on a silver plank. With a gold or silver pen the child is made to write letters on the rice. The following phrases are written: "Salutation to Ganesh, salutation to Sarasvati (goddess of knowledge), salutation to family deities and salutation to Narayan and Lakshmi." The child then writes, "Aum Namah Siddham". He then presents gifts to the acharya, such as a pagh and safo (head adornment of cloth). The acharya then blesses the child.

Upanayan (Yagnopavit) (Sacred thread initiation)

At the age of eight the son is initiated by the acharya with the sacred thread, known as janoi or yagnopavit. Amongst all the foregoing samskaras this is regarded as supreme. It is the dawn of a new life, hence dvija - twice born. The child enters studentship and a life of perfect discipline which involves brahmacharya (celibacy). He leaves the guardianship of his parents to be looked after by the acharya. This samskara is performed by Brahmins, Kshatriyas and Vaishyas, for both boys and girls. Therefore, both the boy and girl received training in discipline, truthful living and physical service. During the course of time this samskara ceased to be given to girls, who thus failed to be formally educated. Today, the tradition of education underlying this samskara has died out. Upanayan only functions to bestow dvijatva to the son.

Upa means 'near.' Nayan means 'to take (him) to,' i.e. to take the son to the teacher. Like the parents, the acharya will mold the student with love and patience into a man of character. He will inculcate in him the invaluable knowledge of the Vedas. This is the second meaning of Upanayan. Among all the cultural systems of the world, none have advocated such a lofty and stringent ideal for studentship than this Hindu samskara. If a student sincerely observes this samskara, he will turn into a successful scholar. Added to this, during this period, he receives from the acharya, a strong background for the householder's life he will later enter. Today, it is obviously not feasible to stay at the acharya's house. But the next best equivalent is to enter a chhatralay - boarding school. The discipline involved infuses in the student a fortitude generally not possible at home. Whereas students wear one janoi, householders could wear two; one for himself and one for his wife.

The three strings of the janoi denote the three gunas - sattva (reality), rajas (passion), and tamas (darkness). They also remind the wearer that he has to pay off the three debts he owes to the seers, ancestors and gods. The three strings are tied by a knot known as the brahmagranthi which symbolises Brahma (creator), Vishnu (sustainer) and Shiva (leveller). One important significance of wearing the janoi is that the wearer would be constantly aware of the different deities which the threads represented.

Therefore, he would be vigilant prior to any action not in accordance with the Dharma Shastras.

Vedarambh (Beginning Vedic study)

This samskara was not mentioned in the earliest lists of the Dharma Sutras, which instead listed the four Vedic vows - Ved Vrats. It seemed that though upanayan marked the beginning of education, it did not coincide with Vedic study. Therefore a separate samskara was felt necessary to initiate Vedic study. In this samskara, each student, according to his lineage, masters his own branch of the Vedas.

Keshant (Godaan) (Shaving the beard)

This samskara is included as one of the four Ved Vrats. When the other three faded, keshant itself became a separate samskara. 'Kesh' means hair and 'ant' means end. This samskara involves the first shaving of the beard by the student at the age of sixteen. It is also called Godaan because it involves gifting a cow to the acharya and gifts to the barber. Since the student now enters manhood he is required to be more vigilant over his impulses of youth. To remind him of his vow of brahmacharya, he is required to take the vow anew; to live in strict continence and austere discipline for one year.

Samavartan (End of Studentship)

This samskara is performed at the end of the brahmacharya phase - the end of studentship. 'Sama vartan' meant 'returning home from the house of the acharya. This involves a ritual sacrificial bath known as Awabhruth Snan. It is sacrificial because it marks the end of the long observance of brahmacharya. It is a ritual bath because it symbolises the crossing of the ocean of learning by the student-hence Vidyasnaatak - one who has crossed the ocean of learning. In Sanskrit literature, learning is compared to an ocean.

Before the bath, the student has to obtain permission from the acharya to end his studentship and give him guru-dakshina - tuition fees. Permission is necessary because it certifies the student as a person fit in learning, habit and character for a married life. Obviously the student is not in a position to pay fees. One Sutra describes the debt of the teacher as unpayable, "Even the earth containing the seven continents is not sufficient for the guru-dakshina." But the formality is a required courtesy and the acharya says, "My child, enough with money. I am satisfied with thy merits." He would elaborate with the impressive statements, known as Dikshant Pravachan, noted in the Taittiriya Upanishad. Those students who wished to remain as lifelong students observing brahmacharya would remain with the acharya. Today, this means accepting a spiritual guru – an Ekantik Satpurush and becoming a sadhu. The student thus bypasses the next two ashrams, to enter sannyas.

Marriage

Vivaha

This is the most important of all the Hindu Samskaras. The Smrutis laud the gruhastha (householder) ashram as the highest, for it is the central support of the other three ashrams. Manu enjoins, "Having spent the first quarter of one's life in the guru's house, the second quarter in one's own house with the wife, and the third quarter in the forest, one should take sannyas in the fourth, casting away every worldly tie." (Manu Smruti). By marriage an individual is able to achieve the four purusharths (endeavors) of life: dharma (righteousness), artha (wealth), kama (desire) and moksha (salvation). He is also able to pay off ancestral debt by having children. Procreation for children is also a primary purpose of marriage.

In addition to being a religious sacrament, Hindu marriage is also regarded as an important social institution. For developing a stable and ideal society, marriage has been regarded as an essential element in all cultures of the world. A society without loyal marital ties tends to degrade. It is said that promiscuity was one reason for the downfall of the Romans. By marriage, both an individual and society, while remaining within the moral norms, can progress together. Simultaneously it does not cause harm to others nor infringe upon one's independence.

Antyesthi (Death rites)

The rishis and Dharma Sutras were at a consensus regarding the final goal of life, which they enjoined in the four ashrams - stages of life. The stalwart poet Kalidas in his classic, Raghuvansha (1-8) stipulates: " *Shaishave abhyastavidyãnãm yauvane vishayaishinãm; Vãrdhakye munivruttinãm yogenãnte tanutyajãm.*" "One studies during childhood (brahmacharya ashram), fulfills his desires during youth (gruhastha ashram), renounces worldly activity for silent contemplation during old age (vanprastha ashram) and then endeavors for God-realisation, after which he leaves his body."

Antyeshti is the final samskara in a Hindu's life. Yajur Veda regards vivaha as the sixteenth samskara while Rig Veda considers antyeshti. Though performed after the death of a person by his relatives, it is of importance because the value of the next world is higher than that of the present. The final rituals are performed with meticulous care with the help of Brahmin priests.

Conclusion: Samskaras like ours have their parallels in the world's other religious denominations-baptism, confirmation, holy matrimony in Christianity; barmitzvahs, and circumcision in Judaism; navjot in Parsis; and circumcision in Islam. These have significance in their own way in the lives of the members of these religions. In the past the sixteen Hindu samskaras formed an integral part of Hindu life. Today, with the encroachment of modern living, especially in urban India, only a few of them have survived: chaul, upanayan, vivaha and antyeshti. Yet these samskaras, with their spiritual import, holistically 'samskarize' (edify) all aspects of an individual's life. Since each samskara ritual makes the individual the focus of the occasion, he/she is psychologically boosted. This strengthens the individual's self-esteem and enriches interaction with those around. The samskaras bring together family members, close relatives and friends, hence increase the cohesiveness of the family unit. Therein the unit harmonizes and strengthens the social structure. The consequence of this is a healthy society with a strong cultural identity which easily refines, boosts and perpetuates its traditional beliefs, customs, morals and values. This has been one of the key reasons for the Hindu Dharma withstanding the rigors and onslaughts of foreign incursions and upheavals through the ages. The ancient rishis and sages enjoined the sixteen samskaras for the eternal benefit of mankind through their direct experience with the Divine. They wove them as into the fabric of daily life of the Hindu. They are 'outward acts,' from pre-birth to postdeath, for inward or spiritual grace. Today, the key samskara which will determine the cohesion and perpetuation of Hindu traditions anywhere in the world is vivaha, if observed sincerely with its pristine and lofty sentiments.

1.2.4.2. Purushartha

The Hindu scriptures declare four goals in human life and they are called the *purushartha.* The term *purushartha* not only denotes what the objectives of life should be but it also means what the objectives of life are as the result of the psychological tendencies of the individual. The *purushartha* consists of dharma, *Artha, Kama* and *Moksha* in the same order.

First, every human being needs to obey the law of nature by strictly following dharma. Dharma is the stability of the society, the maintenance of social order, and the general welfare of mankind. And whatever conduces to the fulfillment of this purpose is called 'dharma'.

Artha is the acquisition of wealth, is regarded as the primary purpose of life, as without it, human existence is impossible. One has to live before one can live well. *Artha* is the foundation upon which the whole structure of life has been built and all the other purushrtha-s can be achieved only by the fulfillment of this primary purpose in life. The acquisition of wealth is through *dharmic* actions and wealth needs to be used in the preservation of dharma.

Kama means desires, desires of varying degrees. It is from dharma that artha and kama result. Man recognises here that *artha* and *kama* satisfy the psychological tendencies of man and they form essentially the two fundamental aspirations of every individual. It is implied what one desires need to be within the threshold of one's wealth and within dharmic values.

Now the word *moksha* means the ultimate freedom from birth and death or the deliverance of the soul from bondage. From the *advaitic* point of view, *moksha* results from the extinction of false knowledge (ignorance). The self-knowledge is the aim and end of man's misery and bondage. In support of the realization of Self, the Upanishads outline several additional explanations. The universe has the natural tendency to guide the realization by the human soul. The natural forces of the universe maintain the balance between the material objects, living plants, conscious animals, and intelligent human beings. The transition from human consciousness into divine (transcendental) consciousness is a long and laborious process. Ordinarily, within the span of a single lifetime, it is not feasible to transit from human to divine. Life is a continuous journey, carried over and continued through the succeeding lives till the attainment of Self realization.

Thus, for the Hindu, the individual's relations with the ultimate principle of the Universal or Primal Cause defines his relations with other men, with his family, with the group or society in which he lives or with which he comes in contact, with his village and his country;-and, indeed, with the entire animate and inanimate creation. The whole of the life of an individual is, for the Hindu, a kind of schooling and self discipline. Now, during the course of this schooling and self discipline, he has to pass through four stages,-four grades of training, as it were-called the *Ashrams.* And, in regard to the *Ashrams,* too, every item and stage and phase has to be defined in terms of the already defined relations between man and God. Here, therefore, practically we start with supernatural basis; upon this we erect the superstructure of man's earthly career. The earthly existence has thus to be defined primarily in terms of dharma; and dharma has to be interpreted in the concrete in terms of karma. The *ashram* scheme, therefore, defines our dharma in and through a life of worldliness, of *samsara,* before it, and beyond its pale; and, in practice it seeks to delineate the implications of dharma in terms of karma. This scheme of transition from one stage to another is prescribed for men of upper castes only, women are supposed to help and support their husbands in proper fulfillment of these goals.

In the opinion of Manu, the good of humanity lies in a harmonious management or co-ordination of the three (*trivarga*), viz, *dharma, artha* and *kama.* Says he: " some declare that the good of man consists in dharma, and *artha*; others opine that it is to be found in *kama* and *artha;* some say that dharma alone will give it; while the rest assert that *artha* alone is the chief good of man here below(on earth). But the correct position is that the good of man consists in the harmonious co-ordination of the three". Thus, on the whole, the *purusharthas* are concerned both with the individual as well as the group. They enunciate and justify the kinds of relation between the individual and the group; they define the just relations between activities of the individual and those of the group; they also state explicitly and by implication, the improper relations between the individual and the group with a view to enabling the individual to avoid them. Thus, the *purushartha* control both the individual and the group, and also their-relations.

Here, it is to be remembered that when we refer to *artha* and *kama* as *purusharthas,* we refer to them in their proper proportions, that is to say, only in the best sense of these words. *Artha* refers to the problem and activities connected with the finding, making, gathering, conserving and organizing of the material necessities of life and all that accompanies the same. Similarly, *kama* refers to the sex and the reproductive aspect, its understanding, its right functions, its functioning, its organization and management both with reference to the individual and the group. As we have pointed out above, *Kama* in the wider sense refers to all the innate desires and urges of man.

Dharma seems to be the arbiter, the conscience keeper, the director, the interpreter, of the properties that govern the right functioning and management of the relations between the inner man and the outer man and between the individual and the group. Dharma is, therefore, the holder of the balance in terms of which *artha* and *kama* have to be dealt with weighed, practiced and apportioned. *Moksha,* on the other hand, seems to be concerned mainly with the individual. It refers, perhaps, to the appeal of the inner man to the individual, unaffected by the group. It is perhaps too personal an outlook that defines the struggle and hope and justification within the individual for *moksha* . But, from the Hindu's point of view, we must also remember, that the inner personality of the individual, at its best, is identified by him not only with the group, nor only with the society, nor with the nation, nor the race, nor even with he entire human race, but with the whole creation, animate and inanimate, seen and unseen, which includes all these and is still much more than all these. In the light of these considerations, the goal of *moksha* does not possess the narrow individual outlook, for the Hindu nor is it to be pursued exclusively and directly by an individual unless and until he has duly satisfied all his social debts (*rinah*) or obligations.

1.2.5. Family in India

The traditional Indian family is a large kinship group commonly described as joint family. A joint family is one in which two or more generations live under one roof or different roofs having a common hearth. All the members own the immovable property of the line in common. This family is generally patriarchal and patrilineal, that is, the father or the oldest male member is the head of the house and administrator of the property and the headship descends in the male line. In modern towns a large number of nuclear families exist which consist of wife, husband and the children. Such families are also partiarchal and patrilineal. But there are many regions where families are matrilineal in which the headship descends in the female line such as in Kerala and the northeastern region of Nagaland and Meghalaya. Whatever be the nature of the family it is the primary unit of the society. The members of the family are bound together by *'shraddha'*, the rite of commemorating the ancestors. *'Shraddha'* defined the family; those who were entitled to participate in the ceremony were *'sapindas'*, members of the family group. The bond between the members of the family gave a sense of social security to its members. In distress a man could rely on the other members of the extended family. At the time of festivals and marriages, the responsibilities were shared reinforcing the family bond. Traditionally the family in India is governed by two schools of sacred law and customs. These are based on *'Mitakshara'* and *'Dayabhaga'*. Most families of Bengal and Assam follow the rules of *'Dayabhaga'* while the rest of India generally follows *'Mitakshara'*. The sacred law made provisions for the break-up of the very large and unmanageable joint families. Such break-ups took place on the death of the patriarch. The joint family property did not include individual properties of the members at least from medieval times onwards and hence such properties could not be divided. In the post-independence period the Constitution provided that each religious community would be governed by their religious personal laws in marters of marriage, divorce, inheritance, succession adoption, guardianship, custody of children and maintenance. Thus, the Hindu, Buddhist, Sikh and Jain communities are governed by the codified Hindu Acts of 1955-56. The Muslim and Christian and Parsi families have their own set of personal laws based on religion.

Joint family is a group of kins of several generations, ruled by a head, in which there is joint residence, hearth and property and whose members are bound with each other by mutual obligations. The chief characteristics of joint family are common residence, common kitchen, joint property, common worship, rule of the *pater familia* and consciousness of mutual obligation among family members. Joint family has been viewed as one of the enduring units of the Indian society which has been undergoing change over time.

According to I. Karve, "A joint family is a group of people who generally live under one roof, who eat food cooked at one hearth, who hold property in common and who participate in common worship and are related to each other as some particular type of kindred." Not only parents and children, brothers and step-brothers live on the common property, but it may, sometimes, include ascendants, descendants and collaterals up to many generations.

A joint family may consist of members related lineally or collaterally or both. A family is essentially defined as "joint" only if it includes two or more related married couples who may be related lineally (as in a father-son relationship or occasionally in a father-daughter relationship), or collaterally (as in a brother-sister relationship). Both these types refer to the compositional aspect of the patrilineal joint family. In matrilineal systems, found in south west and north east India, the family is usually composed of a woman, her mother and her married and unmarried daughters. The mother's brother is also an important member of the family; he is the manager of the matrilineal joint family affairs. The husbands of the female members live with them. In Kerala, a husband used to be frequent visitor to the wife's household and he lived in his mother's household.

1.2.5.1. Characteristics of a joint family

The characteristics of a joint family are as follows:

Commensality: The joint family is characterized by a common hearth; members cook and eat food from the same kitchen.

Common Residence: Members of a joint family have not only the same hearth but share the same dwelling place.

Joint Ownership of Property: Members of a joint family have joint ownership of property and this may be regarded as the most crucial factor in legal terms for the characteristic of a joint family.

Cooperation and Sentiment: In a joint family, the ownership, production and consumption of wealth take place on a joint basis. It is a cooperative institution, similar to a joint stock company in which there is a joint property, and the head of the joint family is like a trustee who manages the property of the family with a view to deriving material and spiritual benefit for the members of the family. I.P. Desai (1964) and K.M. Kapadia (1958) point out that jointness should be looked in functional terms. A functionally joint family lays stress on fulfillment of obligations towards kin. They identify themselves as members of a particular 'family', cooperate in rituals and ceremonies, render financial and other kinds of help; and they cherish a common family sentiment and abide by the norms of joint living.

Ritual Bonds: The ritual bonds of a joint family are considered to be important component of jointness. A joint family, thus, is bound together by periodic propitiation of the dead ancestors. The members perform a '*shraddha*' ceremony in which the senior male member of the joint family propitiates his dead father's or mother's spirit, offering it the '*pinda*' (ball of cooked rice) on behalf of all the members.

Common deity Worship : Another ritual bond among joint family members can be common deity worship. In many parts of South India, each joint family has a tradition of worshipping a particular clan or village deity. Vows are made to this deity in times of joy and trouble. The first tonsure, donning of the sacred thread, marriages etc. are celebrated in or near the deity's temple.

1.2.5.2. Advantages of the joint family

The advantages of the joint family are as follows:

Economic advantage : The joint family system has several economic advantages. It prevents property from being divided. Land is being protected from extreme subdivision and fragmentation. The joint family also assists in economic production where the male members do such work as furrowing, sowing and irrigation while the women assist at the harvest, children graze the cattle, collect fuel and manure. The cooperation of all members helps to save money which would otherwise be paid to a labourer.

Protection of members: the joint family can provide assistance to not only the children but to the old, insane, the widows and helpless. The joint family is capable of providing assistance at times of pregnancy, sickness etc. If a person dies, his wife and children are looked after by the other members of the joint family, and their honour, wealth, and prosperity are protected collectively.

Development of personality : In a joint family the members are able to develop the ideal qualities of a person. The elders care for the children and see to it that they do not engage in undesirable and antisocial behaviours.

Co-operation and Economy : the joint family fosters co-operation and economy to an extent achieved by few, if any, other institution. A sense of cultural unity and an associational feeling exists among the members. There can also be much economy in expenditure.

Socialism in wealth: according to Sir Henry Maine, the joint family is like a corporation the trustee of which is the head of the family. Everyone in the family works according to his capacity but obtains according to his need and in this way achieves the socialistic order from each according to his ability, to each according to his needs.

1.2.5.3. Changes in the joint family

In recent past the joint family has undergone various changes. This can be attributed to the following factors:

Economic Factors: Monetisation (the introduction of cash transactions), diversification of occupational opportunities for employment in varied spheres, technological advancements (in communication and transport) are some of the major economic factors, which have affected the joint family system in India. With the opening of employment in government services and the monetization people left their traditional occupation and moved to cities or towns where jobs are available. Thus they break away from their ancestral place taking their wives and children with them. Since independence opportunities for and diversification of occupations have increased. With a constitutional commitment to promote equality between the sexes, women are being emerged into varied kinds of occupation and role relationships are changed which affects the joint family.

Educational Factors: With the coming of the British opportunity for higher education emerged in which all castes and community had access to the facilities provided by them. Some educated people began to question the Hindu customs and practices relating to child marriage, denial of rights of education to women, property rights, and ill treatment of widows. Marriage for both women and men were desired at a much later age by the educated and this affects the nature of the joint family.

Legal Factors: Legislations regarding employment, education, marriage, and property have affected the family system in many ways. Labour laws, Child Marriage Restraint Act and the Hindu Succession Act affected the joint family in a great way.

Urbanisation: The process of urbanization has also affected the pattern of family life in India. There is a shift from agricultural to non-agricultural occupations. Population pressure on land, education and the prospects for better jobs, medical care and better means of living has led to the migration from rural to urban areas which has affected the joint family.

Changing gender equations: Over last one century gender equations have witnessed major shifts. Traditional joint families had little space for women's autonomy. Women had to bear the brunt of maintaining household work as well as social relations. With expanding horizons of women's education and employment women especially from upper caste families have entered the public sphere with little time for household work and investment in interpersonal relations. Smaller family size also contributes to this phenomenon.

Though the joint family system has seen various changes K.M. Kapadia (1972) has observed that those who migrated to the cities still retain their bonds with their joint family in the village and town. They families may set up residence separately but still retain their kinship orientation and joint family ethic. This is evident in the performance of certain role obligations which include physical and financial assistance to kin members. The industrialization has served to strengthen the joint family because an economic base has been provided to support it or because more hands are needed in a renewed family enterprise or because kin can help one another in striving for upward mobility. Thus, the joint family may seem to be breaking up but it still retains a bond between its members among certain kin groups.

1.2.6. The Marriage in India

Marriage is one of the most fundamental and ancient social institutions. From times immemorial, it has been maintaining order and discipline in human society. Its form, nature and process vary from society to society. Irrespective of these differences this institution has several universally common elements and functions. According to Edward Westermarck, Marriage is a "relation of one or more men to one or more women, which is recognised by custom or law and involves certain rights and duties both in case of parties entering the union and in case of the children born of it." In its essence, it refers to a set of rules and regulations, which determines, who will marry whom, how the marriage union will be established under what conditions and when marriage will take place, what will be the rights and duties of the persons entering into such union and finally how the union will be dissolved. It fulfils the physical, social, psychological and spiritual aims and objectives of both the wife and the husband. Marriage is a socially recognised and normatively prescribed relationship between at least two persons-one female and other male- that defines and estabilishes sexual, economic and other rights and duties which each owes to the other. Marriage gives social and legal recognition to woman and man as wife and husband and their relationship. The children born out of marital relationship are recognised as legitimate children in society. In India different socio-religious and cultural groups have their own traditional concepts, norms and customs of marriage. Let us see some of the most notable forms:

1.2.6.1. Hindu Marriage in India

A distinction has to be made of the book view and field view of marriage. The marriage system of Hindu community has a uniqueness of its own which makes it distinct from other communities. Hindu marriage is not merely a union between a female and a male which is sanctioned by society.

Alongwith the social sanction, it has a religious and divine aspect. What is more important in Hindu marriage is that it is a sacred bond, a religious sacrament. Its aim is not only to secure physical pleasure for the individuals but also to advance their spiritual development. K.M. Kapadia says that—"Hindu marriage is a socially approved union of man and woman aiming at *dharma*, procreation, sexual pleasure and observance of certain obligations." According to P.H.Prabhu the primary object of marriage is the continuity of the family life. Marriage binds the wife and the husband into an indissoluble bond which lasts beyond death. Sociologists have noted the relative stability of marriage relationship in India.

1.2.6.2. Aims of Hindu Marriage

Sociologists and Indologists have discussed about the following aims of Hindu marriage in India.

(1) As a sacrament Hindu marriage aims to fulfil certain religious obligations. During the course of marriage the wife and the husband take an oath to live together. A traditional Hindu passes through four *Ashramas* or stages of life called *Brahamacharya* (student life), *Grihastha*, (family life), *Vanaprastha* (retired life) and *Sannyasa* (renunciation). At the commencemnt of each such *Ashrama*, a Hindu undergoes a sacrament and takes a vow. As a result of this, one becomes purified in body and mind. Marriage is a gateway to *Grihastha Ashrama*.

(2) It is very essential for a Hindu to be married for the fulfilment of religious duties like *dharma* (practice of religion), *praja* (procreation) and *rati* (sexual pleasure). The foremost purpose of Hindu marriage is to practice *dharma* in accordance with '*varna*', '*jati*' and '*kula*' norms.

(3) The Hindus consider *vivah* or marriage as one of the *Samskara* or sacraments sanctifying the body. It is doubly essential for a woman because marriage is the only significant *samskara* for her.

(4) A Hindu *Grihastha* is expected to perform daily fire sacrifies such as *Deva Yajna, Bhut Yajna,* and *Pitriyajna*

by daily chanting vedic *mantras,* offering *ghee* or clarified butter in fire, giving some portion of food to different creatures, extending hospitality to guests and by performing *shraddha* or offering of *pinda* or rice balls to ancestors respectively. Without the active participation of his wife, a man cannot perform these duties.

(5) Hindus believe in a concept of three religious debts or *Rinas.* These are *Pitri Rina, Daiv Rina* and *Guru Rina.* Marriage is essential for repaying *Pitri rina* and the individual repays it by being the father of a son. Role of a wife is essential for the completion of *Grihastha Dharma* and perform religious rites. The wife among the Hindus is called *Ardhangini.*

1.2.6.3. Forms of Hindu Marriage

Hindu scriptures discribed eight forms of marriage. Which are as follows:

Bramha Vivah: This is the most ideal and the most sought after marriage among the Hindus. In this form of marriage the father of the bride invites for marriage the most suitable groom, in terms of learning capacity and character for his daughter who is given to the groom in *kanyadaan.* These days it is called samajik vivah or Kanyadaan vivah as well.

Daiva Vivah: The father of the bride offeres his daughter in the hand of the priest as *Dakshina* and *Yajna,* which has been officiated by him. It was considered as an ideal form of marriage in ancient times but has become irrelevant today.

Arsha Vivah: This was the sanctioned procedure of marriage for sages or renunciators, in case they wanted to lead a family life. They used to gift a pair of cow and a bull to the father of a girl of their choice. In case the father of the girl was in favour of this marriage proposal he accepted the gift and marriage was arranged. Otherwise, the gift was respectfully returned to the sage.

Prajapatya Vivah: This is a modified, less elaborate form of *Brahma vivah.* The main difference lies in the rules of sapinda exogamy.

Asura Vivah: In this form of marriage, the bridegroom pays bride price to bride's father or her kinsmen and marries the bride. Marriage by exchange is also permitted within this marriage.

Gandharva Vivah: It was the traditional form of contemporary love marriage. It was a sanctioned form of marriage in exceptional circumstances and among certain classes but it was not considered as an ideal in the tradition.

Rakshasa Vivah: This is that form of marriage which is known marriage by capture among the tribals. This type of marriage was widely prevalent during the ancient age among the kings as the prizes of war or the machanism to improve relations with the defeated people. It was sanctioned but not an ideal form of marriage.

Paisacha Vivah: This is the least acceptable form of marriage. The man cheats the girl and thereby forces her to marry him. The woman, having lost her chastity, has no other alternative but to marry him. Recognising this form of union as marriage was an attempt to protect the rights of the cheated woman. It also gave legitimacy to the children born of such unions.

1.2.6.4. Rules of Mate Selection

To maintain the purity and distinctive identity of groups in society, the Hindu law-givers have laid down detailed rules and regulations regarding the choice of a partner for the marriage union. These laws are based on two principles i.e., the endogamic rule and the exogamic rules.

(a) Endogamy

While selecting a mate, a person has to choose from her or his own sub-caste and/or caste.

- *(i)* ***Caste Endogamy:*** This rule prescribes marriage within one's own caste and prohibits the members of a caste to marry outside their own caste. The violation of this rule would result into severe social and economic punishments by the 'caste council' or *'panchayat'* amounting to isolation and denial of all sorts of social help and co-operation.
- *(ii)* ***Sub-caste Endogamy:*** Each caste is sub-divided into many small groups, the members of which have feelings of superiority over the others. Each such unit is an endogamous group, directing its members to choose their mates only from that sub-caste. For example, *Brahmanas* are also having some sub-castes like *Saraswat, Gaur, Kanyakubj*, etc. All these groups are endogamous groups.

(b) Exogamy

In exogamy a person is supposed to marry outside one's own group. Though endogamy and exogamy seem to be two contradictory rules, in Hindu society both these rules are practised simultaneously, of course, at different levels. There are two types of exogamous rules in Hindu society:

(i) ***Sagotra Exogamy:*** *Gotra* (sagotra or same *gotra*) is a clan or family group, the members of which are forbidden to marry each other. It is believed that *sagotras* or persons with the same *gotra* have originated from the same ancestor and are, therefore, related by blood. But, this rule has been made legally ineffective by the Hindu Marriage Act, 1955.

(ii) ***Sapinda Exogamy:*** *Sapindas* are supposed to be blood relatives. *Sapindas* are those who are related to one another in ascending or descending order, by five generations from the mother's side and seven generations from the father's side. One cannot select life partner from one's own *Sapindas*. Though the Hindu Marriage Act, 1955 prohibits *Sapinda* marriage in general, it allows this in the form of crosscousin marriages as a peculiar custom of the South India. *Sapinda* exogamy indicates the prohibition placed on inter - marriage of *sapindas*. *Sapinda* represents the relationship between the living member and dead ancestors. The term *sapinda* (saman pind) means (1) Those who share the particles of the same body, and (2) People who are united by offering *pinda* or balls to the same dead ancestor. The Hindu law-givers differ in their definitions of *sagotra*. The Hindu marriage act, however, does not allow marriage within five generations on father's side and three generations on mother's side.

1.2.6.5. Inter-Caste Marriage

It means the marriage between a woman and a man who belong to two different castes. For example, when a woman of *Brahman* caste marries a man from the caste of, say, a weaver that is known as an inter-caste marriage. According to the custom such marriages are not preferred, although in the urban areas this custom is not strictly followed.

1.2.6.6. Other Rules of Marriage

(i) ***Hypergamy or Anuloma:*** Hypergamy is that form of marriage in which the ritual status of a man is higher than that of his prospective wife.

(ii) ***Hypogamy or Pratiloma:*** Hypogamy is that form of marriage in which the ritual status of a woman is higher than that of her prospective husband. The inter-caste marriages have however, been legalised by legislations such as Special Marriage Act 1954, Hindu Marriage Act 1955, Hindu Marriage Laws (Amendment) Act 1976 etc. in Indian society.

1.2.7. Position of Women in Indian Society

Any study of civilization is incomplete without study the status and position of women in it. Women constituted the keystone in the arch of Indian civilization. Indian civilization based on the spirit that women's cause is men; they rise or sink together, dwarfed or godlike, bond or free. One of the best way to understand the spirit of civilization and to appreciate its excellences and to realize its limitations is to study the history of the position and status of women in it. As far as education is concerned, the Ancient Indian Women enjoyed deny them the right to education.

Women enjoyed freedom and participation in public life show that the sense of justice and its play developed in a community. The laws of marriage and customs serve as guide to evaluate partner. His co-operation was must for the happiness and success of the family. The extent to which women were freedom to choose their partners in life. Her management of their household as also the recognition of their proprietary rights indicates man's capacity to control the natural love of self, pelf, power and possession, which is so deeply implanted in the heart of every human being. The position and status of women did not remain constant through the period of our study. Gods are pleased with where women are held at honour remained merely an ideal and in actual practice she was treated as Sudra. She was under the influence where she is given of her parents, as an adult, of her husband and as a widow of her sons. The freedom of women is also circumscribed. If she is girl and a young women or even by an aged one she cannot do anything independently even in herown house. There was gradual deterioration in her status and position. Ancient Indian society was found wanting in establishing the footing equality of man and woman. There was greater erosion in her status and position in medieval and modern period. Those countries which don't respect women have never become great. The main reason why our race is so much degraded is that we have no respect for these living images of Shakti. If we do notraise the women who are living example of the Divine mother, don't think we have another way raise.

A debate is going on regarding the status of women in primitive communities. The ideas that the primitive people were barbaric have led some to conclude that women had been subordinate to men. In early uncivilized societies the communities had not yet emerged from barbarism and there hardly existed any checks on the tyranny of men over women. In primitive life the muscle was an indispensable element in success and the man was stronger in it than women. Physical power, bodily vigour and muscular strength thus naturally established man's permanent superiority over women. So the position women occupied in Hindu society at the dawn of civilization during Vedic age is much better than what we ordinarily expect it to have been.

During Vedic period the society had certainly left behind the state of food gathering and hunting. Women held a position of honour because of her participation was found to be necessary in the production process. During this, the husband and wife are called dampati. It is indicative of the society in which relations between the sexes were based on reciprocity and autonomy in their respective spheres of activity. They took equal part in the sacrificial rites, pressed the Soma, rinsed and mixed it with milk and offered adoration to gods. A woman frequently associated themselves with folk assembly and participated in its deliberations, but in modern time situation is so deteriorate that on Panchayat level government gave thirty three percent reservations to women but after elected by pubic they do not utilize their power, their husband cherish their power and take the decisions, and participate in folk assembly.

If we look in the period of the later samhitas, woman on satisfactory position. A woman was considered as an equal partner with man in the responsibilities and duties at home. She was initiated into Vedic studies after her upanayana (Initiation Ceremony). Sita was described as offering sandhya prayers, i.e. ritual prayers which were offered with mantras in the morning, noon and evening. She was not an obstacle in the path of religion and her presence and co-operation were absolutely necessary in religious rites and ceremonies. At the beginning of 500 B.C. upanayana came to be discouraged for girls and it was declared that marriage was the substitute disastrous consequences on the general status and dignity of women.

The participation of women in productive activity such as agriculture, manufacture of cloth, bows, arrows and other war materials was at the root of freedom and better status of women in the Vedic age. Their position began to deteriorate when the cheap or forced labour of the enslaved population or of the Sudras became available to the society. The lowering of the marriageable age of women from 16 or 17 to 18 or19 and practice of Sati were obviously the consequences of the deterioration in their status. The deterioration in the status and position of women began from 300 B.C. onwards. They come to be considered as fickle-minded, who could be easily, won over by one who is handsome and can sing and dance well. In the *Anusasana Parva* of the Mahabharata we are told that Yudhisthira prayed to Bhishma to enlighten him regarding the nature of women. He prefaced his prayer with the statement. It is said that women is the root of all evils and she is narrow minded. Bhishma agreed and lures. She is not endowed with strength of will enough to resist temptation. She is always stands in need of protection by men. Elsewhere in the Mahabharata we find Bhishma extolling them. Women should always be adored and treated with love. For where women are treated with honour, the very gods are said to be propitiated. Where women are not adored, all acts became fruitless. If the women of a family, on account of the treatment they receive, indulge in grief and tears, that family soon becomes extinct.

Those homes which are cursed by women meet with destruction such homes lose their splendor, their growth and prosperity would cease. This contradiction in Mahabharata shows society's lack of confidence in the nature of women. Though it was forthright in ideal sing women hood and recognizing women as symbol of purity, righteousness and spirituality. Tara, Sita, Draupadi, Ahalya and Mandodari are the five ideal and revered women. The attitude of Buddha, a born democrat, was in no way different though he granted to women the rights to the monastic life and found an order of Nuns. A moral feminine in equality is pointed out in the Jalaka stories. According to the Jatakas "of all the snares of the senses which ignorance sets before the unwary, the most insidious, the most dangerous, and the most attractive is women." The want of sympathy by Buddhism towards women was based on the belief that a woman is nearer to the world than man. Even by founding the order of Nuns, the Buddha does not indicate that he was broad-minded enough to establish the equality of sexes.

Education: In the Rig Vedic Period women took part in the intellectual life of the society. After Upanayana ceremony, this took place as regularly, as that of boys. They devoted their time, till their marriage, to specialize in Vedic theology and philosophy. After marriage both husband and wife took equal part in the sacrificial rites. The authorship of some Vedic hymns is ascribed to women and in fact there are twenty such Women authors. These celebrities attained great eminence as philosophers. In the Upanishadic period there are references to women of high intellectual attainments. Gargi Vacaknavi is one of the example. Maitrey, the wife of Yajnavalkya is represented as holding with her husband philosophical discussion on the relationship of the universal soul (Paramatma)to the individual soul. These examples demonstrate the height of intellectual and spiritual attainments to which as women could rise. Some ladies took teaching carrier and they were known as Upadhyayas. The new term had to be coined to denote lady teacher's shows that Women teachers were numerous. The Puranas also speak of lady teachers and Bhagavata refers to two daughters of Dakshayana as experts in theology and philosophy. This high note about the education of women was not to continue for long. After 300 B.C. the situation changed and the right to study came to be denied for women. It is possible that girls in the well to do families were not denied of educational opportunities. Since higher education was not permissible for girls, they were given training in fine arts like music, dancing and painting from early times. In fact they were recognized as feminine accomplishments.

The ganikas or the courtesans and nautch girls had a recognized place in the social life in South India. They were proficient in fine arts like music and dance. They were even honoured by village assemblies for their public benefaction. In course of time they looked down upon when the dancing girls attached to the temples (devadasis) fell into immorality and these fine arts came to be regarded as fit only to such girls. Some women went in for military and administrative training. Kautilya speaks of a female body guard and directs that the king on getting up from bed shall be received by troops of women armed with bows. Around the beginning of the christen era the doors of Vedic knowledge was closed to women.

Marriage: Hindu writers attach great importance to the marriage of a woman. Womanis the very source of purusharthas, not only Dharma, Artha and Kama, but even Moksa. It was a social and religious duty and necessity. It was obligatory for girls as there will be more pit falls in the path of an unmarried woman. Thinking is same in modern period. Although the society is change, ways of working and living is changed. In the Vedic age girls were normally married after puberty. The Mahabharata favours the marriage of well-developed and grown-up girls. Draupadi, Kunti, Sita, Uttara, as also Devayani were fully grown-up at the time of their marriage though in the early times it was usual for girls to be fully adult before the marriage. There is tendency in the sutra texts to lower the age of marriage for girls. Around 200 A.D. the child marriage was gradually coming into vogue. Marriage usually took place among the couple of the same class and caste but sagotra, sapravara and sapinda marriage were prohibited, as the demands arise in this modern time, the Khap-Panchayata demands the changes in Hindu marriage act 1957 which allows same gotra, and marriage in same village. The sutras permit anuloma (male of higher caste marrying a lower class female) and Smirtis regards such marriages a legal. The progeny of anuloma unions inherited the caste of the father. Marriages were generally arranged by the parents of the couple though there are references to love marriages. Perfect harmony and happiness was expected in conjugal life.

Right to Property: The study of the evolution of the proprietary rights of women is both important and instructive. It is important because the evolution unfolds before us the economic independence and prosperity that women enjoyed in the society. It is instructive because with the gradual decline in her status in the society. The couples were the joint owners of the household as well as the property. At the time of marriage the husband declare that he would not violate the rights and interest of his partner in the economic matters. The joint possession secured her numerous rights and privileges. It gives her an absolute right of maintenance against the husband. By and large the Hindu jurists never made a sincere effort to secure women an absolute equality with their husbands in the ownership of the property of the family. Free India has however corrected this grave injustice to Women. The lawgivers have recognized the claims of wife to Sridhana(Women's Special Property) which consisted of the bride-price, gifts given by the husband even subsequent to the marriages. Later landed property came to be included in the Sridhana. The law relating to the inheritance of Sridhana varied from region to region. If a women died childless and if her marriage was not according to approved forms, the Sridhana devolved on her parents or brother; otherwise it was inherited by her children. In Eastern India brother less daughters were entitled to patrimony. The situation changed after 300 B.C. sisters having brothers denied a share in the patrimony. In free India according to Hindu Succession Act. daughter have equal share in the property inherited from their forefathers. But due to some social pressure and people make the mind set of girls is like that they did not take herown share from the property. This is situation in Middle class of Indian girls in 21st century.

Divorce: The sacred law states that the marriage union was indissoluble once the seven steps had been taken together. There was no place for divorce. An errant wife was denied of most of her rights; still the husband had to maintain her, if demanded. However, she could not remarry. Careful examination of the dharma sutra literature suggests that abandoning of wife/husband was permitted well before the beginning of the Christian era under certain well defined circumstances. Manu does not blame a wife if she left her a husband who is impotent, insane or suffering from an incurable or contagious disease. Manu permits remarriage of such wife. Kautilya is more liberal to women in matters of marriage, contract and divorce. A woman can remarry when her husband was abroad for long time, if he suffered from incurable disease or was sterile, if he had become an out caste, if he was bad in character or was guilty of high treason or was dangerous to her infertility or if she failed to give birth to sons. Divorce on the ground of ill feeling was also possible by mutual consent but not of the will of one party alone. Manu permits the wife to contract a second husband under the defined circumstances, appears to be unsympathetic to the cause of the wife. The above all rules completely forgotten by Gupta time when divorce becomes almost impossible for the people of higher classes. In Moderntime divorce is easily possible. Indian Panel Code gave such rights to women but Indian

Middle class society consider the divorce women inferior in categories and faults lies on her head.

Prostitution: Ancient India contained one class of women who mixed freely with men. They were free from restrains which matrons had to observe. They are called as ganikas (Courtesans) and Vesyas (prostitutes). In the literature the prostitute is depicted as beautiful, accomplished and wealthy women enjoying a position of fame and honour. She was to be thoroughly trained in sixty four Kalas (arts). These included music, dancing, singing and acting etc. the ganikas or the courtesans enjoyed a great social standing and they had nothing in common with such women in modern industrial cities. They were particularly proficient in fine arts like music and dancing. They were honoured by the people for their expertness in those arts as also for their public benefactions. Typically of such respected and honoured courtesans was Ambrapali, the noted courtesan of Vaishali: She was immensely wealthy, highly intelligent and famous throughout the civilized portions of India. She was one of the most treasured possessions of her city, and mixed on equal terms with princes. She was a Sri-ratna (jewel of a woman). South Indian inscriptions record the role that the ganikas played in contemporary society. They suggested how by their charms and wiles the ganikas enslaved and disturbed the courts and cities. The records of the chalukyas, cholas and other dynasties show the been interest the ganikas showed in charities. By the time of the Mauryas the institution of prostitution had come to stay.

We learn from the Arthasastra of Kautilya a prostitute noted for her beauty, youth and accomplishments was appointed superintendent on a salary1000 pans per annum. She not only looked after the welfare of the prostitute but arrange for their education in the relevant arts. Prostitutes were employed by the state as spies. They had to carry a license from the state to carry on their profession by paying two days earning a license fee to the government. They attended the court regularly and also worked in the royal household on a fat salary. As in Indonesia prostitution is legally permitted in modern time. Secular view was favorable to prostitution. The religious view regarded it as an evil and disapproved it.

Widows: A cultured society regarded widows as almost nonentities, humiliated them, and consider their very look an inauspicious. Sati system is disgraceful for living. It is true that they were permitted to holdproperty in their own right, but this did not improve their position. The evidence in the Rig Veda regarding the widow is too meager to form any idea of her position. If the position enjoyed by women in general is any guide, then it can be said that the position of widow was much better. The discussion on the question of widow remarriage and upholding the right of widows in her husband's property is further proofs to the nonprevalence of sati in the Vedic period. The custom of sati was not vogue in India down to 400 B.C. There is no reference to the custom in the Buddhist literature and the Arthsastraof Kautilya.Stray references to sati occur in the Mahabharata. Four wives of Vasudeva and five wives of Krishna committed sati, but Satyabhama, another wife of Krishna retired to the forest. Similarly, Madri, the second wife of Pandu, committed sati, but not Kunti.

The custom of sati began to gain popularity among the ruling classes from around 400 A.D. and some smritkaras make mention of it, though they do not hold it as an ideal for the widow. Even then, itwas not that widespread. Queen Prabhavati Gupta of the Vakataka dynasty did not commit sati, while Yasomati, mother of Harsha did. During the first half of the seventh century A.D. contemporary social thinkers and writers abhorred the custom become evident from the following statement: "To die after one's beloved is most fruitless. It is a custom followed by the foolish. It is mistake committed under infatuation. It is a reckless course followed only on account of haste. It is a mistake of stupendous magnitude. Some thinkers like Angirasa, Harita extolled the custom of sati and it began to gain popularity in north India.

All along the practice was confined to the ruling classes; a few of the brahmana families began to follow it around 1000 A.D. A reference has been made to the practice of Niyoga in the Vedic period. The Vedic literature and the dharma sutras allow remarriage of widow generally those who opposed this were not against the remarriage of child widows. According to Smirtis, a woman can remarry with the recitation of the sacred. Women have contributed to the progress of humanity in every age. They are the agents of change. They have contributed significantly towards nation making. The status of women is a significant reflection of the social justice in the society. In modern Indian society, there are many constitutional guarantees and legislative measures to protect them; but the literacy rate of women is not so high and work participation for women is also low.

The constitution of India has incorporated some special provision for increasing the status of women in India. From 1950 with the introduction of the democratic constitution, it has granted equal social and political rights to women. There are certain constitutional provisions: i. Article 14 guarantees that the State shall not deny equality before the law and equal protection of the laws, ii. Article 15 prohibits discrimination against any citizen on the ground of sex: and Article 15 (3) empowers the state to make positive discrimination in favour of women and child, iii. Article 16 provides for equality of opportunity in matter of public employment. iv. The State to direct its policy towards securing for men and women equally the right to an adequate means of livelihood (Article 39(a)); and equal pay for equal work for both men and women (Article 39(d)), v. The State to make provision for securing just and humane conditions of work and for maternity relief (Article 42), vi. To promote harmony and the spirit of common brotherhood amongst all the people of India and to renounce practices derogatory to the dignity of women (Article 51(A) (e)), vii. Not less than one-third (including the number of seats reserved for women belonging to the Scheduled Castes and the Scheduled Tribes) of the total number of seats to be filled by direct election in every Panchayat to be reserved for women and such seats to be allotted by rotation to different constituencies in a Panchayat (Article 243 D(3)). viii. Not less than one- third of the total number of offices of Chairpersons in the Panchayats at each level to be reserved for women (Article 243 D (4)). ix. Not less than one-third (including the number of seats reserved for women belonging to the Scheduled Castes and the Scheduled Tribes) of the total number of seats to be filled by direct election in every Municipality to be reserved for women and such seats to be allotted by rotation to different constituencies in a Municipality(Article 243 T (3)). x. Reservation of offices of Chairpersons in Municipalities for the Scheduled Castes, the Scheduled Tribes and women in such manner as the legislature of a State may by law provide (Article 243 T (4))

Legislative Provisions: Various legislative measures intended to ensure equal rights, counter social discrimination and various forms of violence and atrocities and to provide support services especially to working women have been enacted by the Govt. to uphold constitutional mandate. Women may be the victims of crimes such as 'Murder, 'Robbery, cheating etc, the crimes which are directed specifically against women, are characterized as 'Crime against Women' which are classified under two categories viz,' The crimes identified under the Indian Panel Code like Rape, Kidnapping or abduction for different purposes, Nomicide for dowry, Dowry deaths, or their attempts, Mental and physical torture, Molestation, Sexual Harassment and Importation of girls etc and (ii) The crimes identified under the special law like: - Employees State Insurance Act, 1948, The plantation labour Act.1951, Family Courts Act, 1954, The special Marriage Act, 1954, The Hindu marriage Act, 1955, The Hindu succession Act, 1956, The Maternity Benefit Act, 1961, Dowry Prohibition Act, 1961, Medical Termination of pregnancy Act, 1971, The Contract Labour Act, 1976, The equal Remuneration Act, 1976, The child Marriage Restraint Act, 1979, Criminal Law (Amendment) Act, 1983, The Factories (Amendment) Act, 1986, Indecent Representation of women (Prohibition) Act, 1986 and Commission of Sati(Prevention) Act,1987and Protection of women under domestic violence Act, 2005.

Special Initiatives for Women: Some special initiations have been taken in recent years in this regards viz: i. National Commission for Women In January 1992, this statutory body with a specific mandate to study and monitor all matters relating to the constitutional and legal safeguards provided for women, review the existing legislation to suggest amendments wherever necessary was set up. ii. Reservation of women in Local Self Govt. The 72nd and 73rd constitutional Amendment Acts passed in 1992 by Parliament ensure one-third of the total seats for women in all elected offices in all Rural and Urban Local Bodies. iii. The National Plan of Action for the Girl Child (1991-2000 AD) The Action Plan is to ensure survival, protection and development of Girl Child with the ultimate objection of building up a letter future for the girl child. iv. National Policy for Empowerment of women, 2001. The Department of Women and Child Development in the Ministry of Human Resources Development has prepared a 'National policy for Empowerment of Women in the year 2001. The goal of this policy is to bring about the advancement, development and empowerment of women.

At present a number of women's organizations have created a sense of consciousness for gender equality but rape, dowry deaths, humiliations, Honour Killing domestic violence and other atrocities against women have become common in our society today. Women constitute half of the population and their contribution to the country's economy is tremendous. But their number in the parliament is just around 8 percent which is highly minimal. Now the government of India has been implementing various schemes and programmes for the welfare and empowerment of women in the area of Poverty, Alleviation, skill up gradation, development and sustainable income generation, education. Health services, awareness generation, legal literacy and support services. Development and empowerment of women has been a thrust area in five year plan. But even after so many implementation and provisions position of women is not satisfactory. Recently the Gang Rape in Delhi, after it gang rape in Mumbai, we heard in news every day at least one news of gang rape, no preventative measure is present in the society. Aarushee Murder Case, Naina Sahni Murder Case, Honour Killing in Rohtak is the taint on humanity. If we consider legal provisions are sufficient to control the crimes against women and it provides safety, security and status to the women then we say modern society is retrogressive on the pole of women status not progressive. Out of universe of 137 countries, India's gender related development ranks 103rd. Life expectancy at birth is 60.7 as compared to 60.7 of males.

As for gender empowerment, India ranks 93rd out of a universe of 174 countries. It had 8.01 % women in the last parliament and the proportion of administrators and managers is only 2.3% while the professional and technical workers are 20.5%. In Indian society, there is very little value for the fact that in the totality of things, men and women have different qualities, they are complementary to each other and their relationship should not be one of superior and subordinate.

As compared to man's greater muscle power, women have greater capacity to care and nurture. Women live longer and can withstand more stress; they have more patience, perseverance and tenacity. They have fewer egos, and more capacity to give service, and these are attributes which form the essence of being.

Conclusion: Women have equal participation in human development. She is half of the human race. But she lack in society. Women is not treated with respect as in the ancient Indian society. Lot of crime against women is seen in modern society. Constitutional provisions are not sufficient to get the respectable position in society. Some certain changes inside mind-set of women as well as man is required. Everybody tries to understand that there is division of labour in society some essential role is played by every pole in society so why we consider women is secondary to men. In Modern times technology developed, globalization and commercialism come in to existence but the status and position of women is rather deteriorated.

1.2.8. Communalism

Indian society is pluralistic from religious point of view. Here, we have the followers of all the great religious systems. Hindus constitute the bulk of the population and they inhabit in all parts of the country. Muslims constitute the largest religious minority. But the adjustment between the Hindus and Muslims has been a failure several times, resulting in violent communal riots. In the communal riots during the period of independence millions of people were rendered homeless while millions of others lost their property. Communalism was responsible for the division of the country into India and Pakistan. The partition was expected to resolve the riddle, but it failed. There is, yet, to develop the neighborhood living pattern between Hindus and Muslims.

1.2.8.1. Meaning of Communalism

Communalism, as we understand it in our country is blind loyalty to one's own religious group. It is described as a tool to mobilize people for or against by raising an appeal on communal lines. Communalism is associated with religious fundamentalism and dogmatism. In other word it can be defined as a social phenomenon characterized by the religion of two communities, often leading to acrimony, tension and even rioting between them. Or Communalism is a political doctrine which makes use of religious and cultural differences to achieve political ends.

Thus, communalism refers to a politics that seeks to unify one community around a religious identity in hostile opposition to another community. It seeks to define this community identity as fundamental and fixed. It attempts to consolidate this identity and present it as natural -as if people were born into the identity, as if the identities do not evolve through history over time. In order to unify the community, communalism suppresses distinctions within the community and emphasises the essential unity of the community against other communities. One could say communalism nurtures a politics of hatred for an identified "other"– "Hindus" in the case of Muslim communalism, and "Muslims" in the case of Hindu communalism. This hatred feeds a politics of violence.

Communalism, then, is a particular kind of politicisation of religious identity, an ideology that seeks to promote conflict between religious communities. In the context of a multi-religious country, the phrase "religious nationalism" can come to acquire a similar meaning. In such a country, any attempt to see a religious community as a nation would mean sowing the seeds of antagonism against some other religion/s.

Defining communalism poses a complex problem for historians in contemporary India. On the one hand is the barrier posited by the communal tradition itself, which has endeavoured, with considerable success, to reduce the 'nation' to the 'community'. The partition of India and the long history of Hindu Rashtravad (Hindu Nationalism) express the formidable successes of this tradition. On the other hand, there is a historical confusion between 'nation' and 'community', which underlies the evolution of the modern nation-state and the subjective reactions to the Industrial Revolution. For instance, Bipan Chandra's definition-"Simply put, communalism is the belief that because a group of people follow a particular religion, they have, as a result, common social, political and economic interests" could be rephrased to define the phenomenon of nationalism as well, leaving us none the wiser. Third, the object of our study distorts and challenges our chronological sensibility.

The substance of communal ideology is historical memory, manifested in myths, symbols and atavistic emotion. The function of communalism is mass mobilization for the authoritarian reconstruction of the state in crisis. This state is a precipitate of a medieval and a colonial past, but is also the organizer of capital accumulation in the context of a world economy. As ideology, communalism achieves the fusion of archaic and modern elements (mythologized memory and Rousseauesque notions of popular sovereignty). The state, too, expresses the fusion of the age-old specialization of power with the modern despotism of capital. A state driven by crises of legitimacy can quite easily and naturally turn to communal institutions and movements to secure an authoritarian popular base. When communalism achieves state-power, the distinction between community and nation seems to vanish, and the task of critical comprehension becomes even more difficult.

1.2.8.2. A Brief history of Communalism in India

The decay of Buddhism and the imperial traditions with which it was associated was accompanied by the gradual resurgence of the Brahmin priesthood. This stratum, for all its pioneering work in assimilation of food-gathering or pastoral tribes into settled agriculture, also contributed to the proliferation of ritual, rule by superstition, caste exclusiveness, and the localisation and autarky of material culture. D.D. Kosambi recounts the process related in some Puranas, known as the *hiranya-garbha* (golden womb) ceremony, by which petty chieftains and kings would acquire high-caste status, agree to maintain the *chaturvarnya* (the four basic castes) and convert the rest of their tribe into a new peasantry.

Counter posed to this priestly culture was the body of differentiated heterodoxy knows as shramanism (asceticism), whose innate hostility to the former grammarian Patanjali (cc 2nd century BC) likened to the enmity between the snake and the mongoose. The shramanic ethic tended to be Universalist, even though it's lay following fell victim to the caste system. The Bhakti movements, which spanned a long period from cc 500 AD onwards, were, in Romila Thapar's view, the inheritors of, the shramanic tradition, and were popular among the 'low' castes. Although they differed widely depending upon time, place, social roots and types of worship, many of them were distinctly opposed to caste divisiveness and the notion of renunciatory salvation, and preached in the vernacular.

Meanwhile, with Islam had arrived the notion of the just and pious Sultan. In theory the Sultan could not be absolutist- he was subservient to and obliged to uphold the divine law (shariah). In practice, since the Sultanat was neither personal property, nor communal property religious law failed to ensure continuity on the basis of de-jure principles, and had perforce to postulate de-facto sovereignty.

Furthermore, the Holy Scriptures enjoined social equality, while orthodoxy at the same time upheld the principle of the supreme leadership of the learned ones; this despite the fact that Islam had never sanctioned a church or a clergy. Having no direct authority in scriptural matters, the ruler could only legitimise his rule by claiming to enforce the shariah; and this could only be done through the ulema. The latter had no means of inducing acceptance of their theological credentials except through the king. A symbiotic interest developed of a state-oriented clergy, who were also tied to the monarch through charitable grants. The tradition of a factional and ambitious ulema, bent upon inculcating among poorer classes of Muslims nothing more than a sense of conformity and inherent superiority, blended well with a culture already engrossed with status and ritual pollution. Orthodoxy, unable to establish the shariah as a normative principle, "made religion a poor dependent of politics and converted a source of moral nourishment into a parasite"

However, establishmentarianism did not go unchallenged. An independent ulema also existed which refused to associate with the institutions of power. The mystics (Sufis) were even further removed from the legalistic tradition. Basing themselves on monistic concepts such as *wahdat-ul-wujud* (the oneness of being), and the union of the self with God, they put forward a more earthy and appealing rendering of the Islamic message. Whereas the orthodox ulema represented the authority of the state and of dogma, the Sufis could provide spiritual sustenance to ordinary people. In so doing, they also had to provide room for belief in the miraculous.

Whereas the state-oriented clergy could quote religious injunctions in favour of obedience to the ruler, equally could their critics use the precepts of conditional obedience, social equality among the faithful, and hostility to ostentation to express their rebellious instincts. An example of this was the Mahdawi movement begun by Saiyyad Mohammad of Jaunpur (1443-1504). The jealous ulema, unable to worst him in discursive combat, concentrated on his messaianic claims. Continual orders of exile, coupled with the Mahdawi accent on hijrat (migration) as a proselytizing mission, led to the setting up of a number of egalitarian 'dairas' (circles) in several parts of western and northern India. The cult lasted till the late sixteenth century, dogged by orthodox and state persecution, which was natural, for if its teachings were to be accepted, the existing social and political system would have to be renounced as subversive of Islam.

Let us now consider developments under Britannic imperialism. The mercantilist interaction with India was already over a century old when colonial conquest began. The latter process took another century, in the course of which the political fragments of the moribund Mughal empire and various predatory polities were brought under a single new political and economic dispensation. Given the highly complex social hierarchies that existed in different areas, the long period of social pacification, the staggered pace of institutional change, and the fact that Britain herself underwent drastic historical transformation during this period, it is not surprising that the reaction to this whole process was highly differentiated.

Conquest of India by the British ended the glorious rule of the Mughals. During the Great Revolt of 1857, the revolutionaries proclaimed Bahadur Shah II as the Emperor of India. With the suppression of the Revolt, the British authority considered the Muslims, their traditional enemy. The Government tried to deal with the Muslims with scorn and contempt. So, communalism emerged among them for their self-protection and survival.

In order to bring awakening' among the Muslims, Sir Slayed Ahmad Khan started the Aligarh Movement. To educate the Muslims, he established Anglo-Mohammedan Oriental College at Aligarh which was later on converted to the Aligarh Muslim University. He envisaged that to be safe, the Muslims should back the British rule. That is why; he wanted to unite the Muslims which made communalism strong.

William Hunter, a British administrator in his book, The Indian Muslimappealed the Britishers to bring a change in their attitude towards the Indian Muslims. On the other hand, Mr. Beck, the principal of the Mohammedan Anglo-Oriental College at Aligarh, advised the Muslims to support the British Government for their safety. He also generated anti-Hindu feelings in the minds of the Muslims and told them to oppose the Indian National Congress. Thus, the British and the Indian Muslims came closer and it contributed to the growth of communalism.

The British policy of 'Divide and Rule' was largely responsible for ' the growth of communalism in India. For gaining the favour of the Muslims, Lord Curzon partitioned Bengal in 1905 and created a Muslim-dominated Province. This policy of Lord Curzon continued with vigor in the -forthcoming years in several ways by the British Government or make the Muslim communalism strong.

Communalism among the Hindus also served as a background for the growth of Muslim communalism. In 1870s, the Hindu landlords, money-lenders and middle-class professionals generated anti-Muslim sentiments. They demanded that seats should be reserved for the Hindus inthe Legislature and government services. This brought the Muslims closer to the British Government and made communalism strong.

In 1906 Sir Agha Khan headed a Muslim delegation and met Viceroy Lord Minot. He convinced the Viceroy that the Muslim minority should be given separate electorate. In the forthcoming elections that was granted to the Muslims. The Morley-M*into reforms and the Montague Chelmsford reforms gave vent to this communalism.

Nawaz Salimulah Khan established the Indian Muslim League in 1906. It aimed at generating better opportunities for the educated Muslims in polities and to put a check to the growing influence of the Indian National Congress. With the gradual march of time, the Muslim League demanded separate electorate and other facilities from time to time and the British Government fulfilled them. The League was instrumental in spreading communalism among the Muslims.

Muhammad Ali Jinnah was an educated Muslim leader who preached that Congress was the Hindu-dominated organisation and it would fail to protect the interest of the Muslims. So, he wanted the partition of the country and gave a clarion call to the Muslims on 16th August, 1946 by saying 'larker lunge Pakistan' (We will take Pakistan by force) and that day was famous as the 'Direct Action Day'. Thus communalism reached its zenith with the demand for Pakistan. In the wake of independence large scale massacre took place in India. Millions of people fro oth Hindu and Muslim communities were butchered.

In free India we have numbers of communal riots. From demolition of the Babri Mosque at Ayodhya to Godhra incidents and subsequent communal riot are shame for humanity.

1.2.8.3. Nature of Indian Communalism

Communalism is the Indian version of fascist populism and racist nationalism. First, it opposes to the time of the present its own ideal time which is an amalgam of the past and the future- both merging to one another in the myth of communal potency. Muslim communalists spoke of the period of 'Muslim sovereignty' as if the medieval Sultanat was the property of every Muslim. Sikh communalists harked back to the reign of Maharaja Ranajit Singh, misrepresenting it as the rule of 'the Khalsa'. And Brahmanical fascists, armed with the doctrine of Hindu Rashtra, dreamt of a new and fantastic monolith the 'majority community', which, as their political property, would enable them to bludgeon all their enemies into submission.

Second, communalism located an internal enemy, deemed to be sapping the strength of the chosen, and makes it the target of mass hatred. In South Asia, since India and Pakistan remain internal to each other's ideological self-consciousness, it could be said that Partition disproved the Two Nation Theory. Thus, for Pakistan, the wickedness of Bharat and the Hindus is the necessary condition for its own existence-Bengalis and Ahmadiyas come a poor second. For Brahmanical fascists in India, the internal enemy are the 'minorities', primarily the Muslims, who are seen as biologically anti-national, Pakistani agents and an unclean element in the body politic. Pakistan is the externalised form of the internal enemy; the Indian Muslims, the internal shadow of Pakistan.

Third, communalism subverts all humanistic rationality and replaces it with romantic, death worshipping cults of unreason whose political functions are the creation of murder squads, the militarisation of civil society and the inculcation of a fragmented morality based on the racist reduction of the hate objects into sub-humans.

Fourth, communalism, like fascism, is capable of using pseudo-radical slogans to mobilize mass support; and of using democratic institutions to seize power and destroy democracy from a position of strength. The numerous occasions on which various brands of communalists made themselves useful to the colonial authorities show up most clearly this anti-democratic nature of communalism, The very early as well as the late history of the Muslim League is an example.

Finally, communalism politicises the underworld, links together goondas and politicians, legitimises criminal violence and institutionalises all these phenomena in stable organizations, creating the symbiosis between the state and the bestial personality which is the hallmark of fascism. Its principal victim is humanity itself.

1.2.8.4. Causes of Communalism:

There are a number of causes which are responsible for the prevalence of communalism. Some of two important causes of communalism are discussed below.

Tendency of the Minorities: The Muslims fail to be intermingled in the national mainstream. Most of them do not participate in the secular nationalistic politics and insist on maintaining tor separate identity the elite among the Muslims have failed to generate the appropriate national ethos.

Orthodoxy and Obscurantism: The orthodox members of minorities feel that they have a distinct entity with their own cultural pattern, personal laws and thought. There are strong elements of conservatism and fundamentalism among the Muslims. Such feeling has prevented them from accepting the concept of secularism and religious tolerance.

Design of the Leaders: Communalism has flourished in India because the communalist leaders of both Hindu and Muslim communities desire to flourish it in the interest of their communities. The demand for separate electorate and the organization of Muslim league were the practical manifestations of this line of thought. The British rule which produced the divide and rule policy, separate electorate on the basis of religion strengthened the basis of communalism in India Ultimately the partition of the country into India and Pakistan provided further an antagonistic feeling towards each other.

Weak Economic Status: A majority of Muslims in India has failed to adopt the scientific and technological education. Due to their educational backwardness, they have not been represented sufficiently in the public service, industry and trade etc. This causes the feeling of relative deprivation and such feelings contain the seeds of communalism.

Geographical Causes: The territorial settlement of different religious groups especially Hindus Muslims and Christians causes in them wide variation in the mode of life, social standards and belief system. Most of these patterns are contradictory and this may cause communal tension.

Historical Causes: The Muslims, all over the subcontinent, are converts from Hinduism, which was facilitated due to the caste-hate relations and under the compulsions of Muslim rulers. The problems of social segregation, illiteracy and poverty that had set apart the low caste people remain unresolved for them, as the foreign elite that rubbed never shared power with them. Their work ended with the conversion of the Indians and the converts began by imitating the masters in thought, speech and dress. It caused their alienation. Gradually, elements of communalism entered in the Muslim community. The separatist elements in the Muslim community, from the very start of the national resurgence had discouraged others of their community, from associating themselves with it. As a result Muslim league was formed which demanded partition of the country.

Social Causes: Cultural similarity is a powerful factor in fostering amicable relations between any two social groups. But the social institutions, customs and practices of Hindus and Muslims are so divergent that they think themselves to be two distinct communities.

Psychological Causes: Psychological factors play an important role in the development of communalism. The Hindus think that the Muslims are fanatics and fundamentalists. They also believe that Muslims are unpatriotic. On the contrary, the Muslims feel that they are being treated as second rate citizens in India and their religious beliefs and practices are inferior. These feelings lead to communal ill-feeing.

Provocation of Enemy Countries: Some foreign countries try to destabilize our country by setting one community against the other through their agents. Pakistan has played a role in fostering communal feeling among the Muslims of our country. Pakistan has been encouraging and promoting communal riots by instigating the militant sections of Indian

Muslim community. Kashmir youths are trained by Pakistan to destabilize India's internal security by spreading communal venom.

Negative Impact of Mass Media: The messages relating to communal tension or riot in any part of the country spread through the mass media. This results in further tension and riots between two rival religious groups.

1.2.8.5. Communalism and threat to Indian Society

India is a secular State. Secular means non-religious, but in the context of Indian polity. It means the co-existence of all religions without any kind of discrimination. Though our constitution safeguards for the minorities, the actual implementations of the provisions is a complex one. Indian people are generally known for their non-violence, tolerance, brotherhood character, that is why number of religion has flourished in India society. After the traumatic partition and bloodshed, during the partition, has given the political parties, several inflammable issues for exploiting communal passions for their political gains. Not only the politicians, but also the religious heads of minorities and majority community instead of trying to mitigate the communal frengy, flared it up with their speeches and actions. The destruction of Babri Masjid and burning alive the Hindu Kar Sewaks in Godhra (Gujarat) and the incidences of violence in Gujrat after Godhra Massacre, have torn the Secular Fabric of Indian Democracy to uncountable pieces. One incidence after another creates more hatred, more incidences, more communalism in the country.

In India, throughout the past century, communal forces have tried to capture the political centre stage. By various means. They have sought to disrupt the unity and integrity of the country,. Tried to gnaw at the very secular foundations of India culture and history. But overtime they have failed. Yet, the consequences of such thought have often been traumatic. One has to but mention the holocaust of 1947, assassination of Mahatma Gandhi demolition of the Babri Mosque at Ayodhya and the riots accompanying it etc. to get a feel of the trauma. The Muslim fundamentalists have made it an issue of their identity and existence. The Hindu fundamentalist are also not behind inciting the gullible masses, to rise against the Muslims, by making them believe that Hindus in Hindustan are being treated as second class citizens.

All groups, whether Hindu or Muslim, which encourage narrow communal identities are adding to the problem. The reality is that real people's identities are fluid and complex, whereas the project of ethnic nationalism requires the construction of narrow identities, and then the use of those identities to mobilize people. In this way, the apparently innocent encouragement of religious identity can be part of a process which culminates in violence.

Riots are rarely spontaneous events. Probably the most incorrect caricature of the recent violence is of spontaneous tit for tat violence. To highlight the organized nature of violence is not to brush away the difficult questions of where exactly mass violence and mass sexual violence comes from and how these are connected with authoritarianism and sexual repression.

The religious right in India exploits to a great extends its multiple faces, from the more respectable to the more extreme. The key point to recognize is that the differences between the organization are tactical rather than ideological. There are no golden pasts. History, especially the pre-British history of India, has become a battle-ground with Hindu Nationalist reminding us of an apparently beautiful pre-Islamic era, and secularists attempting to counter this with examples of peace, progress and cohesion achieved during the time of Mughal rule. The reality is that such simplifications of history are always dangerous. All empires, pre-Islamic, and post-Islamic have been born though brutal conquest and expansion hand have seen great social injustices. Many have also had their times of relative peace and stability, and social progress. Today it is probably more useful to question the overall way the history is caricatured, rather than getting bogged down in detailed debate.

In a country like India, with so much plurality and diversity, talking of Hindu state, or Hindustan for Hindus, shall be a dangerous sign, totally the well-established, secular fabric of Indian Constitution. The un-secular forces organizations must keep in mind that communalizing India will bring horror in the country and the people will eat other and time is near that we will be again under foreign rule. Unless an all-out attempt is made to contain the communal forces, the very unity of India is in danger. A total ban on all types of communal organizations must be put forth. A social and cultural movement should be launched to awaken the people about the reality of the communal violence and their effects on them and on the country as a whole. The process has to start from top. All political parties and religious organizations must stop delivering inflammatory speeches and inciting the general masses in the name of religion. A wrong action on the part of a community cannot be equalized by another wrong action by another community. For the survival of the country, secularism has to survive for the survival of secularism, religious friendship, togetherness and tolerance is must. Communalism can only destroy the unity and integrity of the nation, it can't help in creating friendship, fraternity or togetherness.

1.2.9. Summary

- India is a country of multiple identities based on region, language and religion, each having more or less distinct social structures which have been evolving through the ages.
- Tribes, one of the earliest identifiable social organisations, can be traced to the Vedic period.
- The initial differentiation was based on the colour of the skin which later developed into a complex '*varna* system' with tribes being divided into 'Brahmana', 'Kshatriy', Vaishya' and 'Shudra' categories.
- 'Varna/Jati system' underwent further changes in the post-Vedic societies with the rise of Buddhism and Jainism and later with the arrival of new people in India such as the Shakas, Kushanas, Parthians, and the Indo Greeks.
- Caste system has its regional variations due to the formation of regions and regional consciousness after the eighth century AD and it became more and more complex, multiplying into a number of castes and sub-castes due to a number of factors.
- Untouchability, the most obnoxious practice, took roots during the last phase of the Vedic period and crystallised into a separate identity in the age of the Buddha
- Slavery existed in India though it was different from the classical Greek and Roman slavery,
- *'Purushartha'*, *'ashramas'* and *'samskaras'* are inter-linked concepts.
- The 'Jajmani system was an important institution of complementary relationship between groups of dominant peasant castes on the one hand and service and artisan castes on the other, which continued till modern times in Indian rural society, but is now breaking up under the impact of monetisation, urbranisation and industrialisation.

- Families are the result of a very important *sanskara* ceremony called marriage and different kinds of marriages such as *'anuloma'* and *'pratiloma'* based on the alliances between different *varna/caste;* monogamous, polygamous and polyandrous base on the number of spouses; all can be found in Indian society.
- The traditional Indian family is a joint family governed by two schools of sacred law and customs which are *'Mitakshara'* and *'Dayabhaga'*.
- The position of women in the history of India has been a story of progressive decline until the modern times when, with the spread of western education, efforts were made through social and religious reforms to improve their conditions.

1.2.10. Exercise

1. Explain the origin of the multiple identities in India.

2. Distinguish between the *varna* and the *jsti* system.

3. Discuss the characteristics of the caste system in India.

4. Explain how *'purushartha'*, *'ashrama'* and *'sanskara'* are related to each other.

5. Give an account of the different types of marriage that are prevalent in Indian society.

6. Critically examine the position of women in the history of Indian society.

7. What is Jajmani system? Why is it breaking up in recent times?

8. What is communalism. How communalism is a major threat to Indian society? Discuss.

1.2.11. Further Readings

1. Dube, S.C. 1990.*Indian Society* New Delhi: National Book Trust, India.

2. Dubois, Abbe J.A. 1906. *Hindu manners, customs and ceremonies,* Oxford: Clarendon Press.

3. Dutt, N.K.1986. *Origin and Growth of Caste in India,* Calcutta : Firma KLM.

4. Kapadia, K.M.. 1958. *Marriage and Family in India.* London. : Oxford.

5. Majumdar, R.C. (ed.).1951. *The Vedic Age,* London.

CHAPTER-III
RELIGION AND PHILOSOPHY IN INDIA

PRE-VEDIC AND VEDIC RELIGION, BUDDHISM AND JAINISM, INDIAN PHILOSOPHY-VEDANTA AND MIMANSA SCHOOL OF PHILOSOPHY

Structure

1.3.0. Objectives

This chapter provide you an insight into the different aspects of religion and Philosophy in Indian subcontinent through ages. By the end of this chapter you would be able to:

- *explain the meaning of religion and identify the characteristics of various religions movements in ancient India;*
- *explain the ideas of the six schools of Vedïc philosophy;*
- *explain the Jaina theory of reality;*

- *examine the contributions of Buddhist philosophy.*
- *understand the reasons for the rise of Sufism and Bhakti movements in Medieval India*
- *trace the growth main tenets of the Sufi movement;*
- *explain the philosophy of the Bhakti saints, Sant Kabir and Guru Nanak; rise of Sikhism;*
- *explain the ideology of the Vaishnavite saints;*
- *recognise the contribution of Sufi and Bhakti saints towards the growth of a composite Indian culture.*

1.3.1. Introduction

Religion is the science of soul. Morality and ethics have their foundation on religion. Religion played an important part in the lives of the Indians from the earliest times. It assumed numerous forms in relation to different groups of people associated with them. Religious ideas, thoughts and practices differed among these groups, and transformations and developments took place in the various religious forms in course of time. Religion in India was never static in character but was driven by an inherent dynamic strength.

Indian spirituality is deeply rooted in ancient philosophical and religious traditions of the land. Philosophy arose in India as an enquiry into the mystery of life and existence. Indian sages called Rishis or 'seers', developed special techniques of transcending the sense and the ordinary mind, collectively called yoga. With the help of these techniques, they delved deep into the depths of consciousness and discovered important truths about the true nature of human being and the universe. The sages found that the true nature of the human being is not the body or the mind, which are ever changing and perishable but the spirit which is unchanging, immortal and pure consciousness. They called it the Atman.

The Atman is the true source of human's knowledge, happiness and power. The rishis further found that all individual selves are parts of infinite consciousness which they called Brahman. Brahman is the ultimate reality, the ultimate cause of the universe. Ignorance of human's true nature is the main cause of human suffering and bondage. By gaining correct knowledge of Atman and Brahman, it is possible to become free from suffering and bondage and attain a state of immortality, everlasting peace and fulfillment known as Moksha. Religion in ancient India meant a way of life which enables a human to realize his true nature and attain Moksha.

Thus philosophy provided a correct view of reality, while religion showed the correct way of life; philosophy provided the vision, while religion brought about the fulfillment; philosophy was the theory, and religion was the practice. Thus in ancient India, philosophy and religion complemented each other.

1.3.2. Pre Vedic-Harappan Religion

To understand the religious traditions of India in proper historical will begin with Harappan religion. The archaeological findings from the sites of Harappa, Mohenjodaro, Banwali, Lothal, Kalibangan, have helped us in reconstructing history of Harappan culture which rwhed its mature phase around 2600 B.C. In the absence of definite decipherment of Harappan script the artifacts recovered fiom various excavations at the above sites are the only source of information about Harappan culture. As we all know that town planning and settlement types of Harappan sites speak of a matured urban civilization. So far as Harappan religion is concerned we have scattered knowledge about Mother Goddess, a god similar to Pasupati-Siva, and nature and animal worship. Sir John Marshall first drew our attention to the religious practices of the Harappan people. Later on other archaeologists and researchers have tried to interpret Harappan religion based on their readings of seals and other artifacts. A major debate is centred around whether Harappan religion belonged to Vedic or non-Vedic tradition. In this Unit we will introduce you to historical context and religious beliefs and practices of the Harappans and then show how different scholars have interpreted Harappan religion.

1.3.2.1. Historical context

The Harappan civilization, the earliest known civilization in India, is the culmination of a process and its beginning can be traced in the preceding rural cultures of Neolithic times which are known as Nal, Kulli, Zhob, Quetta culutres. This civilization dates back to about 3000 B.C. and depending on the nature of development it is suggested that there were three distinct phases of Harappan civilization-early Harappan, mature Harappan and 'late Harappan.The Harappan culture matured around 2600 B.C. and it declined around 1700 B.C. The archaeological remains of this civilization were first discovered in the 1920s at Harappa and Mohenjodaro. Initially, it was thought to have been confined to the valley of the river Indus. However, subsequent archaeological excavations established that the contours of this civilization were not restricted to the Indus Valley but speared to a wide area in north western **and** western India. Harappa and Mohenjodaro are now in Pakistan and the major sites in India include Ropar in Punjab, Lothal in Gujarat and Kalibangan in Rajasthan. Excavations at Alamgirpur in Uttarpradesh and Mitathal near Delhi give definite reference of the extension of the civilization towards the Ganges-Yamuna Doab. It is also suggested that a number of Harappan sites existed on the banks of the Ghaggar river which followed through Haryana and Rajasthan before reaching Pakistan.

All the excavations point to a vast area over which this civilization was spread. The amazing similarity right from the grid town, the size of the bricks to the script which is yet to be deciphered speak of unique cultural uniformity prevailing in the Harappan culture over the years. Based on archaeological findings it is believed that this civilization was a developed urban one with the characteristics of a complex society. Society was probably divided according to occupations and in all probability village communities formed the nucleus of the Harappan culture. Though the main occupation of the Harappans was agriculture, there are evidences of a large number of arts and crafts indicating agricultural surplus and existence of an elaborate trade system. The Harappan people had trade relations with other contemporary civilizations of Mesopotamia, Persian Gulf and Egypt. All these suggest the existence of a developed civilization occupying a vast area and it continued for thousand of years. What is of our interest to see here is that in a civilization which is characterized by uniform urban planning, culture, developed agriculture and trade how religious beliefs and practices formed an integral part of culture. **A** large number of human figurines, number of terracotta statues of Mother Goddess, the figures of deities on seals help us in constructing the religious life of the Harappans. In the following section we will introduce you to religious beliefs and practices of the Harappans.

1.3.2.2. Religious beliefs and practices

From the archaeological findings, it may be presumed that the most important - feature of the Indus Valley religion was the cult of Mother Goddess or Nature Goddess. There are quite a few figurines of terracotta or other material which display a standing female figure, with minimum clothing but profusely ornamented, with headdress, collar, etc., wearing a girdle or band round her loins. Seals from Harappa show a female figure turned upside down, with outstretched legs, and a plant emerging fiom her womb. hother representation of a feroali figure standing in a bifurcated tree, probably a pippal (asvattha) tree, may be interpreted to identify the Mother Goddess with the Nature Goddess. Bere are also a few female figures with a number of children which may connect the Mother Goddess with fertility cult. It is interesting to note that some of the figures are smoke-stained. It may, therefore, be inferred that those figures were objects of worship and oil or incense was burnt before them. Among male deities Siva can be identified easily as a principal deity in Harappan religion. Most remarkable representation of this deity is a three-faced figure wearing a three-horned head-dress, seated cross-leged on a throne, the posture being very similar topadmasana, with eyes turned towards the tip of his nose, as described in Yoga texts. This figure is represented withpenis erectus (urdhvarnedhra) which is very significant. Another striking feature of this figure is that the deity is surrounded by a variety of animals, elephant, buffalo, tiger and rhinoceros, with a deer creeping under the seat. This representation brings to light three aspects of Siva, viz. i) three-faced (trimukha), ii) Lord of animals (pasupati) and iii) The Supreme practitioner of Yoga (Yogisvara or Mahayogin).

Two more seals, depicting the same deity, have been discovered from the' excavations in some other sites. The deity is almost nude and has a horned head-dress. One has three faces while the second one has only one face. It also appears that Siva was worshipped both in icon and in linga.

In all probability the Indus Valley people might have been worshipping various animals. Though some of the animal figures might have been used as toys, others were used for religious purpose. Three types of animals are found depicted on the seals and sealings. They are: i) Mythlcal animals, e.g. a) Semi-human semi-bovine, attacking a horned tiger; b) Complex ani-nals- with head of one animal and body of another; ii) Animals neither completely mythical nor completely actual, e.g. the strange unicorn. The great number of unicorns may suggest that it might have been tutelary deity of some of the cities; **iii)** There are actual animals, such **as** bison, tiger, elephant, rhinoceros, buffalo, bull and zebra. Efforts have been made to identify these animals with &vehicles (vahanas) of some Vedic and Puranic deities but such identification are farfetched, and not based on sound proofs.

In all probability the Indus Valley people also worshipped natural objects like water, fire, trees, etc. Various trees, plants and foliage have been depicted on a number of seals. Fire must have been worshipped. But it is not yet very clear whether fire was worshipped as an independent deity or as a messenger to gods as in the Vedic culture. No buildings, which could be identified **as** temples or places of worships have so far been discovered in any site. S.R. Rao, however, has identified a few low structures found in the excavation sites at Lothal and Kalibangan as fire altars and it is assumed that animals were scarified in those altars. S.Ratnagar has written that 'Some aspects of Harappan religious practice would have been highly ceremonial and public, **as** at the Great Bath, but there would also have been domestic worship, as also local cults, village rituals enacted under trees, and so on'.

1.3.2.3. Observations

As our knowledge about Harappan religion is based only on archaeological findings so there are divergent opinions in interpreting Harappan religion. Scholars also differ regarding its relationship with the Vedic tradition. Let us see what the different authors have obserbed about ~arap~raelnig ion. Referring , to the Mother Goddess figurines Sir John Marshall wrote, 'The generally accepted view concerning them is that they represent the Great Mother or Nature Goddess, whose cult is believed to have originated in Anatolia (probably in Phrygia) and spread thence through out most of western Asia. The correspondence, however, between these figurines and those found on the banks of the Indus is such that it is difficult to resist the conclusion that the latter also" represented Mother or Nature Goddess and served the same purpose as their counterparts in the West, viz., either as votive offerings or, less probably, as cult images for household shrines; and this conclusion is strengthened by the fact that the range of these figurines now extends practically without a break from the Indus to the Nile, over tracts that **are** not only geographically continuous but which in the Chalcolithic Age were united by common bonds of culture.

Giving referepce to discoveries at Kalibangan Bridget and Raymond Allchin have suggested that there were several fire altars along with kits containing ashes and this place may be interpreted as ritual centre where animal sacrifice and ritual ablution used to take place. S. Atre is of the opinion that there is continuity in religious beliefs of the Harappans with the religious elements of the hunter-gatherer's cultures. 'Harappan religious ideology and rituals were possibly designed to reassure the bounteousness of life, granted by the Archetypal Mother.. .The main deity of the Harappans was a Great Goddess of animals and vegetation. The Archetypal Motherlthe Great Goddess still holds a prime place in the collective Hindu psyche as well as in Hindu rituals; a phenomenon, more obviously ascribable to the Harappan than to the Vedic cultural traits'.

K.N. Sastri has disagreed with the assumption of female predominance in the Harappan religion and was of the opinion that the Harappan religion was very much within the ambit of the Vedic traditions. It is suggested that the mother Goddess figurines, the linga and yoni symbols, various seals and ritual objects are indicative of primitive tantrik practices. According to N.N. Bhattacharya the yogic posture of 'Proto-Siva' found on the Harappan seals refer to the pre-vedic origin of Yoga. 'The origin of the Sankhya concept of Purusa and Prakrti had been traced to that of the Female and Male principles of creation as was supposed to exist among the Harappans on the suggestiviv of the yoni and linga symbols, the Mother Goddess figures, the male god on the seals and so on'.

S.R. Rao arrives at the conclusion that the religious beliefs and practices of the Harappan people were similar to those of the Vedic Aryans. He postulates that the Mother Goddess was ranked very high. From Kalibangan and Lothal remains, he draws that Agni was accorded a special place and various types of oblations including animals were offered to him. Rao further postulates that the Indus Valley people had a clear conception of Supreme God, whom they mentioned as 'Ka' and **'Eka'.** Bhaga and Brhaspati might have also been known. Yoga was widely practiced as a means to spiritual attainments. in the Harappan sites do not conform to the sacrificial altars of the Vedas' and historically it is not correct to d~awan y analogy between the cultural practices in the Harappan civilization and of those mentioned in the Vedic texts.

S. Ratnagar considers the existence of 'shamanism' in Harappan religion. She explains, 'Shamanism is a form of religious practice that exists among preliterate prehistoric groups, including tribesmen and hunter-gatherers, as well as in the Shang-dominated society of Bronze Age China Central to shamanism is animism, belief in the souls of animals, birds, plants or snakes, and a belief that these souls or spirits can communicate with living people. They do so through the shaman, a person with the rare gift of understanding them as he is able to journey into the world of the spirits-n the waves of frenzied drumming or clapping, on the spirals of smoke, or on the souls of sacrificed animals, by taking part in vigorous dance or by eating hallucinogenic substances. Shamans thus go into ecstasy or trance. While in the other world, they seek out cures for disease or drought.' Ratnagar feels that the copper tablets of Mohenjo-daro, depicting masked figure with horns, animals, material items having association with shamanistic practice, the so-called Pasupati seal and some hybrid personages depicted on Harappan seals suggest the existence of shamanism in Harappan religion.

It is difficult to reach any conclusion based on these observations. However, what can be suggested is that being a highly developed urbanized civilization Harappan people also had developed religious practices and symbolism. But in the absence of proper decipherment of Harappan scripkinferences based on archaeological'findings are very much subjective in nattffe. Establishing any connectivity between Harappan and Vedic religious traditions on thc basis of existing evidences ma always have the possibility of sweeping generalization. This requires further **in**vestigation and corroboration.

1.3.3. Vedic religion

The Vedic tradition at its early stage was primarily a tradition, by priests and priest-craft, with a sizable pantheon of nature deities. There was Vayu, the wind god, Agni, the fire god, Indra, the god of thunder and many others. Sacrifice involving the specialized priests and slaughter of animals was the chief form of religious practice. Sacrifice was originally a rite of hospitality for the gods and this was performed to obtain material rewards on earth and in heaven. In the Vedic texts we find that the sacrifice is symbolic of the selfless, visionary, coordinated, dynamic and creative activity which could be at any level, in any sphere or dimension. Different rituals have deeper meaning of eternal value and universal applications. In the context of the Vedic religion sacrifice needs to be understood with reference to the inner self of man. Ancient seers have suggested two approaches with reference to the Vedic religion – Pravrtti Lakshana (characterized by action) and nivrtti-lakshana (characterized by renunciation). The aim of religion is also two fold: Abhyudaya (prospeSty in the life in this world and enjoyment in heaven in the life after) and Nihsreyasa (permanent freedom from all bondage and sufferings, state of eternal bliss).

The Mantra and Brahmana parts of the Veda which are primarily associated with rites and rituals serve the purpose of Abhyudaya, whereas the Aranyakas and the Upanishads teach the ways and means for Nihsreyasa. In this Unit you will be introduced to sources of the Vedic religion, meaning and classification of various rituals and what do they symbolize.

1.3.3.1. Sources of the vedic religion

The Vedic religion emanates from the Veda. The word 'Veda' is derived from the root 'vid', 'to know' and hence means knowledge. The knowledge contained in and imparted by the Veda is considered to be the knowledge par excellence. The Veda is believed not to be any human composition but to have been revealedto ancient Risis, seers of the truth and hence is Apauruseya, non-human creation.

Our source of knowledge of the Vedic religion is the corpus ofthe Vedic literature which is composed of four great works, the Rig-Veda, the Sama-Veda, the Yajur-Veda and the Atharva-Veda and each of these having fourfold subdivisions the Sarnhitas or Mantras, the Brahmanas, the Aranyakas and the Upanishads. The oldest and most important of all the Vedas is the Rig-Veda which consists of a collection of 1,028 hymns, recited or chanted in the course of a sacrifice. It is divided into ten books, of which the first and the tenth are thought to be somewhat later than the central eight. The Sama-Veda is composed essentially of hymns taken fiom the Rig-Veda (with some seventy-five additional stanzas), rearranged in order to facilitate the singing or chanting of the verses. The Yajur-Veda is a collection of ritual formulae and explanations used by the priests in performing the sacrifice. The Atharva-Veda is a later addition to the other three Vedas and a substantial portion of this text is a collection of magic spells.

Its contents are based on ancient folk religious beliefs. It is believed that the Vedas were compos_ed between 1500 B.C. and 1200 B.C. Several different priestly schools began to record and preserve their expositions of the meaning of the sacrifice, the hymns and the prayers and this led to the development of the texts called the Brahmanas. These are the ritual textbooks intended to guide the priests through the complicated web of sacrificial rites. The Aranyakas, considered as appendices to the Brahmanas, contain the mysticism and symbolism of sacrifice. The Upanishads deal with metaphysical speculations and spiritual teachings. These are in brief the texts which help us in formulating our knowledge about the Vedic religion. In the following section we will discuss the different forms of rituals, particularly the public rites.

1.3.3.2. Rituals - public rites

The formulation of the rites and rituals presupposes the existence of deities who are to bdprobitiated, prayed through the rituals. The Vedas mention quite a good number of deities. The principal deities are classified as belonging to different religions, viz. i) terrestrial, ii) aerial and iii) celestial. Prithivi, Agni, Soma, Brhaspati and the rivers belong to the first order; Indra, Apam-napat, Rudra, Vayu-Vota, Parjanya, Apah and Matarisvan to the second and Dyaus, Varuna, Mitra, Surya, Savitr, Pusan, Visnu, the Adityas, Usas and the Asvins to the third. Performance of ritual was at the centre of philosophy of the early Vedic religion. Ritual and prayer are two expressions in act and word of man's sense of dependence on divine powers. Rituals were performed to enlist the goodwill of divine powers so that they may fulfil the wish of the worshipper.

Sacrifice was considered as an inherent part of the cosmic order. Sacrifice involved the yajamana, the patron of the offering, the god to whom the offering is given, the Brahmana who performs the sacrifice and acts as a link between the yajamana and the god and the bali or the offering which is gifted to the gods. The Vedic sacrifices are performed by offering oblations or Ahutis to fire, since Agni (fire) is believed to be the mouth of all deities. He receives the offerings not only for himself but also for transmissions to the gods. Oblations are offered under different circumstances to three fire altars, containing three sacred fires duly established through rituals, such as Garhaptya, used for warming of dishes and preparation of offerings, Ahavaniya, installed in the east, receives the offerings for the gods and daksina, established in the south, for receiving offering for the ancestors and demons. Vedic rituals are broadly classified into two categories, Public rites (Srauta) and Domestic rites (Grhya or Smarta). In this section we will explain public rites.

The Srauta sacrifices are primarily classified on the basis of the material of the offerings, viz. havir-yajna in which ghee (classified butter-havis) is offered as the main oblation, and Soma-yajna in which the juice of the Soma plant (this plant is now extinct and a substitute called putika is being used since the I st A.D.) is the chief oblation. It is to be noted that in aSoma-yqjna animal sacrifice also forms apart. Different parts of the body of the sacrificial animal, particularly omentum (vapa) are offered to the fire in Soma-yajna. Other objects, which are offered in sacrifices as oblation are sacrificial cakes (purodasa) generally made of barley, milk, curd, etc. Gradually, a section of the adherents of the Vedic lore disliked animal sacrifice and different types of substitutes were in use.

The Srauta rituals require the participation of various types of offioiating priests (rtvij-s). Four are the principal ones, each of them is associated with a particular Veda. They are Hotr (Rgvedic), Udgatr (Samavedic), Adhvaryu (Yajurvedic) and Brahman (Atharvavedic). There are a few subordinate ones, such aspotr; nestr, agnidh, prasastc etc. Among all the priests, Adhvayu performs the manual work, i.e. pouring the offering, while Hotr invokes the gods to be present in the sacrifice. The Udgatr **S** job is chanting the samans in particular tunes and meters. The fourth priest, i.e. Brahman, is entrusted with the general supervision of the sacrifice. Srauta sacrifices are many and varied, and they became more and more complicated. A vast literature, known as Srauta sutras came into being to discuss the details of the performance of the sacrifice. The Srauta sacrifices may be classified as: i) periodic or regularly recurring ones (nitya) and ii) occasional or special (naimittika).

Periodic Sacrifices The first of all periodic sacrifices is the setting up of sacred fire (agnyadhana). This is performed either in a particular season or either on new moon or full moon day. It is a two-day performance. The garhapatya fire is first established on a'circular altar (vedi). The second the dakshina is established on a semicircular altar and the third one, i.e. ahavaniya is established on a square altar. Each of the three fires is established under a separate shed. First the garhapatya fire is lit and a blaze from it is taken to each of the other two fires. The agnihotra is performed daily, morning and evening. The oblation is milk, heated and mixed with water, which is offered to the garhapatya and ahavaniya fires. A part of the evening performance is agnyupasthana, a homage to fire and the cow whose milk is used. The Darsapurnamasa, as its name indicates, is performed on new moon (darsa) and full moon day (purnamasa). Sacrificial cakes (Caturmasya) are performed - at the beginning of spring, monsoon, and autumn seasons. The Maruts are the - most important deities who receive oblations in all these sacrifices alqpg with other. In addition, five oblations to Agni, Soma, Savitr, Sarasvati and Pusan are offered in the beginning of each of the three sacrifices. For the firewood the tree which blossoms in the particular season is selected. In the first four-**12** month sacrifice the five common libations are followed by a cake (purodasa) to Maruts, a milk mixture to the Visvedevas and a cake to heaven and earth (dyavaprthivi).

Another seasonal sacrifice is agrayana-isti, which is the sacrifice of the first. Fruit of the biennial harvest. Apurodasa of barley in spring and ofrice **ig** autumn is offered to Indra, Agni, Visvedevas, Dyau and Prthivi. The first born of the calves during the year is offered as the fee (daksina).

Special Sacrifices: Many sacrifices under this class are known to be variations of the isti type,.on the model of darsapurnamasa. These are performed for the fulfillment of various desires of the yajamana (sacrificer).

First among this type of occasional sacrifices is animal sacrifice (pasuyaga), some times as an independent sacrifice and some times as part of the soma sacrifice. One of the independentpasuvagas is Nirudhapasubandha. However, this has fallen out of practice, even among the Vedic ritualists of today. According to the authoritative texts, Nirudhapasubandha can be performed only by one who has established the sacred fire (ahitagni), because this sacrifice necessitates partaking of meat, which the ahitagni is allowed to. This sacrifice is performed once or twice a year during the northern course of the Sun (uttarayana).

The offering is the same as the Darsa sacrifice, with the exception that an animal replaces milk offered to Indra. A yupa, sacrificial post is erected and the victim (pasu), before it is tied up, is bathed and anointed with butter. Other procedures, following the offering of ajya (clarified butter), are similar to those of the new moon and full moon sacrifices (darsa andpurnamasa).

The ritualistic-texts describe in detail the immolation of the victim and offering the omentum (vapa) and some of the limbs of the victim to the fire. The main ceremony of this animal sacrifice is calledparyagnikarana. At the end of this ceremony, some minor rituals called anuyajas including offering to barhis and the doors are also performed. Somayajnas, i.e. sacrifices in which soma juice forms the main oblation is most important among occasional sacrifices. Since this type of sacrifice is quite expensive, only kings and very wealthy people could perform it. But the Somayajnas are attended by a multitude of people belonging to different strata of the society as a public event.

The Soma sacrifices are performed in Spring, which was the beginning of the year in ancient time. There are seven major Soma sacrifices, the common or class name being Jyotistoma. The seven Soma sacrifices are: Agnistoma, Ukthya, Sodasin, A tiratra, A tyagnistoma, Vajapeya and Aptoryama. This list is not, however, 'exhaustive. The Agnistoma is taken as the model (prakrti) while others are modelled on the form of Agnistoma and hence are known as variatifns.(viktis). The Soma juice offered in Soma sacrifices is pressed in three sessions (savanas), morning, midday and evening @ratah, madhyandina, and trtiya). Offerings in a Soma sacrifices go to a good number of deities of whom Indra is the most prominent. The midday session is exclusively devoted to him while he has shares in the morning and evening sessions also.

Sixteen priests, senior and junior ones, officiate in an Agnistoma. There are various steps or stages of the Agnistoma ceremony. First of them is the selection and commissioning of the priests, which is followed by the consecration (diksa) of the sacrificer (yajamana) and his wife. Then they are supposed to observe silence, abstinence, etc.

The next is the purchase of Soma which is done through a mock fight between the seller and the purchaser. This event is followed by three of actual performances, on each of which pravargya or hot-milk offering is made twice a day. On the second day an altar is constructed to place the cartloads of the Soma plant. An animal sacrifice to Agni and Soma is perforped on the third day. The juice is kxtracted from the Soma plant, with stone or mortar and pestle. After proper purifying through a strainer the Soma juice is mixed with milk. The Soma offerings are accompanied by the chanting of various categories of mantras, known as astras and stotras. Another animal sacrifice, the victim animal, being a goat, is dedicated to Indra and Agni. Oblations, such as sacrificial cakes (purodasas) are also ofired.

The concluding chapter of Agnistoma consists of chanting of particular hymns to Agni and Maruts (Agni-Maruta-sastras) and then immersion of the used Soma shoots, sacrificial implements, etc. in nearby river or tank and finally a bath taken by the sacrificer (yajamana) and his wife. Among the seven Soma sacrifices Vajapeya deserves special mention. It is presumed that this sacrifice shows some traces of popular origin. The purpose of performing this sacrifice is to gain victory and authority. The kings and other wealthy persons from all the three higher castes are entitled to perform the Vaj apeya sacrifice.

Another important Vedic sacrifice was Rajasuya which is related to royal consecration ceremony and, therefore, assumed the character of a public event. The grandeur of the ceremony, very naturally, drew public attention and attendance in a big way. The mantras chanted on this occasion are prayers for the welfare of the state and the people. It is, however, to be borne in mind that the sacrifice was actually performed by the king as the yajamana, and not by the members of the public.

In the performance aspect, Rajasuya was like any other Soma sacrifice, starting from the diksa and to several upasad days. Unlike other sacrifices, the yajamana, i.e. the king has to play a few very important roles and there were a few special features. The Adhvaryu priest would hand over to the king a bow with three arrows; the king should walk a few steps to all the directions. He will sit on a throne made of udumbara wood covered with a tiger-skin, and will be anointed with butter, honey, sacred waters from many rivers and seas.

The real royal grandeur is reflected in the Asvamedha, i.e. horse sacrifice. This sacrifice was performed by powerful kings with imperial ambitions. Prajapati is the chief deity of the Asvamedha rite, though oblations are offered to many other deities. The ceremony starts on the "8 or 9" day of Phalguna and is spread over a year. The procedure of the sacrifice is quite elaborate and complicated. At the outset, a horse of the highest quality is tied and bathed. It is then consecrated near the sacrificial fires and various types of purodasas are offered, during the next three days. Then the horse is set fiee to roam at its free will beyond the boundaries of the king, but it is escorted by the contingerit of army. If the h~rsecr osses the territory of a king unopposed, it will mean that the ruler of the territory concedes to the authority of the former king. If any king obstructs the movement of the horse, it will be rescued by the accompanying army contingent by fighting. During the year of the horse's wandering many types of merry-making continue in capital. On the return of the horse, a Soma sacrifice is performed, in which the Soma is pressed on three days (sutya days). On the second sutya day the horse is sacrificed, alon with a great number of victims, - animals both domestic and wild, - big and small. There are some activities in the ritual which can only be interpreted as a fertility cult. The sacrifice is concluded with the ceremonial both on the third sutya day. If a king succeeds in performing the asvamedha on the return of the horse unopposed, he is acclaimed as an emperor. Though many authors of the Puranas and compilers of later Law digests forbid the performance of the Asvamedha in the Kali Age, the sacrifice continued to be performed till a much later age.

Sautramani is another Vedic sacrifice known for its unique peculiarity that sura, i.e. wine is offered in place of Soma. The Vedic Soma sacrifices are classified by another criterion. If a sacrifice is performed with more than one but upto twelve pressbg (sutya) days, it is called an ahina sacrifice. If the number of the sutya days is more than twelve, it is called a sattra. A sattra may be extended to several years.

1.3.3.3. Rituals - domestic rites

Besides the Srauta sacrifices both regular and occasional, compulsory and optional - a householder belonging to any of the three upper castes is required to perform quite a good number of personal or family rites - as enjoined by the ritualistic texts known as grhya karmans, i.e. domestic rites. The most important distinction between the public rites (srauta) and the domestic rites (grhya) is that while the Srauta rites are performed in three sacred fires, viz. Ahavaniya, Daksinga and Garhapatya, - the grhya rites are performed only in the Garhapatya fire. There are, however, some rites which are both srauta and grhya. The occasions of establishing the Garhapatya fire are marriage, death of the head of the family or division of patemal property, resulting in the setting up of a separate household. The Garhapatya fire is to be maintained uninterruptedly. The auspicious time for the setting up of the Garhapatya fire is any bright fortnight during the northern course of the sun (uttarayana) which rule is of course not very hard and fast. The householder is supposed to perform all the Grhya rites himself, except the Sulagava and Dhanvantari rites which may be performed by a Brahmin priest commissioned for the purpose. During the absence of the householder, however, his wife or a resident pupil may act as his representative. The materials used for the oblations in the Grhya rites are generally the same as those for the srauta rituals, with the exception that Soma is never offered and animals very rarely.

1.3.4. Heterodox Religious Order in Ancient India

The sixth century BC witnessed the emergence and growth of Non-Vedic and Pro-Vedic ideologies. However, one should understand that in the crowd of various types of belief systems, examples of violent religious conflicts were almost absent in India. In fact, these systems resorted to the method of arguments and debates for the propagation of their respective belief system, which is a unique feature of Indian religion, or the ideological system. Against the background of rigid Vedic religion, based on sacrifices & polytheism, the 6th century India witnessed the rise of heterodox & monotheist belief systems like Jainism, Buddhism, and Ajivakas etc. These systems opposed complex and time-labor-money consuming Vedic rituals and sacrifices. Besides, they also rebelled against the growth of Brahmans as a superior socio-religious and economical authority in the society. They provided an ideological alternative and base, on which the society flourished in sixth c. BC.

It should be noted that the non-Vedic religions were not of foreign origin. On the contrary, they were deeply rooted in Indian culture. Initially, they seem to be drastically debating each other, but, in due course of time, they followed similar lines and approaches for the propagation of their respective religions.

There are some causes of the emergence of Non-Vedic cults, as follows: Proliferation of Sacrifices During Later Vedic period, the sacrifices became mandatory for receiving favour of God or fulfilling any wish. The scriptures suggested various types of sacrifices, which were time-money consuming and filled with violence. Besides, similar to the sacrifices, various types of specialized priests and crowd of Gods also emerged in the society. In all, the entire system became very complex and, except favorable to priest class, beyond the limits of common person. Discriminatory institutions The later Vedic culture based on rigid caste-system. The Vedic culture represented with the hierarchy of castes, proliferation of castes and sub castes, humiliating condition of women and Shudras etc. The non-Kshatriya rulers and economical superior trader class, along with common person, found no prestigious place or respect in this system.

Ambiguous scriptures The Vedic literature was varied and specialized. However, it was written in ambiguous Sanskrit language, which was known to only Brahmans. Hence, it was necessary for the common person to know their religion in understandable and clear language and literature. Need of New Thoughts Even among Vedic people, many thinkers were dissatisfied by the ritual extremity of Later Vedic period. Hence, they created a different kind of Vedic literature, i.e. the Upanishads. The Upanishads preferred meditation and introspection to the extravagant sacrifices of Vedic scriptures. However, the meditation of Upanishads was revolving around the subjects like atman, Brahma, dvait-advait etc.; even more abstract than the rituals themselves.

Hence, people were in need of a new, unambiguous, simple thought or beliefsystems. Against the background of such complex nature of Later Vedic rituality, a need was felt of such belief system, which would give simple-clear thought and would suggest cheap, manageable rituals in understandable language. Besides, economically superior Varna like Vaishya and politically superior non-Kshatriya rulers and people were in need of socio-religious sanctions to them or legitimacy in society. Hence, in 6th c BC, Non-Vedic cults emerged who fulfilled all the requirements mentioned above and provided legitimacy to Vaishya and non- Kshatriya powerful people and rulers.

1.3.5. Jainism

By tradition, Jainism is an anadi religion, i.e. the all time/ever-existed religion, and, through tirthankaras, it is retold from time to time. Rishabhdeva was the first among 24 tirthankaras, in which, Neminath was 22nd, whereas, Parshvanatha was 23rd. Parshvanath was the son of Ashvasena, ruler of Banaras and queen Vama. He, at the age of 30, left the throne and resorted to penance. He lived for 100 years and spent his life for the propagation of Jainism. He gave stress on four principles, like, Satya, Brahmacharya, Asteya and Aparigraha. The followers of Parshvanatha, wearing white cloth, consisted of 8 gana, 8 ganadhara and 1000 Shramanas. Vardhaman Mahavir was the 24th tirthankara and most venerated preacher of Jain religion.

1.3.5.1. Vardhaman Mahavir (540 BC to 474 BC): His Life

Vardhaman born at Kundagrama in dist. Muzaffarpur (in present Bihar). He was the son of Siddhartha, king of dnyatrik republic and Trishaladevi, sister of Lichchavi king. Since his childhood, Vardhaman was detached from worldly pleasures and always engaged in meditation. He was married to one Yashoda and had a daughter. After the death of parents, at the age of 30, he took permission from his elder brother and submitted himself to the life of sanyasa (ascetic). Initially he wore cloths, however after 12 months left cloths and remained cloth-less. He resorted to painstaking penance (tapas) for 12 years. On the 13th year, he received enlightenment of supreme knowledge on the banks of Rijipalika at village Jrimbhika and thus become kevalin or arhat. He successfully gained control on all his senses (indriyas). Hence, he is called the Jina, i.e. Jitendriya (who won over his senses). As he was freed from all the bondages, he was called as Nigranth. Afterwards, he propagated his thought in public up to 72 years. Then, at Pavapuri he received Nirvana.

1.3.5.2. His Work

Mahavira reinterpreted the then existed philosophy and code of conducts of Jainism. He contributed a new principle of non-violence (ahimsa) to the four principles, told by Parshvanatha. He, based on non-violence, framed a new set of philosophy and codes of conduct. Then, he consolidated his disciples. Besides, he refreshed Jain monachism (monasticism) and put rules of hierarchy of Jain-preachers or Shramanas. Besides, he provided such rules, which would be suitable for the laymen. For the propagation of his religion, he accepted ardhamagadhi-a language of people as a medium of preaching and methods of dialogue and debates to preach.

Due to his simple codes of conducts and use of people-language, Mahavira could successfully propagated Jainism, which, within a short span of time, received popularity among common person-as also among kings and traders. Hence, Mahavira considered as an actual founder of Jainism.

1.3.5.3. Basic Principles of Jainism

The basic principles of Jainism surmised as follows:

1. Negations of Vedas, Vedic rituals, sacrifices and its concept of God
2. To achieve moksha, one should control his own senses instead of depending on the favours of God
3. Universe is created due to jiva (soul) which is immortal
4. To achieve moksha, jiva should freed from actions
5. Belief in equality

1.3.5.4. The Vratas: *Maha-vrata & Anu-vrata:*

Ahimsa: This is the centre-thought of Jainism. It means to abstain from troubling any living thing with any sort of violence, like, physical, verbal and mental. Satya To speak truth and create such a situation in which other would speak truth. Asteya Not to possess the thing, which is not belonged to us Aparigraha To possess only those things, which are most needed Brahmacharya Abstain from sexual relations These five principles were mandatory for Jain monks and nuns. Hence, these are called as 'maha-vrata'. However, it is not possible for laymen to follow such strict codes of conduct. Hence, Jainism made provision of the same principles for them but in a soft or limited form. They are called as 'anu-vrata', like ahimsa-anuvrata, satyaanuvrata etc.

Guna-vrata: To inculcate patience and sacrifice among laymen and women (shravaka and shravika), three guna-vrata were provided for them, like, Dig-vrata While traveling one should limit his directions and maintain that limitation. Kal-vrata While traveling one should limit the duration and maintain that limitation Anarth-dandavat While following ones occupation one should respect the limits and values of that occupation.

Shiksha-vrata: To increase the tendency of detachment from worldly pleasures and for the social-health, some principles are told, like, Samayika To follow habit of seating calmly at one place and meditate Proshadhopavasa To observe fast on fifth (panchami), eighth (ashtami), fourteenth (chaturdashi) day of every fortnight; or, on eighth and fourteenth day during chaturmasa (Ashadh to Ashvin i.e June-September/rainy season) On the day of fast one should seat in Jain temples and recite scriptures and follow meditation

Bhogopabhoga parinama Decide limitation on food consumption and pleasure for each day and follow that limitation. Atithi samvibhag To give part of our cooked food to the truthful and worthy guest.

Types of Disciples: According to Jainism, there are five types of disciples, comprised of 1. Tirthankara (free), 2. Arhata (a soul flowing to nirvana), 3. Acharya (Great Disciple), 4. Upadhyaya (Teacher), 5. Sadhu (general disciple) Jain Scriptures. According to tradition, the original preaching of Mahvira compiled in 14 volumes, called as Parva. In the first grand-assembly, held at Pataliputra, Sthulabhadra classified Jainism into 12 Anga. These Angas included famous angas like Acharanga sutra and Bhagavati sutra. Further in the second grand-assembly, held at Vallabhi, these supplemented by the Upangas. The original Jaina canons (85) comprised of sutragrantha (41), prakirnakas (31), Niyukti/Bhashya (12), Mahabhashya (1). These are called as Agama, written in ardhamagadhi script.

1.3.5.5. The Spread of Jainism

By tradition, Jainism was existed before Mahavira. However, due to tenuous efforts of Mahavira and his new contributions like consolidation, reinterpretation of philosophy and codes of conduct, a separate set of codes for laymen, hierarchical systemized monachism; he was credited as an actual founder of Jaina religion. Among his 11 disciples or ganadharas, Arya Sudharma became the first mainpreacher or thera. During the period of Nanda dynasty, Sambhutavijaya propagated Jainism. Bhadrabahu, the sixth thera, was contemporary to Chandragupta Maurya. The basic reason of the spread of Jainism was the support and favours of contemporary rulers. Great rulers like Bimbisara, Ajatshatru, Chandragupta Maurya, Kharvela (north) and southern dynasties like Ganga, Kadamba, Chalukya, Rashtrakuta, and Shilahara accepted Jainism as their personal and royal religion. They extended their support to Jain for their propagation and consecutive spread. The Jain were mainly concentrated in the region of Mathura; however, due to the favour of Chalukya rulers of Gujarat and notable dynasties of South, it spread in Gujarat and south India.

Apart from rulers, the trader and artisan's class also accepted Jainism. It spread on the financial base provided by these classes. Due to the favour of rulers, Jaina literature and art also flourished. Vast collections of Jaina literature created in the public-language like ardhamagadhi and then Sanskrit, too. Besides, caves-viharas-temples constructed to accommodate the worshipers for large congregations. These places served as educational centres where renowned works and researches on Jainism were undertook by various scholars, like, Mathura and Shravanbelagola were the most renowned research institutions of Jainism.

The stress of Jainism on the adherence of strict codes of conduct hampered its spread; however, on the other hand, by these, it could retain its oldest form until today. Especially, the concept of 'ahimsa' and 'anekantavada', were the immortal gift of Jainism to the India culture.

1.3.5.6. Grand Assemblies

During the draught of 12 years in Magadha, Bhadrabahu, with his disciples departed to Shravanbelagola, in South India, whereas, some Jain, mostly Shvetambaras, remained in Magadha under the leadership of Sthulbahubhadra. Around 300 BC, he organized first grand assembly at Pataliputra. The assembly came up with the classification of Mahavira's preaching in 12 Angas. When, Jain from south India, mostly Digambaras, returned to Magadha, they refuted these Angas and stated that all the original scripture were lost.

After many years, in 512 AD, second grand assembly was held at Vallabhi (Gujarat) presided by Deavardhimani Kshamashramana. Meanwhile, the 12th Anga was lost. Hence, the assembly tried to consolidate and compile the scripture. They created new texts like Upanga and supplemented to remaining Angas.

1.3.5.7. Dissensions

Earlier, Jaina remained without cloths. During Chandragupta Maurya's time, most of the Jaina under the leadership of Bhadrabahu left Magadha towards south India. After some period,

they returned to Magadha. Meanwhile, the Jaina at Magadha were resorted & become habitual to cover their body with white cloth. Besides, they have softened some codes of conduct, like permission of women in Jain monachism, whereas, the Jaina, who returned from south were attached to earlier strict rules and remained cloth-less. Obviously, their arrival created dissensions among Jaina. It divided between the two cults, the Shvetambaras (clad in white-dress) and Digambaras (cloth-less). The Digambara Jaina believed remaining cloth-less and they are against permitting women in the fold of religion, whereas, the Shvetambara Jaina supports participation of women and accepted the white (shveta) cloth to wear. In due course of time, both these major cults came up with their own version and scriptures of Jainism. Generally, the Digambaras were mostly concentrated in the southern part of India whereas north populated by the Shvetambaras.

1.3.6. Buddhism

1.3.6.1. Gautama Buddha (566 to 486 BC): His life

Siddhartha was born at Lumbini in present Nepal. He was son of Shuddodana, the King of Shakya gana of Kapilvastu and Mayadevi, princess of Koliya gana. In his childhood he was taken care by Gautami, hence he also called as Gautama. After his enlightenment, he called as Buddha. Shuddodana provided all kinds of comforts and pleasure to Siddhartha. However, since his childhood, Siddhartha was detached from worldly pleasure and engrossed in meditation. When he arrived to his youth, he deeply moved by the misery and agony of human life. Traditions inform us about the effects on Siddhartha of the sight of old man, a sick man, a dead body and meditative sage. He became restless to seek the cause of such agony and real meaning of truth. Hence, at 29, he left his wife Yashodhara and son Rahul and, moved to forests to know the real meaning of truth and reason of sorrow. His departure from material pleasure for the welfare of humanity engraved in history as maha-bhi-ni-shkramana. He spent his six years on experimenting in various methods of penance supervised under various scholars. However, he felt such methods as fruitless hence left them. At the end, on the banks of Uruvela, at Gaya, he received enlightenment under the pipal (bodhi)- tree. He became the Buddha-the enlightened one and Tathagath-who knew the truth. He refuted the known methods and authority of knowledge and put forth his new version of truth. He decided to share his knowledge with the people, basedon simple code of conducts and in the languages of people, i.e. Pali. He gave his first sermon at Sarnath and introduced his dhamma. This sermon refuted the earlier versions of truth and introduced a new beginning in the philosophical history of Indian culture; and hence, memorized as dhamma-chakra-parivartana. His knowledgeable, simple and sacrificial character and his teaching in simple tone impressed people.

Initially there were five disciples-Ashvajit, Upali, Mogalalana, Shreyaputra and Anand. However, within a short span of period crowds and crowds of people gathered around him and accepted his knowledge. He was followed by, along with common person, wealthy merchants-traders, artisans and kings like Ajatshatru (Magadha), Prasenjit (Kosala) and Udayana (Kaushambi) of that time. Then, Buddha organized his disciples into a specific monachism rested on definite rules and codes of conduct. This is called the Sangha. The Buddhists express their devotions by submitting themselves to Buddha, his Sangha and his dhamma.

After painstaking propagation and travels through distant lands, in the age of 80, Buddha rested at Kusinagar (Kasaya, dist. Devriya, present Uttar Pradesh) in peace. His departure commemorated as maha-pari-nirvana.

Buddhist Monasticism or Sangha: For the propagation of Buddhism, Buddha created a disciplined mechanism of missionaries, called as Bhikshus and Bhikshunis. He organized the missionaries and his disciples in a specific organization, called as Sangha.

Membership of Sangha (Monastery): Any person (male or female) who is above 18 and left his possessions could become member of Sangha based on equality. Initially women were not permitted in Sangha, but thanks to persistent efforts and convincing by Ananda (disciple) and Gautami (foster mother); the doors were opened for women. Besides, after the permission of owner, slaves, soldiers and debtors could also become member of Sangha. However, criminals, lepers and contagious patients not permitted into Sangha. At the outset, one has to take oath (loyalty towards Buddha-Dhamma-Sangha), then shave his head (mundana) and wear yellow dress. Then, after one month, he could take a diksha called as upasampada. In addition, after upasampada he is taken as a member of Sangha. However, the member is expected to follow the codes of conduct (dasha-shila), comprised of, abstaining from: consuming alcohol, taking untimely food, dance-songs, using perfumes, using mattress for sleep, wearing gold & silver ornaments, indulging in adultery etc.

The organizational base of Sangha was a democratic one. The monks are expected to travel for eight months for the propagation of Buddhism. Then, during the four months of rainy season, they gathered at one place, called as varshavasa.During varshavasa, they discuss, share their experiences, and gave confessions, take prayashcita (expiation). Hence, they were expected to frequently gather, behave unanimously and respect the elders in Sangha.

The monks assemble in upasabhas on specific days like eighth, fourteenth, full moon, no-moon days of the month. They submitted their reports, gave confessions and-in a situation of breach-of-rules, follow prayaschita. Due to such a disciplinary and chaste character of monks, they received a great respect in the society. It helped the increase in Buddhism in large population. Besides, the Sangha also functioned as a socio-religious legitimization for the traders, for which, the latter generously gave donations for the constructions of Buddhist place of worships and residence. In need of support of superior economical class of that period and the support of religion of people, the rulers also provided favours, donations and protections to the Sangha.

1.3.6.2. Buddhist Scriptures

Buddha's preaching collected and classified into three volumes, collectively called as pitakas. The three volumes are like these, Sutta-pitaka It is a collection of Buddha's preaching in dialogue form, which mainly made for common people. It has five nikayas, in which, the stories of Buddha's rebirth (the jatakas) collected in the fifth nikaya. Vinaya pitaka It is a collection of rules and codes of conduct for Buddhist monks and nuns.

Abhi-dhamma-pitaka It is a collection of Buddha's philosophical thought in the form of Question & answers. It mainly meant for scholars of Buddhism.

Dharmaparishadas: The Grand Assemblies After the mahaparinirvana of Buddha, Buddhism witnessed the crowd of various versions of Buddha's preaching. Hence, to remove such discrepancy and reach to unanimous platform, a need was felt to rearrange and compile Buddha's original preaching and codify them. For this purpose, grand assemblies of Buddhist followers organized from time to time.

Immediately after the death of Buddha, around 483 BC, during the reign of Ajatshatru of Haryaka dynasty, the first grand assembly organized in the caves of Saptaparni, close to Rajgriha. It was presided by Mahakashyapa. The assembly came up with collection of Buddha's preaching in pitakas. Under the supervision of Upali, Vinaya Pitaka compiled whereas Sutta-pitaka compiled under the supervision of Ananda.

Then during the reign of Kalashoka of Shishunaga dynasty, in 387 BC, second grand assembly organized at Vaishali. In this, monks of Pataliputra and Vaishali introduced some rules, however, debated by monks of Avanti and Kaushambi. The debate not reached to any conclusion; hence, Buddhism witnessed its first major division under the names of Mahasanghika and Sthavirvadis. The Mahasanghik supported new rules whereas the Sthavirvadi decided to stick to the rules, compiled under Vinaya pitaka.

During the reign of Ashoka of Maurya dynasty, in 251 BC, third grand assembly organized at Pataliputra, presided by Moggaliputta Tisya. The assembly came up with the collection of Buddha's philosophy under the volume called as Abhidhammapitaka. The assembly also drove away 60000 monks who were not following Buddha's rules.

In the background of waves of new thinking, Kanishka of Kushana dynasty called the fourth grand assembly at Kundalvana (Kashmir). The assembly came up with the collection of treaties on three pitakas. However, due to the debates between new thinking and traditional scholars, the earlier division was dissolved and united under the name of Hinayana, whereas the new thinkers known as Mahayana.

1.3.6.3. Dissensions

During second grand assembly at Vaishali, Buddhism witnessed its major dissensions due to the intense arguments by the monks of Kaushambi and Avanti and those of Pataliputra and Vaishali. They are called as Sthavirvadis (those who stressed on strict observance of Vinaya-rules) and

Mahasanghikas (those who wished to introduce new rules and changes), respectively.

After Mauryas, the rulers started favoring Vedic religion than Buddhism. Besides, Vedic religion, in reaction to the popularity of Buddhism, started introspecting itself and making improvisation in their philosophical and practical approaches. At this time, foreign rulers and concepts of art were making entry into Indian soil. Besides, to enlarge mass base, every belief systems were adhering to the process of deification and idol-worship. Hence, these systems started considering Sanskrit language for their scriptures to compete Vedic religion.

Against this background, forth grand assembly was organized at Kundalvana. Many Buddhists thinkers, to enlarge mass base were inclined to idol-worship and appealing for other drastic changes in Buddhism. To oppose them, the earlier divisions of Sthavirvadis and Mahasanghikas united under Hinayana, whereas, the new thinkers were called as Mahayana.

Decline of Buddhism : As mentioned earlier, Buddhism witnessed clash of philosophy and stress on codes among various versions. In due course of time, it gradually declined and, around the end of 7th century, became almost invisible from the Indian land. What were the causes of such a decline? Let us find out. Shift of kings'-favor As we know that the favour and support of rulers were one of the causes for the spread of Buddhism. However, after the Mauryas, India was mushroomed with those kings who favoured Vedic religion. In fact, the rulers and their officers started resurrecting Vedic religion by performing huge sacrifices and giving donations. It hampered the support of Buddhism.

Introspection of Vedic religion The speedy growth of non-Vedic religions forced Vedic religion to introspect within their own belief systems. Thus, they made some reforms in the erstwhile rigid ritualistic Vedic religion. It became people oriented. It introduced concepts like temples for mass-congregation, idol-worships, devotional mode of prayers, simple code of conducts, establishment of monasteries, pilgrimages etc.

Hence, crowds of people were attracted to Vedic religion. Dissensions in Buddhism Immediately after the departure of Buddha, Buddhism faced with dissensions. To curb such conflicts and reach to unanimity, contemporary rulers organized grand assemblies from time to time. However, they proved in vain. Besides, for the peopleorientation, Buddhism also accepted the concepts like idol-worship, Sanskrit-language, concept of heaven & hell, cycle of birth etc. Such concepts marred the individualistic identity of Buddhism, which was originally revolutionary and heterodox in nature.

Foreign invasion Except Menander and Kanishka, almost all foreign rulers were followers of the Vedic religion. Especially, the aggressive Huna tribe was the follower of Shaiva cult. It destroyed Buddhist monastery and learning centres. It was a final blow of dispersed Buddhists at that time.

In summing up, we can say that, by introducing religion based on simple philosophy and codes of conduct Buddhism presented a challenge to the then ritualistic, complex and isolated Vedic religion. Due to Buddhism, India witnessed the true religion of common person. Besides, it is credited of spreading Indian culture into distant foreign lands.

1.3.7. The Ajivakas

During the birth of heterodox religions like Jainism and Buddhism, the cult of Ajivakas was emerged in north India. We do not have the scriptures of this belief system; hence, based on references scattered in Buddhist and Jain literature we can collect some information about Ajivakas.

One Makkhaliputra Goshal is perceived as the founder of this cult. According to some, before Goshala, since 117 years, this cult was existed under the leadership of Nandabachcha, Kisasankichcha etc. Goshal's father was Makkhali (Sanskrit: Maskari) which means who holds cane-stick. He lived on begging alms. Goshala was born in cattle pen (goshala) and hence his name. Makkhaliputra Goshala was contemporary to Mahavira. In fact, he was the initial disciple of Mahavira and spent six years with him. However, due to debates on the issues of codes of conduct, Goshala left Jainism and founded his new cult-the Ajivaka at Shravasti. Within short span of time, we informed that large crowds of people were attracted towards Ajivakas. Especially he had considerable amount of followers in potter community.

It expanded in the area from Avanti (western Madhya Pradesh) to Anga (Bihar). We know that Ashoka and his grandson donated rock-cut caves for Ajivakas in the hills of Baravara and Nagarjuni. These were the earliest known caves in the history of rock-cut cave architecture in India. It is told that the Goshala indulged in illicit activities with one potter-lady. He became addicted to various kinds of intoxication. However, in due course of time, he came out of such engagements and again revived his cult. In 500 BC he departed.

1.3.7.1. Philosophy of Ajivakas

Ajivaka means one who disregards restrictions, has faith upon destiny, live by his natural tendencies and thus follows free life.

- They have faith that every being has soul within it, which takes rebirth after each life.

- However, they disregard the importance of any action and have faith on destiny.
- According to them,
- 'Any thing reaches to its predetermined destination without any force of supportive action'.
- 'natural and spiritual progress is a process happened through the continuous cycle of birth & rebirth'
- 'No thing/being/quality is caused by human action; in fact, it is to be existed due to its own destiny.
- Whatever happiness and sorrow is there they do not have any cause and cannot avoided.

These concepts gave birth to the philosophy of akarmanyavada i.e. believing on no-action. Goshala says, natthi karmya, natthi kiriyam, natthi viriyam (no action, no deeds, and no power). Hence, he called as maskari=ma-karanshila means one who does no action. The determinism of Goshala gave rise to his concept of amorality. He refutes the kriyavada, i.e. who believes in actions. That leads to his protest against the principle, which believes that due to moral behaviour an individual and society progress.

In short, if one agrees that the things happened without any action, then, the criteria of moral or immoral conscious are naturally remained useless. Hence, Goshal's reliance on destiny and concept of non-action naturally led to the defense of immoral behaviour.

1.3.8. Other Brahmanical Cult

The worship of Yakshas and Nagas and other folk deities constituted the most important part of primitive religious beliefs, in which Bhakti had a very important role to play. There is ample evidence about the prevalence of this form of worship among the people in early literature as well as in archaeology.

1.3.8.1. Vasudeva/Krishna Worship

A Sutra in Panini's *Ashtadhyayi* refers to the worshippers of Vasudeva (Krishna). The Chhandogya Upanishad also speaks of Krishna, the son of Devaki, a pupil of the sage Ghora Angirasa who was a sun-worshipping priest. A large number of people worshipped Vasudeva Krishna exclusively as their personal God and they were at first known as Bhagavatas. The Vasudeva-Bhagavata cult grew steadily, absorbing within its fold other Vedic and Brahminic divinities like Vishnu (primarily an aspect of the sun) and Narayana (a cosmic God). From the late Gupta period the name mostly used to designate this Bhakti cult was Vaishnava, indicating the predominance of the Vedic Vishnu element in it with emphasis on the doctrine of incarnations *(avataras).*

1.3.8.2. Vaishnava movement in the south

The history of the Vaishnava movement from the end of the Gupta period till the first decade of the thirteenth century AD is concerned mainly with South India. Vaishnava poet-saints known as *alvars* (a Tamil word denoting those drowned in Vishnu-bhakti) preached single-minded devotion *(ekatmika bhakti)* for Vishnu and their songs were collectively known as *prabandhas.*

1.3.8.3. Shaivism

Unlike Vaishnavism, Shaivism had its origin in antiquity. Panini refers to a group of Shivaworshippers as Shiva-bhagavatas, who were characterised by the iron lances and clubs they carried and their skin garments. Shaiva Movement in the South: The Shaiva movement in the South flourished at the beginning through the activities of many of the 63 saints known in Tamil as Nayanars (Siva-bhakts). Their appealing emotional songs in Tamil were called *Tevaram Stotras,* also known as *Dravida Veda* and ceremonially sung in the local Shiva temples. The Nayanars hailed from all castes. This was supplemented on the doctrinal side by a large number of Shaiva intellectuals whose names were associated with several forms of Shaiva movements like Agamanta, Shudha and Vira-shaivism.

1.3.8.4. Minor religious movements

Worship of the female principle (Shakti) and of Surya did not achieve equal importance as the other two major brahminical cults. The female aspect of the divinity might have been venerated in the pre-Vedic times. In the Vedic age respect was shown also to the female principle as the Divine Mother, the Goddess of abundance and personified energy (Shakti). However, clear reference to the exclusive worshippers of the Devi is not to be found until a comparatively late period. As mentioned earlier, Surya has been venerated in India from the earliest times. In Vedic and epic mythology, Sun and his various aspects played a very important part. The East Iranian (Shakadvipi) form of the solar cult was introduced in parts of northern India in the early centuries of the Christian era. But it was only at a comparatively late period that god figured as the central object in religious movements.

1.3.9. Philosophy in Ancient India

In classical India, philosophy was understood as contributing to human well-being by freeing people from misconceptions about themselves and the world. Ultimate well-being was conceived as some sort of fulfilment outside the conditions of space and time. Philosophies, as well as religious traditions, understood themselves as paths to that final goal. Where the religious contexts of those who engaged in critical, reflective and argumentative philosophy are concerned we have to reckon with a tremendous variety of beliefs and practices. Neither 'Hinduism' nor 'Buddhism' are really homogenous. It is difficult to know where to begin: you can always go back further. In the course of the second millennium B.C. the Aryan migrations into north west of the sub-continent introduced the Vedic religious culture and the four-fold hierarchy of *varn. as* (Brahmins, Warriors, Farmers and Servants) that was superimposed on the indigenous system of *jātis*. It appears that originally the ritual cult was concerned with the propitiation by offerings of the many deities in the Vedic pantheon. Their favour thus secured would yield mundane and supra-mundane rewards. Rituals performed by members of the Brahmin caste were understood as yielding benefits for both the individual and the community. But there developed an outlook that the continuation of the cosmos, the regularity of the seasons and the rising of the sun, were not merely marked or celebrated by ritual acts but actually depended upon ritual. What the rituals effected was too important to be left to the choices of ultimately uncontrollable capricious divinities. So rituals came to be thought of as automatic mechanisms, in the course of which the mention of the deities' names was but a formulaic aspect of the process. The relegated gods existed only in name. The Brahmins unilaterally declare themselves the gods in human form. From the point of view of the individual, the benefit of the ritual was understood in terms of the accumulation of merit or good *karma* that would be enjoyed at some point in the future, in this or a subsequent life perhaps in a superior sphere of experience for those with sufficient merit.

1.3.9.1. Vedic philosophy

Religion of the Rig Vedic people was very simple in the sense that it consisted mainly of worship of numerous deities representing the various phenomena of nature through prayers. It was during the later Vedic period that definite ideas and philosophies about the true nature of soul or Atman and the cosmic principle or Brahman who represented the ultimate reality were developed. These Vedic philosophical concepts later on gave rise to six different schools of philosophies called *shada darshana*. They fall in the category of the orthodox system as the final authority of the Vedas is recognised by all of them. Let us now find outmore about these six schools of Indian philosophy.

Samkhya System: The Samkhya philosophy holds that reality is constituted of two principles one female and the other male i.e. Prakriti, Purusha respectively. Prakriti and Purusha are completely independent and absolute. According to this system, Purusha is mere consciousness; hence it cannot be modified or changed. Prakriti on the other hand is constituted of three attributes, thought, movement and the change or transformation of these attributes brings about the change in all objects. The Samkhya philosophy tries to establish some relationship between Purusha and Prakriti for explaining the creation of the universe. The propounder of this philosophy was Kapila, who wrote the *Samkhya sutra.* Infact Samkhya school explained the phenomena of the doctrine of evolution and answered all the questions aroused by the thinkers of those days.

Yoga: Yoga literally means the union of the two principal entities. The origin of yoga is found in the *Yogasutra* of Patanjali believed to have been written in the second century BC. By purifying and controlling changes in the mental mechanism, yoga systematically brings about the release of purusha from prakriti. Yogic techniques control the body, mind and sense organs. Thus this philosophy is also considered a means of achieving freedom or *mukti.* This freedom could be attained by practising self-control (*yama*), observation of rules (*niyama*), fixed postures *(asana),* breath control *(pranayama*), choosing an object (*pratyahara*) and fixing the mind *(dharna),* concentrating on the chosen object *(dhyana)* and complete dissolution of self, merging the mind and the object *(Samadhi*). Yoga admits the existence of God as a teacher and guide.

Nyaya: Nyaya is considered as a technique of logical thinking. According to Nyaya, valid knowledge is defined as the real knowledge, that is, one knows about the object as it exists. For example, it is when one knows a snake as a snake or a cup as a cup. Nyaya system of philosophy considers God who creates, sustains and destroys the universe. Gautama is said to be the author of the Nyaya Sutras.

Vaisheshika: Vaisheshika system is considered as the realistic and objective philosophy of universe. The reality according to this philosophy has many bases or categories which are substance, attribute, action, genus, distinct quality and inherence. Vaisheshika thinkers believe that all objects of the universe are composed of five elements–earth, water, air, fire and ether. They believe that God is the guiding principle. The living beings were rewarded or punishedaccording to the law of *karma,* based on actions of merit and demerit. Creation and destruction of universe was a cyclic process and took place in agreement with the wishes of God. Kanada wrote the basic text of Vaisheshika philosophy.

A number of treatises were written on this text but the best among them is the one written by Prashastapada in the sixth century AD. Vaisheshika School of philosophy explained the phenomena of the universe by the atomic theory, the combination of atoms and molecules into matter and explained the mechanical process of formation of Universe.

Mimamsa: Mimamsa philosophy is basically the analysis of interpretation, application and the use of the text of the *Samhita* and *Brahmana* portions of the Veda. According to Mimamsa philosophy Vedas are eternal and possess all knowledge, and religion means the fulfilment of duties prescribed by the Vedas. This philosophy encompasses the Nyaya-Vaisheshika systems and emphasizes the concept of valid knowledge. Its main text is known as the Sutras of Gaimini which have been written during the third century BC. The names associated with this philosophy are Sabar Swami and Kumarila Bhatta. The essence of the system according to Jaimini is Dharma which is the dispenser of fruits of one's actions, the law of righteousness itself. This system lays stress on the ritualistic part of Vedas.

Vedanta: Vedanta implies the philosophy of the Upanishad, the concluding portion of the Vedas. Shankaracharya wrote the commentaries on the Upanishads, *Brahmasutras* and the *Bhagavad Gita*. Shankaracharya's discourse or his philosophical views came to be known as Advaita Vedanta. Advaita literally means non-dualism or belief in one reality. Shankaracharya expounded that ultimate reality is one, it being the Brahman. According to Vedanta philosophy, 'Brahman is true, the world is false and self and Brahman are not different, Shankaracharya believes that the Brahman is existent, unchanging, the highest truth and the ultimate knowledge. He also believes that there is no distinction between Brahman and the self. The knowledge of Brahman is the essence of all things and the ultimate existence. Ramanuja was another well known Advaita scholar. Among different schools of philosophy was found one philosophy which reached the climax of philosophic thought that the human mind can possibly reach, and that is known as the Vedantic philosophy.

Vedanta philosophy has ventured to deny the existence of the apparent ego, as known to us, and in this respect Vedanta has its unique position in the history of philosophies of the world. Vedanta is a philosophy and a religion. As a philosophy it inculcates the highest truths that have been discovered by the greatest philosophers and the most advanced thinkers of all ages and all countries. Vedanta philosophy teaches that all these different religions are like so many roads, which lead to same goal. Vedanta (the end of the Vedas or knowledge) refers to the Upanishads which appeared at the end of each Veda with a direct perception of reality. The core message of Vedanta is that every action must be governed by the intellect – the discriminating faculty. The mind makes mistakes but the intellect tells us if the action is in our interest or not. Vedanta enables the practitioner to access the realm of spirit through the intellect. Whether one moves into spirituality through Yoga, meditation or devotion, it must ultimately crystallize into inner understanding for atitudinal changes and enlightenment.

Charvaka school: Brihaspati is supposed to be the founder of the Charvaka School of philosophy. It finds mention in the Vedas and Brihadaranyka Upanishad. Thus it is supposed to be the earliest in the growth of the philosophical knowledge. It holds that knowledge is the product of the combination of four elements which leaves no trace after death. Charvaka philosophy deals with the materialistic philosophy. It is also known as the *Lokayata* Philosophy – the philosophy of the masses. According to Charvaka there is no other world. Hence, death is the end of humans and pleasure the ultimate object in life. Charvaka recognises no existence other than this material world. Since God, soul, and heaven, cannot be perceived, they are not recognised by Charvakas. Out of the five elements earth, water, fire, air and ether, the Charvakas do not recognise ether as it is not known through perception. The whole universe according to them is thus consisted of four elements.

1.3.9.2. Jain philosophy

Like the Charvakas, the Jains too do not believe in the Vedas, but they admit the existence of a soul. They also agree with the orthodox tradition that suffering (pain) can be stopped by controlling the mind and by seeking right knowledge and perception and by observing the right conduct. The Jaina philosophy was first propounded by the *tirthankar* Rishabha Deva. The names of Ajit Nath and Aristanemi are also mentioned with Rishabha Deva.

There were twenty-four *tirthankaras* who actually established the Jaina *darshan.* The first *tirthankar* realised that the source of Jaina philosophy was Adinath. The twenty fourth and the last *tirthankar* was named Vardhaman Mahavira who gave great impetus to Jainism. Mahavira was born in 599 BC. He left worldly life at the age of thirty and led a very hard life to gain true knowledge. After he attained Truth, he was called Mahavira. He strongly believed in the importance of celibacy or *brahamcharya.*

Jain Theory of Reality: Seven Kinds of Fundamental Elements: The Jainas believe that the natural and supernatural things of the universe can be traced back to seven fundamental elements. They are *jiva, ajivaa, astikaya, bandha, samvara, nirjana,* and *moksa.* Substances like body which exist and envelope (like a cover) are *astïkaya. Anastikayas* like 'time' have no body at all. The substance is the basis of attributes (qualities). The attributes that we find in a substance are known as *dharmas.* The Jainas believe that things or substance have attributes. These attributes also change with the change of *kala* (time). From their point of view, the attributes of a substance are essential, and eternal or unchangeable. Without essential attributes, a thing cannot exist. So they are always present in everything. For example, consciousness *(chetana)* is the essence of the soul; desire, happiness and sorrow are its changeable attributes.

1.3.9.3. Philosophy of the Buddha

Gautama Buddha, who founded the Buddhist philosophy, was born in 563 BC at Lumbini, a village near Kapilavastu in the foothills of Nepal. His childhood name was Siddhartha. His mother, Mayadevi, died when he was hardly a few days old. He was married to Yashodhara, a beautiful princess, at the age of sixteen. After a year of the marriage, he had a son, whom they named Rahul. But at the age of twenty-nine, Gautama Buddha renounced family life to find a solution to the world's continuous sorrow of death, sickness, poverty, etc. He went to the forests and meditated there for six years. Thereafter, he went to Bodh Gaya (in Bihar) and meditated under a pipal tree. It was at this place that he attained enlightenment and came to be known as the Buddha. He then travelled a lot to spread his message and helped people find the path of liberation or freedom. He died at the age of eighty.

Gautama's three main disciples known as Upali, Ananda and Mahakashyap remembered his teachings and passed them on to his followers. It is believed that soon after the Buddha's death a council was called at Rajagriha where Upali recited the *Vinaya Pitaka* (rules of the order) and Ananda recited the *Sutta Pitaka* (Buddha's sermons or doctrines and ethics). Sometime later the *Abhidhamma Pitaka* consisting of the Buddhist philosophy came into existence.

Main Characteristics: Buddha presented simple principles of life and practical ethics that people could follow easily. He considered the world as full of misery. Man's duty is to seek liberation from this painful world. He strongly criticised blind faith in the traditional scriptures like the Vedas. Buddha's teachings are very practical and suggest how to attain peace of mind and ultimate liberation from this material world.

Realization of Four Noble Truths. The knowledge realized by Buddha is reflected in the following four noble truths:

There is suffering in human life. When Buddha saw human beings suffering from sickness, pain and death, he concluded that there was definitely suffering in human life. There is pain with birth. Separation from the pleasant is also painful. All the passions that remain unfulfilled are painful. Pain also comes when objects of sensuous pleasure are lost. Thus, life is all pain.

There is cause of suffering, The second Noble Truth is related to the cause of suffering. It is desire that motivates the cycle of birth and death. Therefore, desire is the fundamental cause of suffering.

There is cessation of suffering. The third Noble Truth tells that when passion, desire and love of life are totally destroyed, pain stops. This Truth leads to the end of sorrow, which causes pain in human life. It involves destruction of ego *(aham or ahamkara),* attachment, jealousy, doubt and sorrow. That state of mind is the state of freedom from desire, pain and any kind of attachment. It is the state of complete peace, leading to *nirvana.*

Path of Liberation. The fourth Noble Truth leads to a way that takes to liberation. Thus, initially starting with pessimism, the Buddhist philosophy leads to optimism. Although there is a constant suffering in human life, it can be ended finally. Buddha suggests that the way or the path leading to liberation is eight-fold, through which one can attain *nirvana.*

Eight-fold Path to Liberation *(Nirvana)*

(i) Right Vision. One can attain right vision by removing ignorance. Ignorance creates a wrong idea of the relationship between the world and the self. It is on account ofwrong understanding of man that he takes the non-permanent world as permanent. Thus, the right view of the world and its objects is the right vision.

(ii) Right Resolve. It is the strong will-power to destroy thoughts and desires that harm others. It includes sacrifice, sympathy and kindness towards others.

(iii) Right Speech. Man should control his speech by right resolve. It means to avoid false or unpleasant words by criticizing others.

(iv) Right Conduct. It is to avoid activities which harm life. It means to be away from theft, excessive eating, the use of artificial means of beauty, jewellery, comfortable beds, gold etc.

(v) Right Means of Livelihood. Right livelihood means to earn one's bread and butter by right means. It is never right to earn money by unfair means like fraud, bribery, theft, etc.

(vi) Right Effort. It is also necessary to avoid bad feelings and bad impressions. It includes self-control, stopping or negation of sensuality and bad thoughts, and awakening of good thoughts.

(vii) Right Mindfulness. It means to keep one's body, heart and mind in their real form. Bad thoughts occupy the mind when their form is forgotten. When actions take place according to the bad thoughts, one has to experience pain.

(viii) Right Concentration. If a person pursues the above seven Rights, he will be able to concentrate properly and rightly. One can attain *nirvana* by right concentration (meditation).

Except for Charvaka School, realisation of soul has been the common goal of all philosophical schools of India. I am sure you would like to know more about Buddhism. We will go to Bodhgaya in Bihar. Tread reverently along this ancient path. Begin with the Mahabodhi tree where something strange happened - realization of truth or spiritual illumination. Tradition states that Buddha stayed in Bodhgaya for seven weeks after his enlightenment. There you must also see the Animeshlocha Stupa which houses a standing figure of the Buddha with his eyes fixed towards this tree. Bodhgaya is also revered by the Hindus who go to the Vishnupada temple to perform 'Pind-daan' that ensures peace and solace to the departed soul.

It was from Rajgir that Buddha set out on his last journey. The first Buddhist Council was held in the Saptaparni cave in which the unwritten teachings of Buddha were penned down after his death. Even the concept of monastic institutions was laid at Rajgir which later developed into an academic and religious centre.

1.3.10. Religion and philosophy in Medieval India

Nearly every month a programme is going on in any auditorium in the city where songs of the Sufi saints and Bhakti saints are sung. The popularity of these programems can be seen from the attendance that is there. They are patronized by the government, by big business houses and even by individuals. The songs and the teachings of the Sufi and the Bhaki saints are relevant even today. Do you know the medieval period in India saw the rise and growth of the Sufi movement and the Bhakti movement. The two movements brought a new form of religious expression amongst Muslims and Hindus. The Sufis were mystics who called for liberalism in Islam. They emphasised on an egalitarian society based on universal love. The Bhakti saints transformed Hinduism by introducing devotion or bhakti as the means to attain God. For them caste had no meaning and all human being's were equal. The Sufi and Bhakti saints played an important role in bringing the Muslims and Hindus together. By using the local language of the people, they made religion accessible and meaningful to the common people.

1.3.10.1. The Sufi movement

You will recall that Islam was founded by Prophet Muhammad. Islam saw the rise of many religious and spiritual movements within it. These movements were centered mainly around the interpretation of the Quran.

There were two major sects that arose within Islam – the Sunnis and Shias. Our country has both the sects, but in many other countries like Iran, Iraq, Pakistan etc. you will find followers of only one of them. Among the Sunnis, there are four principal schools of Islamic Law, These are based upon the Quran and Hadis (traditions of the Prophet's saying and doings). Of these the Hanafi school of the eighth century was adopted by the eastern Turks, who later came to India. The greatest challenge to orthodox Sunnism came from the rationalist philosophy or *Mutazilas,* who professed strict monotheism. According to them, God is just and has nothing to do with man's evil actions. Men are endowed with free will and are responsible for their own actions. The *Mutazilas* were opposed by the Ashari School. Founded by Abul Hasan Ashari (873-935 AD), the Ashari school evolved its own rationalist argument in defence of the orthodox doctrine *(kalam).* This school believes that God knows, sees and speaks. The Quran is eternal and uncreated. The greatest exponent of this school was Abu Hamid al-Ghazali (1058-1111 AD), who is credited with having reconciled orthodoxy with mysticism. He was a great theologian who in 1095 began to lead a life of a Sufi. He is deeply respected by both orthodox elements and Sufis. Al-Ghazali attacked all non-orthodox Sunni schools. He said that positive knowledge cannot be gained by reason but by revelation. Sufis owed their allegiance to the Quran as much as the *Ulemas* did. The influence of the ideas of Ghazali was greater because of the new educational system set up by the state, It provided for setting up of seminaries of higher learning (called *madrasas)* where scholars were familiarised with Ashari ideas. They were taught how to run the government in accordance with orthodox Sunni ideas. These scholars were known as *ulema. Ulema* played an important role in the politics of medieval India.

The Sufis: Contrary to the *ulema* were the Sufis. The Sufis were mystics. They were pious men who were shocked at the degeneration in political and religious life. They opposed the vulgar display of wealth in public life and the readiness of the *ulema* to serve "ungodly" rulers. Many began to lead a retired ascetic life, having nothing to do with the state. The Sufi philosophy also differed from the *ulema.* The Sufis laid emphasis upon free thought and liberal ideas. They were against formal worship, rigidity and fanaticism in religion. The Sufis turned to meditation in order to achieve religious satisfaction. Like the Bhakti saints, the Sufis too interpreted religion as 'love of god' and service of humanity. In course of time, the Sufis were divided into different *silsilahs* (orders) with each *silsilah* having its own *pir* (guide) called *Khwaja* or *Sheikh.* The *pir* and his disciples lived in a *khanqah* (hospice). A *pir* nominated a successor or *wali* from his disciples to carry on his work. The Sufis organised *samas* (a recital of holy songs) to arouse mystical ecstasy. Basra in Iraq became the centre of Sufi activities. It must be noted that the Sufi saints were not setting up a new religion, but were preparing a more liberal movement within the framework of Islam. They owed their allegiance to the Quran as much as the *ulema* did.

Sufism in India: The advent of Sufism in India is said to be in the eleventh and twelfth centuries. One of the early Sufis of eminence, who settled in India, was Al-Hujwari who died in 1089, popularly known as *Data Ganj Baksh* (Distributor of Unlimited Treasure). In the beginning, the main centres of the Sufis were Multan and Punjab. By the thirteenth and fourteenth centuries, the Sufis had spread to Kashmir, Bihar, Bengal and the Deccan. It may be mentioned that Sufism had already taken on a definite form before coming to India. Its fundamental and moral principles, teachings and orders, system of fasting, prayers and practice of living in *khanqahs* had already been fixed. The Sufis came to India via Afghanistan on their own free will. Their emphasis upon a pure life, devotional love and service to humanity made them popular and earned them a place of honour in Indian society.

Abul Fazl while writing in the *Ain-i-Akbari* speaks of fourteen *silsilahs* of the Sufis. However, in this lesson we shall outline only some of the important ones. These *silsilahs* were divided into two types: *Ba-shara* and *Be-shara*. *Ba-shara* were those orders that followed the Islamic Law (Sharia) and its directives such as *namaz* and *roza*. Chief amongst these were the Chishti, Suhrawardi, Firdawsi, Qadiri and Naqshbandi *silsilahs*. The *beshara silsilahs* were not bound by the *Sharia*. The Qalandars belonged to this group.

The Chishti Silsilah: The Chishti order was founded in a village called Khwaja Chishti (near Herat). In India, the Chishti *silsilah* was founded by Khwaja Muinuddin Chishti (born *c.* 1142) who came to India around 1192. He made Ajmer the main centre for his teaching. He believed that serving mankind was the best form of devotion and therefore he worked amongst the downtrodden. He died in Ajmer in 1236. During Mughal times, Ajmer became a leading pilgrim centre because the emperors regularly visited the Sheikh's tomb. The extent of his popularity can be seen by the fact that even today, millions of Muslims and Hindus visit his *dargah* for fufilment of their wishes. Among his disciples were Sheikh Hamiduddin of Nagaur and Qutubuddin Bakhtiyar Kaki. The former lived the life of a poor peasant, cultivated land and refused Iltutmish's offer of a grant of villages. The *khanqah* of Qutubuddin Bakhtiyar Kaki was also visited by people from all walks of life. Sultan Iltutmish dedicated the Qutub Minar to this Saint. Sheikh Fariduddin of Ajodhan (Pattan in Pakistan) popularised the Chishti *silsilah* in modern Haryana and Punjab. He opened his door of love and generosity to all. Baba Farid, as he was called, was respected by both Hindus and Muslims. His verses, written in Punjabi, are quoted in the *Adi Granth.*

Baba Farid's most famous disciple Shaikh Nizamuddin Auliya (1238-1325) was responsible for making Delhi an important centre of the Chishti *silsilah.* He came to Delhi in 1259 and during his sixty years in Delhi, he saw the reign of seven sultans. He preferred to shun the company of rulers and nobles and kept aloof from the state. For him renunciation meant distribution of food and clothes to the poor. Amongst his followers was the noted writer Amir Khusrau. Another famous Chishti saint was Sheikh Nasiruddin Mahmud, popularly known as Nasiruddin *Chirag-i-Dilli* (The Lamp of Delhi). Following his death in 13 56 and the lackof a spiritual successor, the disciples of the Chishti *silsilah* moved out towards eastern and southern India.

***The Suhrawardi** Silsilah:* This *silsilah* was founded by Sheikh Shihabuddin Suhrawardi. It was established in India by Sheikh Bahauddin Zakariya (1182-1262). He set up a leading *khanqah* in Multan, which was visited by rulers, high government officials and rich merchants. Sheikh Bahauddin Zakariya openly took Iltutmisht's side in his struggle against Qabacha and received fromhim the title *Shaikhul Islam* (Leader of Islam). It must be noted that unlike the Chishti saints, the Suhrawardis maintained close contacts with the state. They accepted gifts, jagirs and even government posts in the ecclersiastical department. The Suhrawardi *silsilah* was firmly established in Punjab and Sind. Besides these two *silsilahs* there were others such as the Firdawsi *Silsilah,* Shattari *Silsilah,* Qadiri *Silsilah,* Naqshbandi *Silsilah.*

The importance of the Sufi movement: The Sufi movement made a valuable contribution to Indian society. Like the Bhakti saints who were engaged in breaking down the barriers within Hinduism, the Sufis too infused a new liberal outlook within Islam. The interaction between early Bhakti and Sufi ideas laid the foundation for more liberal movements of the fifteenth century. You will read that Sant Kabir and Guru Nanak had preached a non-sectarian religion based on universal love.

The Sufis believed in the concept of *Wahdat-ul-Wajud* (Unity of Being) which was promoted by Ibn-i-Arabi (1165-1240). He opined that all beings are essentially one. Different religions were identical. This doctrine gained popularity in India. There was also much exchange of ideas between the Sufis and Indian yogis. In fact the *hatha-yoga* treatise *Amrita Kunda* was translated into Arabic and Persian. A notable contribution of the Sufis was their service to the poorer and downtrodden sections of society. While the Sultan and *ulema* often remained aloof from the day to day problems of the people, the Sufi saints maintained close contact with the common people.

Nizamuddin Auliya was famous for distributing gifts amongst the needy irrespective of religion or caste. It is said that he did not rest till he had heard every visitor at the *khanqah*. According to the Sufis, the highest form of devotion to God was the service of mankind. They treated Hindus and Muslims alike. Amir Khusrau said "Though the Hindu is not like me in religion, he believes in the same things that I do". The Sufi movement encouraged equality and brotherhood. It fact, The Islamic emphasis upon equality was respected far more by the Sufis than by the *ulema*. The doctrines of the Sufis were attacked by the orthodoxy. The Sufis also denounced the *ulema*. They believed that the *ulema* had succumbed to world by temptations and were moving away from the original democratic and egalitarian principles of the Quran. This battle between the orthodox and liberal elements continued throughout the sixteenth, seventeenth and eighteenth centuries. The Sufi saints tried to bring about social reforms too.

Like the Bhakti saints, the Sufi saints contributed greatly to the growth of a rich regional literature. Most of the Sufi saints were poets who chose to write in local languages. Baba Farid recommended the use of Punjabi for religious writings. Shaikh Hamiduddin, before him, wrote in Hindawi. His verses are the best examples of early Hindawi translation of Persian mystical poetry. Syed Gesu Daraz was the first writer of Deccani Hindi. He found Hindi more expressive than Persian to explain mysticism. A number of Sufi works were also written in Bengali. The most notable writer of this period was Amir Khusrau (l 252-1325) the follower of Nizamuddin Auliya. Khusrau took pride in being an Indian and looked at the history and culture of Hindustan as a part of his own tradition. He wrote verses in Hindi (Hindawi) and employed the Persian metre in Hindi. He created a new style called *sabaq-i-hindi*. By the fifteenth century Hindi had begun to assume a definite shape and Bhakti saints such as Kabir used it extensively.

1.3.10.2. The Bhakti movement

The development of Bhakti movement took place in Tamil Nadu between the seventh and twelfth centuries. It was reflected in the emotional poems of the Nayanars (devotees of Shiva) and Alvars (devotees of Vishnu). These saints looked upon religion not as a cold formal worship but as a loving bond based upon love between the worshipped and worshipper. They wrote in local languages, Tamil and Telugu and were therefore able to reach out to many people. In course of time, the ideas of the South moved up to the North but it was a very slow process. Sanskrit, which was still the vehicle of thought, was given a new form. Thus we find that the Bhagavata Purana of ninth century was not written in the old Puranic form. Centered around Krishna's childhood and youth, this work uses Krishna's exploits to explain deep philosophy in simple terms. This work became a turning point in the history of the Vaishnavite movement which was an important component of the Bhakti movement.

A more effective method for spreading of the Bhakti ideology was the use of local languages. The Bhakti saints composed their verses in local languages. They also translated Sanskrit works to make them understandable to a wider audience. Thus we find Jnanadeva writing in Marathi, Kabir, Surdas and Tulsidas in Hindi, Shankaradeva popularising Assamese, Chaitanya and Chandidas spreading their message in Bengali, Mirabai in Hindi and Rajasthani. In addition, devotional poetry was composed in Kashmiri, Telugu, Kannad, Odia, Malayalam, Maithili and Gujarati.

The Bhakti saints believed that salvation can be achieved by all. They made no distinction of caste, creed or religion before God. They themselves came from diverse backgrounds. Ramananda, whose disciples included Hindus and Muslims, came from a conservative brahman family. His disciple, Kabir, was a weaver. Guru Nanak was a village accountant's son. Namdev was a tailor.

The saints stressed equality, disregarded the caste system and attacked institutionalised religion. The saints did not confine themselves to purely religious ideas. They advocated social reforms too. They opposed sati and female infanticide. Women were encouraged to join *kirtans.* Mirabai and Lalla (of Kashmir) composed verses that are popular even today.

Amongst the non-sectarian Bhakti saints, the most outstanding contribution was made by Kabir and Guru Nanak. Their ideas were drawn from both Hindu and Islamic traditions and were aimed at bridging the gulf between the Hindus and the Muslims. Let us read in some detail about them. Kabir (1440-1518) is said to have been the son of a brahman widow, who abandoned him. He was brought up in the house of a Muslim weaver. Kabir believed that the way to God was through personally experienced bhakti or devotion. He believed that the Creator is One. His God was called by many names - Rama, Hari, Govinda, Allah, Rahim, Khuda, etc. No wonder then that the Muslims claim him as Sufi, the Hindus call him Rama-Bhakta and the Sikhs incorporate his songs in the *Adi Granth.* The external aspects of religion were meaningless for Kabir. His beliefs and ideas were reflected in the *dohas* (Sakhi) composed by him. One of his dohas conveyed that if by worshipping a stone (idol) one could attain God, then he was willing to worship a mountain. It was better to worship a stone flour-grinder because that could at least fill stomachs.

Kabir emphasised simplicity in religion and said that bhakti was the easiest way to attain God. He refused to accept any prevalent religious belief without prior reasoning. For him, a man could not achieve success without hard work. He advocated performance of action rather than renunciation of duty. Kabir's belief in the unity of God led both Hindus and Muslims to become his disciples. Kabir's ideas were not restricted to religion. He attempted to change the narrow thinking of society. His poetry was forceful and direct. It was easily understood and much of it has passed into our everyday language.

Another great exponent of the *Nankana* school was Guru Nanak (1469-1539). He was born at Talwandi (Nakana Sahib). From an early age, he showed leanings towards a spiritual life. He was helpful to the poor and needy. His disciples called themselves Sikhs (derived from Sanskrit *sisya,* disciple or Pali *sikkha,* instruction). Guru Nanak's personality combined in itself simplicity and peacefulness. Guru Nanak's objective was to remove the existing corruption and degrading practices in society. He showed a new path for the establishment of an egalitarian social order. Like Kabir, Guru Nanak was as much a social reformer as he was a religious teacher. He called for an improvement in the status of women. He said that women who give birth to kings should not be spoken ill of. His *vani* (words) alongwith those of other Sikh Gurus have been brought together in the Guru Granth Sahib, the holy book of the Sikhs.

1.3.10.3. The importance of the Bhakti and Sufi movements

You will recall that the Bhakti movement was a socio-religious movement that opposed religious bigotry and social rigidities. It emphasised good character and pure thinking. At a time when society had become stagnant, the Bhakti saints infused new life and strength. They awakened a new sense of confidence and attempted to redefine social and religious values. Saints like Kabir and Nanak stressed upon the reordering of society along egalitarian lines. Their call to social equality attracted many a downtrodden. Although Kabir and Nanak had no intention of founding new religions but following their deaths, their supporters grouped together as Kabir *panthis* and Sikhs respectively.

The importance of the Bhakti and Sufi saints lies in the new atmosphere created by them, hich continued to affect the social, religious and political life of India even in later centuries. Akbar's liberal ideas were a product of this atmosphere in which he was born and brought up. The preaching of Guru Nanak were passed down from generation to generation. This resulted in the growth of a separate religious group, with its separate language and script Gurmukhi and religious book, Guru Granth Sahib. Under Maharaja Ranjit Singh, the Sikhs grew into a formidable political force in the politics of North India.

The interaction between the Bhakti and Sufi saints had an impact upon Indian society. The Sufi theory of *Wahdat-al-Wujud* (Unity of Being) was remarkably similar to that in the Hindu Upanishads. Many Sufi poet-saints preferred to use Hindi terms rather than Persian verses to explain concepts. Thus we find Sufi poets such as Malik Muhamniad Jaisi composing works in Hindi. The use of terms such as Krishna, Radha, Gopi, Jamuna, Ganga etc. became so common in such literature that an eminent Sufi, Mir Abdul Wahid wrote a treatise *Haqaiq-i-Hindi* to explain their Islamic equivalents. In later years this interaction continued as Akbar and Jahangir followed a liberal religious policy. The popular verses and songs of the Bhakti saints also served as forerunners of a musical renaissance. New musical compositions were written for the purpose of group singing at *kirtans.* Even today Mira's *bhajans* and Tulsidas's *chaupais* are recited at prayer meetings.

1.3.10.4. Philosophy in Medieval India

The major religious movements were brought about by the mystics. They contributed to the religious ideas and beliefs. Bhakti saints like Vallabhacharya, Ramanuja, Nimbaraka brought about new philosophical thinking which had its origin in Shankaracharya's *advaita* (non-dualism) philosophy.

Vishistadvaita **of Ramanujacharya:** *Vishistadvaita* means modified monism. The ultimate reality according to this philosophy is Brahman (God) and matter and soul are his qualities.

Sivadvaita **of Srikanthacharya:** According to this philosophy the ultimate Brahman is Shiva, endowed with Shakti. Shiva exists in this world as well as beyond it.

Dvaita **of Madhavacharya:** The literal meaning *of dvaita* is dualism which stands in opposition to non-dualism and monism of Shankaracharya. He believed that the world is not an illusion *(maya)* but a reality full of differences.

Dvaitadvaita **of Nimbaraka:** *Dvaitadvaita* means dualistic monism. According to this philosophy God transformed himself into world and soul. This world and soul are different from God (Brahman). They could survive with the support of God only. They are separate but dependent.

Suddhadvaita **of Vallabhacharya:** Vallabhacharya wrote commentaries on Vedanta Sutra and Bhagavad Gita. For him. Brahman (God) was Sri Krishna who manifested himself as souls and matter. God andsoul are not distinct, but one. The stress was on pure non-dualism. His philosophy came to be known as *Pushtimarga* (the path of grace) and the school was called Rudrasampradaya.

1.3.11. Summary

- It is difficult, at the present state of our knowledge, to form a clear idea about the true contents of the Harappan religion or religions.
- It can, be presumed that some features of religions common to other ancient civilizations existed in the Indus valley also. These features consisted in worshipping Mother Goddess, deification of trees and their spirits, certain animal figures, a prototype of Siva and *svastika.*
- We find in the Vedic in texts elaborate description of public and domestic rites. Sacrifice was the chief act of worship which had significant religious and social connotation.
- In course of time, the liturgical details of the Vedic rituals became more and more complicated and technical and lots of sutra works were written to formulate the procedures of the rites.
- In the Vedic Age, the performance of the rituals became the professional monopoly of the priests. followers of the Vedic religion. This of public apathy resulted in considerable decline in the cult of sacrifice.
- The elaborate sacrifices were replaced to a great extent by another mode of religious performance, namelypuja, taught by the Puranas and the Tantras. On the other hand thinkers laid more emphasis on philosophic speculation, penance and meditation as means towards the attainment of emancipation (moksa), i.e. fieedom from all bondage and sufferings.
- This new trend gave rise to the Upanisadic philosophy on one hand and schools like Buddhism and Jainism on the other.
- Changes that were coming in material life of people because of pastoral society being replaced by agriculture and growth of trade and commerce as well as the reactions created by ritualism and driestly dominance paved the ground for looking of alternative paths to realize the ultimate truth.
- Following this trend we find that sixth century B.C. witnessed the development of two important religious

traditions in India, Jainism and Buddhism. The Jains believe that there were twenty four Tirthankaras and Mahavira was the last Tirthankara.

- It is believed that Mahavira and his predecessor Parsva mainly shaped Jainism. According to Jainism the universe is eternal and god has nothing to do with creation of the universe.
- The resolution to take five vows: Ahimsa, Satya, Asteya, Brahmacharya, Aparigraha provide the frame work for an ascetic or householder towards the progressive march of the soul to higher planes.
- By the seventh century A.D. having spread through out East Asia and South- East Asia, Buddhism probably had the largest religious following in the world.
- For centuries, Buddhism enjoyed patronage of the royal houses and merchants in India. However, Buddhism in India died out gradually after the seventh century, though it did not disappear completely.
- It is suggested that shifts in royal patronage from Buddhist to Hindu religious institutions, deviation fiom original teachings of the Buddha and adoption of popular religious forms fiom Hindu religious traditions, origin and development of new Hindu religious orders, etc. contributed to the gradual decline of Buddhism in India.
- We have explained the circumstances in which Buddhism developed in India. Then we have explained the important features of the Buddhist philosophy, followed by discussion on how in the absence of the Buddha Buddhism developed in India.
- The systems of Indian philosophy that originated from the Vedas are called Orthodox systems. Samkhya philosophy holds that reality is constituted of the self and non-self that is *purusha* and *prakriti,* Yoga is a very practical philosophy to realise the 'Self', Nyaya presents a technique of logical thinking, Vaisheshika gives us the principles of reality which constitute the universe.
- Mimamsa philosophy is basically the analysis of the Vedic scriptures

- Charvakism, Jainism and Buddhism are known as the unorthodox systems.
- The Bhakti and Sufi movements were liberal movements within Hinduism and Islam emphasising a new and more personalised relationship between the human being and God. The message of the Sufi movement was universal love and brotherhood of man.
- The Bhakti movement grew amongst Nayanars and Alvars of the south and stressed a new method of worship of God based upon devotional love.
- The Bhakti saints were divided into the *Nirgun* and *Sagun* believers.

1.3.12. Excercise

1. Which is the most important principle of Jainism?

2. Which was the way to solve the grief according to Buddha?

3. What are the distinctive features of Buddhism? What is the urban basis of the origin of Buddhism?

4. How does Hinayana Buddhism differ fiom Mahayana Buddhism? Make a comparison between the Upanishads and the Buddhist doctrines.

5. Write a note on religious practices of the Harappans.

6. How will you differentiate the Chisti Silsilah with the Subrawardi Silsilah?

7. The Bhakti Saints and the Sufi Saints were the two faces of a coin. Elaborate.

8. What was the role played by Charvaka School in the religious movement of India?

9. How does Buddhist philosophy contribute to become a better human being?

10. How can you say that Mimamsa philosophy is basically the analysis of Vedic scriptures?

1.3.13. Further Readings

- Romila Thapar, Cultural Pasts: Essays in Early Indian History.
- Shirin Ratnagar, Understanding Harappa: Civilization in **the** Greater Indus Valley.

- Bridget and Raymond Allchin, The Rise of Civilization in India and Pakistan.
- Cultural Heritage of India, Vol.1, The Ramkrishna Mission Institute of Culture, Golpark, Kolkata.
- S. Radhakrishnan, Indian Philosophy, Vol.1.
- A.K. Warder, Indian Buddhism. J.E. Cort, Jains in the World: Religious Values and Ideology in India.
- A.L. Basharn (ed.), A Cultural History of India. P.D. Mehta, Early Indian Religious Thought.

UNIT-II

CHAPTER-I
INDIAN LANGUAGES AND LITERATURE

EVOLUTION OF SCRIPT AND LANGUAGES IN INDIA: HARAPPAN SCRIPT AND BRAHMI SCRIPT.

Structure

2.1.0. Objective

The chapter deals with Indian languages and literature. The entire chapter will discuss the evolution of script, dissemination of Indian languages and role of Harappan and Brahmi script for subsequent development of Indian writing. The objectives of this unit are to.

- *examine the rich literary heritage of India;*
- *develop an awareness of the variety of languages and literature in India;*
- *list the different kinds of languages and literature in India; and*
- *trace the evolution of script in India.*

2.1.1. Introduction

Language is a medium through which we express our thoughts while literature is a mirror that reflects ideas and philosophies which govern our society. Hence, to know any particular culture and its tradition it is very important that we understand the evolution of its language and the various forms of literature like poetry, drama and religious and non-religious writings. This lesson talks about the role played by different languages in creating the composite cultural heritage that characterizes our country, India.

2.1.2. Indian languages: Their classification

The Indian people, composed of diverse racial elements, now speak languages belonging to four distinct speech families—'the Aryan, the Dravidian, the Sino-Tibetan (or Mongoloid), and the Austric. It has been suggested by some that over and above these four groups, there might have been one or two more there seems to be some evidence from linguistics for this idea. But nothing definitely has yet been found, and we are quite content to look upon these four groups as the basic ones in the Indian scene. People speaking languages belonging to the above four families of speech at first presented distinct culture groups; and the Aryans in ancient India were quite conscious of that. Following to some extent the Sanskrit or Indo-Aryan nomenclature in this matter, the four main 'language-culture' groups of India, namely, the Aryan, the Dravidian, the Sino- Tibetan, and the Austric, can also be labelled respectively as Arya, Dramida or Dravida, Kirata, and Nisada. Indian civilization, as already said, has elements from all these groups, and basically it is pre-Aryan, with important Aryan modifications within as well as Aryan super-structure at the top. In the four types of speech represented (by these, there were, to start with, fundamental differences in formation and vocabulary, in sounds and in syntax. But languages belonging to these four families have lived and developed side by side for 3,000 years and more, and have influenced each other profoundly-'particularly the Aryan, the Dravidian, and the Austric speeches; and this has led to either a general evolution, or mutual imposition, in spite of original differences, of some common characteristics, which may be called specifically *Indian* and which are found in most languages belonging to all these families.

Overlaying their genetic diversity, there is thus in the general run of Indian languages at the present day, an *Indian* character, which forms one of the bases of that 'certain underlying uniformity of life from the Himalayas to Cape Comorin', of that 'general Indian personality', which has been admitted by an Anglo-Indian scholar like Sir Herbert Risley, otherwise so sceptical about India's claim to be considered as one people.

2.1.2.1. Aryan

Of these linguistic and cultural groups, the Aryan is the most important, both numerically and intrinsically. As a matter of fact, Indian civilization has found its expression primarily through the Aryan speech as it developed over the centuries—'through Vedic Sanskrit (Old Indo-Aryan), then Classical Sanskrit, then Early Middle Indo-Aryan dialects like Pali and Old Ardha-Magadhi, then Buddhist and Jaina Sanskrit and after th at the various Prakrits and Apabhramsas, and finally in the last phase, the different Modern Indo-Aryan languages of the country. The hymns and poems collected in the four Vcdas, probably sometime during the tenth century b. c,, represent the earliest stage of the Aryan speech in India, known as thc Old Indo-Aryan.

Of these again, the language of the Rg-Vedic hymns gives us the oldest specimens of the speech. From the Punjab, the original *nidus* of the Aryans in India, Aryan speech spread east along the valley of the Ganga, and by 600 B.C., it was well established throughout the whole of the northern Indian plains up to the eastern borders of Bihar. The non-Aryan Dravidian and Austric dialects (and in some places the Sino-Tibetan speeches too) yielded place to the Aryan language, which, both through natural change and through its adoption by a larger and larger number of people alien to it, began to be modified in many ways; and this modification was largely along the lines of the Dravidian and Austric speeches. The Aryan speech entered in this way into a new stage of development, first in eastern India (Bihar and the eastern U.P. tracts) and then elsewhere. The Punjab, with a larger proportion of born Aryan-ppeakers, remained true to the spirit of the older Vedic speech-the Old Indo-Aryan-to the last, to even as late as the third century B.C., and possibly still later. This new stage of development, which became established during the middle of the first millennium B.C., is known as that of Middle Indo-Aryan or Prakrit. The spoken dialects of Aryan continued to have their own lines of development in the different parts of North India, and these were also spreading over Sind, Rajasthan, Gujarat, and northern Deccan, as well as Bengal and the sub-Himalayan regions. The whole country in North, East, and Central India was thus becoming Aryanized through the spread of the Prakrit or Middle Indo-Aryan dialects. While spoken forms of the Aryan speech of this second stage were spreading among the masses in this way, a younger form of the Vedic speech was established by the Brahmanas in northern Punjab and in the 'Midland' (i.e. present day eastern Punjab and western U.P.) as a fixed literary language, during the sixth-fifth centuries B.C. This younger form of Vedic or Old Indo-Aryan, which was established just when the Middle Indo-Aryan (Prakrit) dialects were taking shape, later came to be known as Sanskrit or Classical Sanskrit. Sanskrit became one of the greatest languages of Indian civilization, and it has been the greatest vehicle of Indian culture for the last 2,500 years (or for the last 3,000 years, if we take its older form Vedic also). Its history-'that of Vedic-cum-Sanskrit-as a language of religion and culture has been longer than that of any other language-with the exception possibly of written Chinese and Hebrew.

It may be noted that Vedic and later (Classical) Sanskrit stand in the same relation to each other as do Homeric and Attic Greek. Sanskrit spread with the spread of Hindu or ancient Indian culture (of mixed Austric, Mongoloid, Dravidian, and Aryan origin) beyond the frontiers of In d ia : and by a .d . 400, it became a great cultural link over the greater part of Asia, from Bali, Java, and Borneo in the South-East to Central Asia in the North-West, China too falling within its sphere of influence. Gradually, it acquired a still wider currency in the other countries of Asia wherever Indian religion (Buddhism and Brahmanism) was introduced or adopted. A great literature was built up in Sanskrit-'epics of national import, *belles letters* of various sorts including the drama, technical literature, philosophical treatises-every department of life anc[thought came to be covered by the literature of Sanskrit. The range and variety of Sanskrit literature is indeed an astonishing phenomenon, unmistakably testifying to the uniqueness of the wisdom and genius of the ancient Indian masterminds and the expressiveness of the language in a style which has been universally acclaimed as one o f the richest and the most elegant the world has ever seen.

The various Prakrits or Middle Indo-Aryan dialects continued to develop and expand. Some of these were adopted by Buddhist and Jaina sects in ancient India as their sacred canonical languages, notably Pali among the Buddhists (of the Hlnayana School) and Ardha-Magadhi among the Jains. The literature produced in these languages particularly in Pali (and also Gandhari Prakrit) migrated to various Asian countries where original contributions in them came into existence. The process of simplification of the Aryan speech which began with the Second or Middle Indo-Aryan stage, continued, and by A.D. 600 we come to the last phase of Middle Indo-Aryan, known as the Apabhramsa stage. Further modification of the regional Apabhramsas of the period A.D. G00-1000 gave rise, with the beginning of the second millennium A.D., to the New Indo-Aryan or Modern Indo-Aryan languages, or *bhasas,* which arc current at the present day.

The New Indo-Aryan languages, coming ultimately from Vedic Sanskrit (or 'Sanskrit', in a loose way), are closely related to each other, like the Neo-Romanic languages derived out of Latin. It is believed that in spite of local differences in the various forms of Middle Indo-Aryan, right up to the New Indo-Aryan development, there was a sort o f pan-Indian vulgar or koine form of Prakrit or Middle Indo-Aryan. But local differences in Middle Indo-Aryan grew more and more pronounced during that centuries round about A.D. 1000, and this led to the provincial New Indo-Aryan languages taking shape and being born. Taking into consideration these basic local characteristics, the New Indo-Aryan speeches have been classified into a number of local groups, viz. (i) North-Western group, (ii) Southern group, (iii) Eastern group, (iv) East-Central or Mediate group, (v) Central group, and (vi) Northern or Himalayan group. The major languages of the New or Modern Indo-Aryan speech family are: Assamese, Bengali, Gujarati, Hindi, Marathi, Odia, Punjabi, Sindhi, and Urdu. Kashmiri, one of the major modern Indian languages, belongs to the Dardic branch of the Indo-Iranian group within the Aryan family. Although Dardic by origin, Kashmiri came very early under the profound influence of Sanskrit and the later Prakrits which greatly modified its Dardic bases. Most scholars now think that Dardic is just a branch of Indo-Aryan.

2.1.2.2. Dravidian

Dravidian is the second important language family of India and has some special characteristics- of its own. After the Aryan speech, it has very largely functioned as the exponent of Indian culture, particularly the earlier secular as well as religious literature of Tamil. It forms a solid bloc in South India, embracing the four great literary languages, Kannada, Malayalam, Tamil, and Telugu and a number of less important speeches all of which are, however, overshadowed by the main four. It is believed that the wonderful city civilization of Sind and South Punjab as well as Baluchistan (fourth-third millennium B.C.) was the work of Dravidian speakers. But we cannot be absolutely certain in this matter, so long as the inscribed seals from the city ruins in those areas like Harappa, Mohenjo-daro, etc. remain undeciphered.

The art of writing would appear to have been borrowed from the pre-Aryan Sind and South Punjab people by the Aryan speakers, probably in the tenth century B.C., to which period the beginnings of the Brahmi alphabet, the characteristic Indian system of writing connected with Sanskrit and Prakrit in pre-Christian centuries, may be traced.

The Dravidian speech in its antiquity in India is older than Aryan, and yet (leaving apart the problematical writings on the seals found in Sind and South Punjab city ruins) the specimens of connected Dravidian writing or literature that we can read and understand are over a millennium later than the oldest Aryan documents. Of the four great Dravidian languages, Tamil has preserved its Dravidian character best, retaining, though not the old sound system of primitive Dravidian, a good deal of its original nature in its roots, forms, and words. The other three cultivated Dravidian speeches have, in the matter of their words of higher culture, completely surrendered themselves to Sanskrit, the classical and sacred language of Hindu India. Tamil has a unique and a very old literature, and the beginnings of it go back to about 2,000 years from now. Malayalam as a language is an offshoot of Old Tamil. From the ninth century A.D. some Malayalam characteristics begin to appear, but it is from the fifteenth century that Malayalam literature took its independent line of development. Kannada as a cultured language is almost as old as Tamil; and although we have some Telugu inscriptions dating from the sixth/seventh century A.D., the literary career of Telugu started from the eleventh century. Tamil and Malayalam are very close to each other, and are mutually intelligible to a certain extent. Kannada also bears a great resemblance to Tamil and Malayalam. Only Telugu has deviated a good deal from its southern neighbours and sisters. But Telugu and Kannada use practically the same alphabet, which is thus a bond of union between these two languages.

2.1.2.3. Sino-Tibetan and Austric

Peoples of Mongoloid origin, speaking languages of the Sino-Tibetan family, were present in India at least as early as the tenth century B.C, when the four Vedas appear to have been compiled. The Sino-Tibetan languages do not have much numerical importance or cultural significance in India, with the exception of Manipuri or Meithei of Manipur. Everywhere they are gradually receding before the Aryan languages like Bengali and-Assamese.

The Austric languages represent the oldest speech family of India, but they are spoken by a very small number of people, comparatively. The Austric languages of India have a great interest for the student of linguistics and human culture. They are valuable relics of India's past, and they link up India with Burma, with Indo-China, with Malaya, and with Indonesia, Melanesia, and Polynesia. Their solidarity is, however, broken as in most places there has been penetration into Austric blocs by the more powerful Aryan speeches with their overwhelming numbers and their prestige. Speakers of Austric in all the walks of life (they are mostly either farmers, or farm and plantation, or colliery labourers) know some Aryan language. In some cases they have become very largely bilingual. Their gradual Aryanization is a process which started some 3,000 years ago when the first Austrics (and Mongoloids as well as Dravidians) in North India started to abandon their native speech for Aryan. But in the process of abandoning their own language and accepting a new one, namely the Aryan, the Austrics (as well as the Dravidians and the Sino-Tibetans) naturally introduced some of their own speech habits and their own words into Aryan. In this way, the Austrics and other non-Aryan peoples helped to modify the character of the Aryan speech in India, from century to century, and even to build up Classical Sanskrit as the great culture speech of India. As the speakers of the Sino-Tibetan and Austric languages had been in a backward state living mostly a rather primitive life in out-of-the-way places, their languages do not show any high literary development excepting, as already said, in the ease of Meithei or Manipuri belonging to Sino-Tibetan, which has quite a noteworthy and fairly old literature. They had, however, some kind of village or folk-culture, connected with which there developed in all these languages an oral literature consisting of folk-songs, religious and otherwise, of folk-tales, and of their legends and traditions. And a literature, mainly of Christian inspiration, has been created in some of these speeches by translating the *Bible* in its entirety or in part.

Songs, legends, and tales of the Austric languages have been collected and published, particularly in Santali and Mundari, and in Khasi. Munda and Santali lyrics give pretty, idyllic glimpses of tribal life, some of the Munda love poems having a rare freshness about them; and a number of Santali folk-tales are very beautiful. A few of the folk-tales prevalent in the Sino-Tibetan speeches are also beautiful, but they do not appear to compare favorably with the Santali and Mundari languages in the matter of both lyric poems and stories. A systematic study of these languages started only during the nineteenth century when European missionaries and scholars got interested in them. I have discussed in detail the speeches of the Sino-Tibetan and Austric families prevalent in the country in my contribution to this volume, entitled 'Adivasi Languages and Literatures of India'.

There is, as already said, a fundamental unity in the literary types, *genres*, and expressions among all the modern languages of India in their early, medieval, and modern developments. The reason of this unique phenomenon is that there has been a gradual convergence of Indian languages belonging to the different linguistic families, Aryan, Dravidian, Sino-Tibetan, and Austric, towards a common Indian type after their intimate contact with each other for a t least 3,000 years. This volume of *The Cultural Heritage o f India* is indeed an encyclopedia in its scope and range, and it will certainly provide an authentic and valuable contribution towards the study of Indian languages and literatures in their glory and grandeur; it will also afford a spectacular display of the genius of India reflected in various branches of knowledge. It is needless to add that the literary heritage of India constitutes a priceless possession covetable to any nation, however great it may be by any standard.

2.1.3. Evolution of Writing in Ancient India

The sub-continent of India is a vast region, now embracing the three independent States of India proper (or Bharat), Pakistan and Nepal. It shows, in its natural of geographical setup as well as in its population, a unique diversity against the background of a remarkable unity which is basic or fundamental. Almost all the various types of climate, excepting the arctic, are found here; and in her population India is a veritable museum of races and languages, cultures and religions. Yet, there is an underlying unity behind all this variety. Different people came to India at different times, each with its special racial type, language, region and culture, but after they settled down side by side, a great intermingling of races and cultures started from prehistoric times, resulting in the emergence of a mixed Indian people with a composite culture of its own, in the evolution of which all the component elements were represented. In the evolution of development of languages in India we see this process of miscegenation at work. The Aryan speech, after it came to India, assimilated with the pre-Aryan languages- the Dravidian, the Austric and the Indo-Mangoloid- and a common speech, gradually evolved. It had some common characteristics, although in their own region, in their roots and formative elements, as well as in their words- their *sprachgut* or "Speech-commodity"- they were different.

Until the discovery of the Indus Valley Civilization in 1920, ancient India seemingly had two main scripts in which languages were written, Brahmi and Kharosti. The Brahmi script developed under Semitic influence around 7th c. BC, and was originally written from right to left. The Kharosti script came into being during the 5th c. BC in northwest India which was under Persian rule.

Although the origin of the Brahmi script is uncertain, the Kharosti script is commonly accepted as a direct descendant from the Aramaic alphabet.

The direction of writing in the Kharosti script is as in Aramaic, from right to left, and there is also a likeness of many signs having similar phonetic value.

In the later centuries of its existence, Brahmi gave rise to eight varieties of scripts. Three of them - the early and late Mauryas and the Sunga - became the prototypes of the scripts in northern India in the 1st c. BC and AD. Out of these developed the Gupta writing which was employed from the 4th to the 6th c. AD.

The Siddhamatrka script developed during the 6th c. AD from the western branch of the eastern Gupta character. The Siddhamatrka became the ancestor of the Nagari script which is used for Sanskrit today. The Nagari developed in the 7th to 9th c. AD, and has remained, since the 7th to 9th centuries, essentially unaltered.

However, certain other factors need to be considered to get the complete picture of script development in India. In 1920 archaeologists announced the discovery of extensive urban ruins in the Indus Valley which pre-dated the earliest literary sources and which caused scholars working on ancient texts to re-examine their views on the different phases of Indian culture. The Rig Veda which speaks in such derogatory terms of the enemies subdued by the Aryan tribes, gives the impression that they were all savage barbarians. The Brahmins for centuries have degraded the original inhabitants of India with the intention of self elevation, preservation and oppression. These ancient dwellers in India were Dravidian, and in fact, their culture had developed a highly sophisticated way of life which compares favorably with that of contemporary urban civilizations in Egypt and Mesopotamia.

The extensive excavations carried out at the two principal city sites, Harappa and Mohenjo-Daro, both situated in the Indus basin, indicates that this Dravidian culture was well established by about 2500 B.C., and subsequent discoveries have revealed that it covered most of the Lower Indus Valley. What we know of this ancient civilization is derived almost exclusively from archaeological data since every attempt to decipher the script used by these people has failed so far. Recent analyses of the order of the signs on the inscriptions have led several scholars to the view that the language is not of the Indo-European family, nor is it close to the Sumerians, Hurrians, or Elamite, nor can it be related to the structure of the Munda languages of modern India. If it is related to any modern language family it appears to be Dravidian akin to Old Tamil, presently spoken throughout the southern part of the Indian Peninsula.

What this points to is the existence of a system of writing far more ancient than what was originally considered. For instance when the Indian scripts are grouped, the southern scripts form a class of their own. The Grantha alphabet, which belongs to the writing system of southern India, developed in the 5th c. AD and was mainly used to write Sanskrit. Inscriptions in Early Grantha, dating from the 5th to 6th c. AD are on copper plates and stone monuments from the kingdom of the Pallavas near Chennai (Madras).

The influx of foreign invaders through the northwest over the centuries, forced the Dravidians, the original inhabitants of India, south. Scholars have indicated that the south has been the gateway for religious and cultural developments in India. Originally Grantha was used for writing Sanskrit only, and Sanskrit was later transliterated with Nagiri after the 7th c. AD. Scholars over the years have indicated that many Hindu writings have been tampered with, and certainly this could have happened during the transliteration process. The later varieties of the Grantha script were used to write a number of Dravidian Languages, and the modern Tamil script certainly seems to be derived from Grantha.

The bibliographical evidences indicate that the Vedas are written in the Grantha and Nagari scripts, and according to tradition Veda Vyasa, a Dravidian, compiled and wrote the Vedas. The Grantha script belongs to the southern group of scripts and Veda Vyasa being a Dravidian would certainly have used it. Since the earliest evidence for Grantha is only in the 5th c. AD, the Vedas were written rather late.

Another important fact is brought out in the account of the religion, philosophy, literature, geography, chronology, astronomy, customs, laws and astrology of India about AD 1030 by Alberuni. He states that, "The Indian scribes are careless, and do not take pains to produce correct and well-collated copies. In consequence, the highest results of the author's mental development are lost by their negligence, and his book becomes already in the first or second copy so full of faults, that the text appears as something entirely new, which neither a scholar nor one familiar with the subject, whether Hindu or Muslim, could any longer understand. It will sufficiently illustrate the matter if we tell the reader that we have sometimes written down a word from the mouth of Hindus, taking the greatest pains to fix its pronunciation, and that afterwards when we repeated it to them, they had great difficulty in recognising it."

This is a clear opposite to Yuan Chwang's time in the 7th c AD, when this young Chinese Buddhist scholar came to India in search of authentic sacred books which he accomplished. However, scholars indicate that the same is not true with early Tamil classics like the Sangam literature (3rd c. BC - 3rd c. AD) which are remarkably helpful in the reconstruction of history.

Thus, in the matter of writing, we find a long history from prehistoric times before the coming of the Aryans down to recent years. Until the discovery by excavations of the pre-historic and pre-Aryan city cites of Mohen-jo-Daro in northern Sind and Harappa in South Punjab, the oldest writings known in India was the Maurya script, used in inscriptions of Ashoka and in a few old coins and inscriptions which date back to the 3rd Century B.C. Here we are in broad daylight, although it was only over century ago, in 1837, that the Brahmi script could be read and understood for the first time. Throughout the whole of India, we have inscriptions of Emperor Ashoka in different forms of Prakrit in Brahmi script and decade-by-decade and century by century, this script has gone on evolving on the soil of India. In North India, through various stages like Kusana Brahmi; Gupta Brahmi and Siddhamatraka of 7th century A.D., we arrive through the Nagara style of writing at the Siddhamatraka and through the Sharada and the Kutila styles at modern North India scripts. All these are related to each other as distant cousins and going back to their common source, the Brahmi of Ashoka-scripts like the Nagari (or Devanagari) Bengali, Assamese, Odia, Maithili, Sharada, Gurumukhi etc.

In South India, there was a similar development of Brahmi, and by the middle of the 6th century we come to the Pallava script, whence originated the modern Telugu and Kannada scripts, the Malaylam and the Grantha script (Sanskrit is written and printed in the Grantha script in the Tamil country) and the Tamil script. We have no inscriptions or other writing prior to the Ashokan Brahmi of the 3rd Century B.C. Long ago, there were discovered in grave sites in South India, painted on potsherds, certain letters like symbols or signs, mostly occurring singly. They do not seem to be letters of any alphabet or syllabary or system of writing, but rather appear to be individual signs or marks, such as are, for example, used in branding cattle to indicate ownership. Similar symbols are found on the oldest coins of India-the square or oblong pieces in silver or copper known as puranas which go back to the centuries just before the Christian era. Then quite a mass of short inscriptions came to light after the Mohen-jo-Daro site was discovered in North Sind, and in Harappa in South Punjab. These were found on seals of soft stones, and they look like simple letters and combinations of letters. An inventory has been made of these letters, and their number comes up to over a hundred. In the Mohen-jo-Daro script, which goes back to 3500 B.C.

and beyond, several strata are noticed. The one which is supposed to be the youngest or most advanced in development (following the first stratum in which the signs appear to be pictograms or crude pictures of objects, and the second stratum which might represent syllables rather than pictures or simple alphabetical letters) has simple shapes for the signs, depicted like linear writing. There is a superficial agreement between this youngest or linear phase of Mohen-jo-Daro writing of the period before 1500 or 2000 B.C. and the Brahmi script of the 3rd century B.C. Some of the Mohen-jo-Daro signs resembles or are almost identical with Brahmi letters. Some others are a bit complicated. What is most important, in some of Mohen-jo-Daro signs, it would appear that the Brahmi characteristic of tagging on vowel signs to the consonant letters is also found, besides combinations of two or more consonants.

This brings us to the question of the origin of the Brahmi script. Most scholars until recently thought that the Brahmi scripts was derived from the ancient Phoenician script of, say, 1200 B.C., itself a derivative of the still more ancient Egyptian hieroglyphic writing, through the later Demotic style. A direct Mesopotamia was thought possible. About the middle of the first millennium B.C., or little earlier, it was believed that Indian merchants who used to go by sea to Baveru or Babylon saw that writing was in vogue there, and got both the idea and the very simple Phoenician letters in Babylon and modified it to suit the Indian Prakrit they spoke, and so evolved the Brahmi writing. Others thought that the South Arabian form of Phoenician was the immediate source of Brahmi. But there are some basic divergences between Phoenician writing on the one hand and Brahmi on the other, which make this affiliation a little difficult to accept. On the other hand, the agreements between the linear and later Mohen-jo-Daro script and Brahmi would suggest that Brahmi was derived from the former, and was gradually perfected by 300 B.C. it would appear very reasonable to think that sometime in the 10th Century B.C. the compilers of the Vedic literature of songs and hymns and short prose directives in connection with the ritual of their predecessors evolved a kind of Proto-Brahmi script from the latest linear Mohen-jo-Daro writing, and this is how Brahmi come into existence. Of course, to start with, it could not be a perfect or full system of writing, expressing in all its niceties the entire sound-system or Phonological habits of the Aryan speech of the time, which was a late form of Vedic. There was also a suggestion that the Brahmi letters originated independently in India from pictures of objects, the initial sound of the Sanskrit names of which was associated with the picture, which finally became the letter for the sound. Thus the Brahmi letter for *dh*, which was shaped like the Roman capital D, was a picture of the bow, Dhanu, and then this picture became a letter and the value of *dh*. So Brahmi n is shaped like the Roman capital inverted T, L, and this denoted the nose-nasa; and so on with most of the letters. But this is extremely fanciful, and there is no evidence to establish this kind of derivation.

The Brahmi letters have the great beauty of simplicity-they stand bold and clear, statuesque and columnar, like Greek and Latin letters (capitals) or ancient Phoenician letters. There is no matra of top-line or flourish and compared with Brahmi, Nagari or Telugu, Sharada or Grantha, are very complicated and cumbersome scripts indeed. Brahmi letters are so simple in their structure that an Indian familiar with any of the modern descendants of Brahmi can pick it up in a few hours. It lends itself to decorative treatment in its grandeur of simplicity, and the acquisition of Brahmi by an Indian intellectual of to-day can be a very easily acquired accomplishment with its attendant historical and cultural value.

So far as we know, the Aryans had no system of writing of their own when they came to India and all their literature was, as in the case of many primitive people, entirely oral. But there is evidence that, as in some of the most ancient countries outside India like Egypt and Babylon, Asia Minor and China, pre-Aryan India, too, had her own system of writing. The oldest Sanskrit script goes back to the early centuries of the Christian era and Sanskrit inscriptions are written in the characters of that period which are but modifications of the earlier ancient Indian Brahmi of the 3rd Century B.C. and between the coming of the Aryans which might have happened round about 1500 B.C. and the use of Brahmi as in the Ashoka inscriptions of the 3rd Century B.C. what was the script in which the Aryan speakers wrote their language? Until now, European scholars thought that Indian merchants going to Mesopotamia and to some of the western countries like Egypt from the beginning of the first millennium B.C. learnt the art of writing from there and that they modified some form of Phoenician writing into the ancient Indian script-Brahmi, which may have taken its rise sometime before 500 B.C. But we have now found out that there was this Mohen-jo-Daro system of writing in its various stages of development and in the last stage, there appears to be some agreement with the Brahmi writing of the 3rd century B.C. It would be most reasonable to assume that the Brahmi script in its very ancient form as a sort of Proto-Brahmin was developed out of the youngest form of the Mohenjo-jo-Daro script. Thus, the origin of the Brahmi script and its subsequent developments in the succeeding centuries was native Indian. Step by step, thus original Brahmi went on changing. It was ordinary Ashokan Brahmi in the 3rd Century B.C. about time of Christ, it became modified into what is known as Kusana Brahmi, then about 400 A.D. it became Gupta Brahmi and then in the 7th Century A.D. it came to be known as the Siddhamatraka form of writing. Ultimately, by about 1000 A.D. it became a kind of Proto-Nagari and a Proto-Kutila script, which is the ultimate mother of Bengali-Assamese, Maithili, Newari and Odia and also of the ancient Sharada script of Kashmir, and of both the Kashmir scripts still known as Sharada and Gurumukhi. In South India, the history was somewhat analogous. In the middle of the 7th century A.D., it became the developed Pallava script which is the ultimate mother of the four great systems of writing in the South - the Telugu, the Kannada, the Tamil including Grantha and the Malayalam.

2.1.4. Brahmi Script

Brahmi is the modern name given to the one of the oldest scripts used on the Indian Subcontinent and in Central Asia, during the final centuries BCE and the early centuries CE. Like its contemporary, Khasosthi, which was used in what is now Afghanisthan, Pakisthan and India.

The best-known Brahmi inscriptions are the rock-cut edicts of Asoka in north-central India, dated to 250-232 BCE. The script was deciphered in 1837 by James Princep, an archaeologist, philologist, and official of the British East India Company. The origin of the script is still much debated, with current Western academic opinion generally agreeing (with some exceptions) that Brahmi was derived from or at least influenced by one or more contemporary Semitic scripts, but a strong current of opinion in India favors the idea that it is connected to the much older and as-yet undecipered Indus Script.

The Gupta Script of the 5th century is sometimes called "Late Brahmi". The Brahmi script diversified into numerous local variants, classified together as theBrahmanic family script. Dozens of modern scripts used across South Asia have descended from Brahmi, making it one of the world's most influential writing traditions.

While the contemporary and perhaps somewhat older Kharosthi script is widely accepted to be a derivation of the Aramic Script, the genesis of the Brahmi script is less straightforward. An origin in the Imperial Aramaic script has nevertheless been proposed by some scholars since the publications by Albrecht Weber (1856) and George Buhler's *On the origin of the Indian Brahma alphabet* (1895). Bühler's ideas have been particularly influential, though even by the 1895 date of his great opus on the subject; he could identify no less than five competing theories of the origin, one positing an indigenous origin and four deriving it from various Semitic models.

Like Kharosthi, Brahmī was used to write the early dialects of Prakrit. Surviving records of the script are mostly restricted to inscriptions on buildings and graves as well as liturgical texts. Sanskrit was not written until many centuries later, and as a result, Brahmi is not a perfect match for Sanskrit; several Sanskrit sounds cannot be written in Brahmi.

2.1.4.1. Origin of Brahmi script

The most disputed point about the origin of the Brahmī script is whether it was a purely indigenous development or was inspired or derived from scripts that originated outside India. Saloman noted that the indigenous view is strongly preferred by Indian scholars, whereas the idea of Semitic borrowing is preferred most often by Western scholars. He agreed with S.R. Goyal that biases have influenced both sides of the debate. Buhler curiously cited a passage by Sir Alexander Cunningham, one of the earliest indigenous origin proponents, that indicated that, at the time, the indigenous origin was a preference of English scholars in opposition to the "unknown Western" origin preferred by continental scholars.

Among scholars who have taken the origin to have been purely indigenous is Raymond Allchin, who speculated in a personal communication that Brahmi perhaps had the Harappan script (i.e. Indus script) as its predecessor. However, Allchin and Erdosy later in 1995 expressed the opinion that there was as yet insufficient evidence to resolve the question, though they were confident that the development of Brahmi was earlier than and "quite independent" of the Aramaic derivation of Kharosthi. G.R. Hunter in his book *The Script of Harappa and Mohenjodaro and Its Connection with Other Scripts* (1934) proposed a derivation of the Brahmi alphabets from the Indus Script, the match being considerably higher than that of Aramaic in his estimation.

The most prominent alternative view in the indigenous origin category is that Brahmi was invented entirely independently of either foreign scripts or the Indus script. This view usually accepts that the Mauryans were previously aware of the art of writing in general but proposes that Brahmi was created anew for the purposes of writing Prakrit, based on well established theories of Vedic grammar and phonetics, and probably on the order of the reform-minded King Asoka. From this point of view, Brahmi might be seen as a successful attempt to remedy some of the apparent limitations of Kharosthi as a vehicle for writing Prakrit.

There is little intervening evidence for writing during the millennium and a half between the collapse of the Indus Valley Civilisation c. 1900 BCE and the first appearance of Brahmi in the 3rd century BCE and there is no accepted decipherment of the Indus script, but similarities to the Indus script have been nonetheless claimed by scholars such as Kak, who did not even acknowledge the existence of the Semitic-origin theory. A promising possible link between the Indus script and later writing traditions may be in the graffiti of the South Indian megalithic culture, which may have some overlap with the Indus symbol inventory and persisted in use up at least through the appearance of the Brahmi and Tamil Brahmi scripts up into the 3rd century CE. These graffiti usually appear singly, though on occasion may be found in groups of two or three, and are thought to have been family, clan, or religious symbols.

There appears to be general agreement at least that Brahmi and Kharosthi are historically related, though much disagreement persists about the nature of this relationship. Trigger considered them, as a pair, to be one of four instances of the invention of an alpha-syllabary, the other three being Old Persian Cuneiform, the Merotic script, and the Geez Script. All four of these have striking similarities, such as using short /a/ as an inherent vowel, but Trigger (who accepted the Aramaic inspiration of Brahmi with extensive local development, along with a pre-Ashokan date) was unable to find a direct common source among them. Gnanadesikan also posited a stimulus diffusion view of the development of Brahmi and Kharosthi, in which the idea of alphabetic sound representation was learned from the Aramaic-speaking Persians, but much of the writing system was a novel development tailored to the phonology of Prakrit.

2.1.4.1. 1. Aramaic hypothesis

The Semitic theory (Phoenician or Aramaic) is the more strongly supported by the available data. According to the Aramaic hypothesis, the oldest Brahmi inscriptions shows striking parallels with contemporary Aramaic for the sounds that are congruent between the two languages, especially if the letters are flipped to reflect the change in writing direction. For example, both Brahmi and Aramaic *g* resemble Λ; both Brahmi and Aramaic *t* resemble *ʎ*, *etc.*

Brahmi does feature a number of extensions to the Aramaic alphabet, as it was required to write more sounds. For example, Aramaic did not distinguish dental stops such as d from retroflex stops such as ḍ, and in Brahmi the dental and retroflex series are graphically very similar, as if both had been derived from a single Aramaic prototype. Aramaic did not have Brahmi's aspirated consonants (kh, th, *etc.*), whereas Brahmi did not have

Aramaic's emphatic consonent (*q*, ṭ, ṣ), and it appears that these unneeded emphatic letters filled in for Brahmi's aspirates: Aramaic *q* for Brahmi *kh*, Aramaic ṭ (Θ) for Brahmi *th* (ʘ), *etc.* And just where Aramaic did not have a corresponding emphatic stop, *p*, Brahmi seems to have doubled up for the corresponding aspirate: Brahmi *p* and *ph* are graphically very similar, as if taken from the same source in Aramaic *p*. The first letters of the two alphabets also match: Brahmi *a*, which resembled a reversed κ, looks a lot like Aramaic alef, which resembled Hebrew א. The following table compares Brahmi with Phoenician and Aramaic.

Both Phoenician/Aramaic and Brahmi had three voiceless sibilants, but because the alphabetical ordering was lost, the correspondences among them are not clear. Not accounted for are the six Brahmi consonants 𑀪 *bh*, 𑀖 *gh*, 𑀳 *h*, 𑀚 *j*, 𑀛 *jh*, 𑀜 *ny*, some of which could conceivably derive from the three Aramaic consonants with no obvious correspondence, *he*, *heth*, and *ayin*. (Brahmi [*ng* was a later development.) Salomon (1998), for example, states that *gh* probably derives from *heth*.

The earliest likely contact of the Hindu Kush region with the Aramaic script occurred in the 6th century BCE with the expansion of the Achaemenid Empire under Darius the great to the Indus valley. It appears that no use of any script to write an Indo-Aryan language occurred before the reign of Emperor Ashoka in the 3rd century BCE, despite the evident example of Aramaic. Meghasthenes, an ambassador to the Mauryan court in Northeastern India only a quarter century before Ashoka, noted explicitly that the Indians "have no knowledge of written letters". This might be explained by the cultural importance at the time (and indeed to some extent today) of Oral literature for history and Hindu scripture. Another Greek, Nearchus, a few decades earlier observed that in northwestern India letters were written on cotton cloth. Authors have variously speculated that this might have been Kharosthi or Aramaic, but Salomon thus regarded the evidence from Greek sources to be inconclusive.

There have been claims that fragments of Brahmi epigraphy found in Tamil Nadu and Sri Lanka date as far back as the 5th or 6th century BCE. Recent claims for earlier dates include fragments of pottery from the trading town of Anuradhapura in Sri Lanka, which have been dated to the early 4th century BCE; from Bhattiprollu and on pieces of pottery in Adichanallur, Tamil Nadu, which were associated with radiocarbon dates to the 6th century BCE. The claimed pre-Ashokan Bhattiprolu and Adichanallur inscriptions have been widely reported in the press, but do not appear to have been academically published so far. Saloman recognized the potential significance of the Anuradhapura inscriptions with respect to dating the origin of Brahmi but was cautious in accepting the early dates. Coningham et al., in their thorough analysis of the Anuradhapura inscriptions, found that the language was Prakrit rather than Dravidian, and they were unwilling to draw any conclusions about the affinities of the script beyond its being Brahmi; no claim was made that it is Tamil Brahmi. The historical sequence of the specimens was interpreted to indicate an evolution in the level of stylistic refinement over several centuries, and they concluded that the Brahmi script may have arisen out of "mercantile involvement" and that the growth of trade networks in Sri Lanka was correlated with its first appearance in the area.

A date for Tamil-Brahmi inscriptions in Palani as early as the 6th century has also been claimed, but as of its 2011 announcement, Iravatham Mahadevan, "a leading authority on the Tamil-Brahmi and Indus scripts," and Dr. Y. Subbarayalu, Head of the Department of Indology at the French Institute of Pondicherry, cautioned that it was difficult to reach a conclusion on the basis of one single scientific dating.

Overall, evidence for pre-Mauryan Brahmi inscriptions remains inconclusive, restricted to pottery fragments with possible individual glyphs. The earliest complete inscriptions remain the 3rd-century-BCE Ashokan texts. Many early post-Ashokan remains show regional variation thought to have developed after a period of unity across India during the Ashokan period.

Brahmi is clearly attested from the 3rd century BCE during the reign of Ashoka, who used the script for imperial edict. It has commonly been supposed that the script was developed at around this time, both from the paucity of earlier dated examples, the alleged unreliability of those earlier dates, and from the geometric regularity of the script, which some have taken to be evidence that it had been recently invented.

2.1.4.2. Early Regional Varient

The earliest Ashokan inscriptions are found across India-apart from the Kharosthi-writing northwest-and are highly uniform. By the late third century BCE regional variants had developed, due to differences in writing materials and to the structures of the languages being written. For example, Tamil Brahmi had a divergent system of vowel notation.

The earliest definite evidence of Brahmi script in south India comes from Bhattiprolu in Andhra Pradesh. The Bhattiprolu was written on an urn containing Buddhist relics, apparently in Prakrit and old Telugu. Twenty-three letters have been identified. The letters *ga* and *sa* are similar to Mauryan Brahmi, while *bha* and *da*resemble those of modern Telugu script.

Unlike the edicts of Ashoka, however, the majority of the inscriptions from this early period in Sri Lanka are found above caves, are only a few words in length and "rarely say anything more than the name of the donor (who paid for the renovation of the cave, presumably); sometimes the donor's profession and village-of-origin are added, and sometimes the reader may be unable to guess if they are looking at the name of a person, profession or village, but can see that it is a name in any case (and not a philosophical statement)." Earliest writing in Brahmi was found in Anuradhapura, Sri Lanka in Prakrit language, ancestor of Sinhalese language.

2.1.4.3. Characteristics

Brahmi is usually written from left to right, as in the case of its descendants. However, a coin of the 4th century BCE has been found inscribed with Brahmi running from right to left, as in Aramaic.

Brahmi is an abugida, meaning that each letter represents a consonant, while vowels are written with obligatory diacritics called *mātrās* in Sanskrit, except when the vowels commence a word. When no vowel is written, the vowel /a/ is understood. This "default short a" is a characteristic shared with Kharosthī, though the treatment of vowels differs in other respects. Special conjunct consonent are used to write consonant clusters such as /pr/ or /rv/. In modern Devanagari conjunct consonant are written left to right to join them as one composite character whereas in Brahmi characters are joined vertically downwards.

Vowels following a consonant are inherent or written by diacritics, but initial vowels have dedicated letters. There are three vowels in Brahmi: /a/, /i/, /u/; long vowels are derived from the letters for short vowels. However, there are only five vowel diacritics, as short /a/ is understood if no vowel is written.

It has been noted that the basic system of vowel marking common to Brahmi and Kharosthī, in which every consonant is understood to be followed by a vowel, was well suited to Prakrit, but as Brahmi was adapted to other languages, a special notation called the virama was introduced to indicate the omission of the final vowel.

Punctuation can be perceived as more of an exception than as a general rule in Asokan Brahmi. For instance, distinct spaces in between the words appear frequently in the pillar edicts but not so much in others. ("Pillar edicts" refers to the texts that are inscribed on the stone pillars oftentimes with the intention of making them public.) The idea of writing each word separately was not consistently used.

In the early Brahmi period, the existence of punctuation marks is not very well shown. Each letter has been written independently with some space between words and edicts occasionally.

In the middle period, the system seems to be in progress. The use of a dash and a curved horizontal line is found. A flower mark seems to mark the end, and a circular mark appears to indicate the full stop. There seem to be varieties of full stop.

In the late period, the system of interpunctuation marks gets more complicated. For instance, there are four different forms of vertically slanted double dashes that resemble "//" to mark the completion of the composition. Despite all the decorative signs that were available during the late period, the signs remained fairly simple in the inscriptions. One of the possible reasons may be that engraving is restricted while writing is not.

2.1.4.4. Descendant

Over the course of a millennium, Brahmi developed into numerous regional scripts, commonly classified into a more rounded Southern India group and a more angular Northern India group. Over time, these regional scripts became associated with the local languages. A Northern Brahmi gave rise to the Gupta script during the Gupta period, sometimes also called "Late Brahmi" (used during the 5th century), which in turn diversified into a number of cursives during the Middle Ages, including Siddham (6th century), Sharada (9th century) and Nagari (10th century).

Southern Brahmi gave rise to the Pallave Grantha (6th century), Vatteluttu (8th century) scripts, and due to the contact of Hinduism with South-East Asia during the early centuries CE also gave rise to the Babybayin in Philippines, the Javanese script in Indonesia and the Khmer script in Cambodia, and the Mon script in Burma.

Also in the Brahmic family of scripts are several Central Asian scripts such as Tibetan and Khotanese. Gary Ledyrad has suggested that the basic letters of hangual were taken from the Phagspa script of the Mongol Empire, itself a derivative of the Brahmic Tibetan alphabet.

The *varga* arrangement of Brahmi was adopted as the modern order of Japanese kana, though the letters themselves are unrelated.

2.1.5. The Harappan Script

The **Indus script** (also **Harappan script**) is a corpus of symbols produced by the Indus valley civilisation during the Kot Diji and Mature Harappan periods between the 26th and 20th centuries BC. Most inscriptions are extremely short. It is not clear if these symbols constitute a script used to record a language, and the subject of whether the Indus symbols were a writing system is controversial. In spite of many attempts at decipherment, it is undeciphered, and no underlying language has been identified. There is no known bilingual inscription. The script does not show any significant changes over time.

The first publication of a seal with Harappan symbols dates to 1873, in a drawing by Alexnader Cunningham. Since then, over 4,000 inscribed objects have been discovered, some as far afield as Mesopotamia. In the early 1970s, Iravatham Mahadevan published a corpus and concordance of Indus inscriptions listing 3,700 seals and 417 distinct signs in specific patterns. The average inscription contains five signs, and the longest inscription is only 17 signs long. He also established the direction of writing as right to left.

Some early scholars, starting with Cunningham in 1877, thought that the system was the archetype of the Brahmi script. Cunningham's ideas were supported by scholars, such as G.R. Hunter, S.R Rao, F. Raymond Allchin, John Newberry and Iravatham Mahadevan, some of whom continue to argue for an Indus predecessor of the Brahmic script.

Early examples of the symbol system are found in an Early Harappan context, dated to possibly as early as the 33rd century BC. In the Mature Harappan period, from about 2600 BC, strings of Indus signs are most commonly found on flat, rectangular stamp seals, but they are also found on at least a dozen other materials including tools, miniature tablets, copper plates, and pottery.

2.1.5.1. Late Harappan

After 1900 BC, the systematic use of the symbols ended, after the final stage of the Mature Harappan civilization. A few Harappan signs have been claimed to appear until as late as around 1100 BC. Onshore explorations near Bet Dwarka in Gujrat revealed the presence of late Indus seals depicting a 3-headed animal, earthen vessel inscribed in what is claimed to be a late Harappan script, and a large quantity of pottery similar to Lustrous Red Ware bowl and Red Ware dishes, dish-on-stand, perforated jar and incurved bowls which are datable to the 16th century BC in Dwaraka, Rangpur and Prabhas. The Thermoluminescence date for the pottery in Bet Dwaraka is 1528 BC. This evidence has been used to claim that a late Harappan script was used until around 1500 BC.

In May 2007, the Tamil Nadu Archaeological Department found pots with arrow-head symbols during an excavation in Melaperumpallam near Poompuhar. These symbols are claimed to have a striking resemblance to seals unearthed in Mohenjo-Daro in the 1920s.

In one purported decipherment of the script, the Indian archeologist S.R Rao argued that the late phase of the script represented the beginning of the alphabet. He notes a number of striking similarities in shape and form between the late Harappan characters and the Phoenician letters, arguing than the Phoenician script evolved from the Harappan script, challenging the classical theory that the first alphabet was Proto-Sinatic.

The characters are largely pictorial but include many abstract signs. The inscriptions are thought to have been mostly written from right to left, but sometimes follow a boustrophedonic style. The number of principal signs is about 400, comparable to the typical sign inventory of a logo-syllabic script.

2.1.5.2. Decipherment

In a 2004 article, Farmer, Sproat, and Witzel presented a number of arguments that the Indus script is nonlinguistic, principal among them being the extreme brevity of the inscriptions, the existence of too many rare signs (increasing over the 700-year period of the Mature Harappan civilization), and the lack of the random-looking sign repetition typical of language, as seen, for example, in Egyptian cartouches. Though it remains controversial, many authorities found the article plausible or convincing.

Asko Parpola, reviewing the Farmer, Sproat, and Witzel thesis in 2005, states that their arguments "can be easily controverted". He cites the presence of a large number of rare signs in Chinese, and emphasizes that there is "little reason for sign repetition in short seal texts written in an early logo-syllabic script". Revisiting the question in a 2007 lecture, Parpola takes on each of the 10 main arguments of Farmer *et al.*, presenting counterarguments for each. He states that "even short noun phrases and incomplete sentences qualify as full writing if the script uses the rebus principle to phonetize some of its signs".

A 2009 paper published by Rajesh P.N.Rao, Iravatham Mahadevan, and others in the journal science challenged the argument that the Indus script might have been a nonlinguistic symbol system. The paper concludes that the conditional entropy of Indus inscriptions closely matches those of linguistic systems like the Sumerian logo-syllabic system, Old Tamil, Rig Vedic Sanskrit etc., though they are careful to stress that this does not mean that the script is linguistic. A follow-up study elaborated on these claims. Sproat in turn notes a number of misunderstandings in Rao *et al.*, a lack of discriminative power in their model, and that applying their model to known non-linguistic systems such as Mesopotamian deity symbols produces similar results to the Indus script.

Over the years, numerous decipherements have been proposed, but none have been accepted by the scientific community at large. The following factors are usually regarded as the biggest obstacles for a successful decipherment:

- The underlying language has not been identified though some 300 loanwords in the Rigveda are a good starting point for comparison.
- The average length of the inscriptions is less than five signs, the longest being only 17 signs (and a sealing of combined inscriptions of just 27 signs).
- No bilingual texts (like a Rosetta stone) have been found.
- The topic is popular among amateur researchers, and there have been various (mutually exclusive) decipherment claims. None of these suggestions has found academic recognition.

2.1.5.3. Dravidian hypothesis

The Russian scholar Yuri Knorozov surmised that the symbols represent a logosyllabic script and suggested based on computer analysis, an underlying agglutinative Dravidian language as the most likely candidate for the underlying language. Knorozov's suggestion was preceded by the work of Henry Heras, who suggested several readings of signs based on a proto-Dravidian assumption.

The Finnish scholar Asko Parpola led a Finnish team in the 1960s-80s that vied with Knorozov's Soviet team in investigating the inscriptions using computer analysis. Based on a proto-Dravidian assumption, they proposed readings of many signs, some agreeing with the suggested readings of Heras and Knorozov (such as equating the "fish" sign with the Dravidian word for fish "min") but disagreeing on several other readings. A comprehensive description of Parpola's work until 1994 is given in his book *Deciphering the Indus Script.* The discovery in Tamil Nadu of a late Neolithic (early 2nd millennium BC, i.e. post-dating Harappan decline) stone celt allegedly marked with Indus signs has been considered by some to be significant for the Dravidian identification.

Iravatham Mahadevan, who supports the Dravidian hypothesis, says, we may hopefully find that the proto-Dravidian roots of the Harappan language and South Indian Dravidian languages are similar.

2.1.5.4. "Sanskritic" hypothesis

Indian archeologist Shikaripura Raghunatha Rao claimed to have deciphered the Indus script. Postulating uniformity of the script over the full extent of Indus-era civilization, he compared it to the Phenician Alphabet, and assigned sound values based on this comparison. His decipherment results in an Saskritic reading, including the numerals *aeka, tra, chatus, panta, happta/sapta, dasa, dvadasa, sata* (1, 3, 4, 5, 7, 10, 12, 100).

John E. Mitchiner, after dismissing some more fanciful attempts at decipherment, mentions that a more soundly-based but still greatly subjective and unconvincing attempt to discern an Indo-European basis in the script has been that of Rao.

2.1.6. Summary

- Language is a medium through which we express our thoughts while literature is a mirror that reflects ideas and philosophies which govern our society.
- The Indian people, composed of diverse racial elements, now speak languages belonging to four distinct speech families-'the Aryan, the Dravidian, the Sino-Tibetan (or Mongoloid), and the Austric.
- Indian civilization has found its expression primarily through the Aryan speech as it developed over the centuries-'through Vedic Sanskrit (Old Indo-Aryan), then Classical Sanskrit, then Early Middle Indo-Aryan dialects like Pali and Old Ardha-Magadhi, then Buddhist and Jaina Sanskrit and after th at the various Prakrits and Apabhramsas, and finally in the last phase, the different Modern Indo-Aryan languages of the country.
- Dravidian is the second important language family of India and has some special characteristics- of its own. After the Aryan speech, it has very largely functioned as the exponent of Indian culture, particularly the earlier secular as well as religious literature of Tamil. It forms a solid bloc in South India, embracing the four great literary languages, Kannada, Malayalam, Tamil, and Telugu.
- The Dravidian specch in its antiquity in India is older than Aryan, and yet the specimens of connected Dravidian writing or literature that we can read and

understand are over a millennium later than the oldest Aryan documents.

- The Sino-Tibetan languages do not have much numerical importance or cultural significance in India, with the exception of Manipuri or Meithei of Manipur. Everywhere they are gradually receding before the Aryan languages like Bengali and-Assamese.
- The Austric languages represent the oldest speech family of India, but they are spoken by a very small number of people, comparatively. The Austric languages of India have a great interest for the student of linguistics and human culture. They are valuable relics of India's past, and they link upIndia with Burma, with Indo-China, with Malaya, and with Indonesia, Melanesia, and Polynesia.
- Until the discovery of the Indus Valley Civilization in 1920, ancient India seemingly had two main scripts in which languages were written, Brahmi and Kharosti.
- The Brahmi script developed under Semitic influence around 7th c. BC, and was originally written from right to left. The Kharosti script came into being during the 5th c. BC in northwest India which was under Persian rule.
- Although the origin of the Brahmi script is uncertain, the Kharosti script is commonly accepted as a direct descendant from the Aramaic alphabet. The direction of writing in the Kharosti script is as in Aramaic, from right to left, and there is also a likeness of many signs having similar phonetic value.
- In the later centuries of its existence, Brahmi gave rise to eight varieties of scripts. Three of them - the early and late Mauryas and the Sunga - became the prototypes of the scripts in northern India in the 1st c. BC and AD. Out of these developed the Gupta writing which was employed from the 4th to the 6th c. AD.
- The Siddhamatrka script developed during the 6th c. AD from the western branch of the eastern Gupta character. The Siddhamatrka became the ancestor of the Nagari script which is used for Sanskrit today.

- In the matter of writing, we find a long history from prehistoric times before the coming of the Aryans down to recent years. Until the discovery by excavations of the pre-historic and pre-Aryan city cites of Mohen-jo-Daro in northern Sind and Harappa in South Punjab, the oldest writings known in India was the Maurya script, used in inscriptions of Ashoka and in a few old coins and inscriptions which date back to the 3rd Century B.C.
- In 1837, that the Brahmi script could be read and understood for the first time. Throughout the whole of India, we have inscriptions of Emperor Ashoka in different forms of Prakrit in Brahmi script and decade-by-decade and century by century, this script has gone on evolving on the soil of India.
- An inventory has been made of these letters, and their number comes up to over a hundred. In the Mohen-jo-Daro script, which goes back to 3500 B.C. and beyond, several strata are noticed. The one which is supposed to be the youngest or most advanced in development has simple shapes for the signs, depicted like linear writing.

2.1.7. Exercise

1. Discuss the different language of India.
2. Trace the evolution of writing in India.
3. Write an essay on the origin and development of Brahmi script in India.
4. Give an account on the Harappan script of India.
5. Write short notes on: Harappan script, Dravidian language, Brahmi script, Austric language.

2.1.8. Further Reading

- Daniels, Peter T. & William Bright (eds.) 1996. *The world's writing systems.* New York: Oxford University Press.
- Driem, George van 1999. "On the Austroasiatic Indus theory." [Review of Witzel 1999], *Mother Tongue,* Special issue (October): 75–83.
- Kenoyer, Jonathan Mark 1998. *Ancient cities of the Indus Valley Civilization.* Karachi: Oxford University Press & American Institute of Pakistan Studies.

- Kochhar, Rajesh 2000. *The Vedic people: Their history and geography*. New Delhi: Orient Longman Limited.
- Parpola, Asko 1975. "Tasks, methods and results in the study of the Indus script." *Journal of the Royal Asiatic Society* 1975: 178–209.
- Rogers, Henry 2005. *Writing systems: A linguistic approach*. (Blackwell textbooks in linguistics, 18.) Oxford: Blackwell Publishing Ltd.

CHAPTER-II
SHORT HISTORY OF THE SANSKRIT LITERATURE

THE VEDAS, THE BRAHMANAS AND UPANISHADS & SUTRAS, EPICS: RAMAYANA AND MAHABHARATA & PURANAS.

2.2.0. Objectives

In this chapter we intended providing you an insight into the long history of Sanskrit language and literature that flourished in India since the Vedic Age. The lesson will briefly discuss the vast corpus of Vedic and Vedic allied literature and other Brahminical scripture composed in early age in chaste Sanskrit. By the end of this chapter the learners would be able to:

- *understand the vast corpus of Sanskrit Religious and secular literature;*
- *trace the development of vedic and ancillary vedic literature*
- *survey the brahminical post vedic Sanskrit literature.*
- *describe the content and characteristic features of Ramayana and Mahabharata;*
- *discuss the content,characteristics and value of Puranic literature; and*
- *trace the growth dharma sastras, strotras and other Sanskrit literature.*

2.2.1. Introduction

Ever since human beings have invented scripts, writing has reflected the culture, lifestyle, society and the polity of contemporary society. In the process, each culture evolved its own language and created a huge literary base. This literary base of a civilization tells us about the evolution of each of its languages and culture through the span of centuries. Sanskrit is the mother of many Indian languages. The Vedas, Upanishads, Puranas and Dharmasutras are all written in Sanskrit. There is also a variety of secular and regional literature. By reading about the languages and literature created in the past, we shall be able to understand our civilization better and appreciate the diversity and richness of our culture. All this was possible because of the language that developed during that time.

Sanskrit is the most ancient language of our country. It is one of the twenty-two languages listed in the Indian Constitution. The literature in Sanskrit is vast, beginning with the most ancient thought embodied in the Rig Veda, the oldest literary heritage of mankind, and the Zend Avesta. It was Sanskrit that gave impetus to the study of linguistics scientifically during the eighteenth century. The great grammarian Panini, analysed Sanskrit and its word formation in his unrivalled descriptive grammar *Ashtadhyayi.* The Buddhist Sanskrit literature includes the rich literature of the Mahayana school and the Hinayana school also. The most important work of the Hinayana school is the Mahavastu which is a storehouse of stories. While the Lalitavistara is the most sacred Mahayana text which supplied literary material for the Buddhacarita of Asvaghosa. Sanskrit is perhaps the only language that transcended the barriers of regions and boundaries. From the north to the south and the east to the west there is no part of India that has not contributed to or been affected by this language. Kalhan's *Rajatarangini* gives a detailed account of the kings of Kashmir whereas with *Jonaraja* we share the glory of Prithviraj. The writings of Kalidasa have added beauty to the storehouse of Sanskrit writings.

2.2.2. The Vedic Literature

The Vedas are the earliest known literature in India. The Vedas were written in Sanskrit and were handed down orally from one generation to the other. The preservation of the Vedas till today is one of our most remarkable achievements. To be able to keep such a literary wealth as the Vedas intact when the art of writing was not there and there was a paucity of writing material is unprecedented in world history. The word 'Veda' literally means knowledge. In Hindu culture, Vedas are considered as eternal and divine revelations. They treat the whole world as one human family Vasudev Kutumbakam.

There are four Vedas, namely, the- Rig Veda, Yajur Veda, Sama Veda and Atharva Veda. Each Veda consists of the Brahmanas, the Upanishads and the Aranyakas.

2.2.2.1. The Rig-veda Samhita

The *Rig-Veda Samhita* which has come down to us belongs to the branch known as the Sakala Sakha. It consists of 1,028 *suktas* (hymns) including eleven additional hymns. These hymns, which are made up of a varying number of *mantras* in the form of metrical stanzas, are distributed in ten books called *mandalas.* The formation of the *mandalas* was governed mainly by the principle of homogeneity of authorship. Among the classes of the Vedic Aryans certain families had already acquired some measure of socio-religious importance. The *mantras,* or hymns, which the progenitor and the members of any of these families claimed to have 'seen' were collected in the book of that family. The nucleus of the *Rig- Veda mandalas* two to seven is formed of six such family books, which are respectively ascribed to the families of Grtsamada, Visvamitra, Vamadeva, Atri, Bharadvaja, and Vasistha. The eighth *mandala* laRigely belongs to the Kanvas. The ninth *mandala* is governed by the principle of the homogeneity not of authorship but of subject-matter, for all the *suktas* in this *mandala* relate to *soma* (an intoxicating juice). The first and the tenth *mai.ulalas,* cach of which has 191 hymns, are miscellaneous collections of long and short *suktas.*

Within a *mandala,* the *suktas* are arranged according to the subject-matter. That is to say, the *suktas* are grouped according to the divinities to whom they relate, and then these *devata* groups are arranged in some set order. Within a *devata* group, again, the *suktas* are normally arranged in the descending order of the number of their stanzas The *Rig-Veda* has also been arranged by another method. In this the whole collection is divided into eight *astakas* (books). Each *astaka* is subdivided into eight *adhyayas* (chapters), and each *adhyaya* is further subdivided into about thirty-three *vaRigas* (sections) consisting of about five *mantras* each. This arrangement, however, is obviously mechanical and intended mainly to serve the practical purpose of Vedic study.

Tradition requires that before starting the study of any *sukta* one should know four essential items about it: *rsi,* authorship; *devata,* subject-matter; *chandas,* metre; and *viniyoga* ritualistic application. The poets of the *Rig-Veda* show themselves to have been conscious artists and they sometimes employed various stylistic and rhetorical devices. The majority of the *suktas* in the *Rig-Veda* are of the nature of prayers addressed to different divinities usually with background descriptions of their various exploits and achievements. Apart from these prayers and their mythology, however, we do get in some *suktas* the *Rig-Veda* intimations of the further development of Vcdic thought in the directions of ritualism and philosophical speculation. In connection with the latter, special mention may be made of the *Hiranyagaibha-sukta* and the *Purusa-sukta*.

2.2.2.2. The Atharva-veda Samhita

In contrast to the *Rig- Veda,* the *Alharva- Veda* is essentially a heterogeneous collection of *mantras.* It concerns itself mostly with the everyday life of the common man, from the pre-natal stage to the post-mortem. It portrays that life with all its light and shade, and highlights the generally obscure human emotions and relations. Truly, there is an aura of mystery and unexpectedness about it. The interest of the *Atharva-Veda* is varied and its impact is irresistible.

A distinctive feature of the *Atharva-Veda* is the laRige number of names by which it has been traditionally known. All these names are significant, and together give a full idea of the nature, extent, and content of this Veda. The name *Atharvangirasah* (an abbreviated form of this, *Atharva-Veda,* has, in the course of time, come to be the one most commonly used) is, for example, indicative of the twofold character of the Atharvanic magic: the wholesome, auspicious, 'white' magic of the Atharvans and the terrible, sorcerous, 'black' magic of the Angirasas. The substitution of BhRigu for Atharvan in the name *BhRigvangirasah* is presumably the result of the dominant role played by the family of the BhRigus in a certain period of India's cultural history. The *purohita* (priest) of a Vedic king was expected to be an adept in both white and black magic, and in order to dischaRige adequately the duties of his responsible office he naturally depended on the *mantras* and practices of the *Atharva-Veda.* Thus it was that this Veda also came to be called the *Purohita-Veda.* It was also called the *Ksatia-Veda,* because it included within its scope many practices specifically relating to the Ksatriya rulers.

The *Atharva-Veda* consisted of *Brahmans* (magically potent *mantras*) and was therefore, according to one view, called the *Brahma-Veda.* But there is another reason why it is called the *Brahma-Veda,* which is far more significant. On account of the peculiar character of the contents of the *Atharva-Veda,* it was, for a long time, not regarded as being on a par with the other three Vedas, called *trayi.* As a reaction against this exclusive attitude of the Vedic hierarchy, the Atharva-Vedins went to the other extreme and claimed that their Veda not only enjoyed, by right, the full status of a Veda, but actually comprehended the other three Vedas. The view had already been independently gaining ground that the *Rig-Veda,* the *Yajur-Veda,* and the *Sama-Veda* were essentially limited in scope and that *Brahman* alone was truly limitless. The sponsors of the *Atharva-Veda* claimed that this *Brahman* was adequately embodied in their Veda, and that the *Atharva-Veda* was therefore the *Brahma-Veda.*

However, it is not unlikely that the name *Brahma-Veda* became stabilized because the priest of the *Atharva-Veda* in the Vedic ritual was called *Brahman.* The *Atharva-Veda* is usually considered to be a Veda of magic, and magic bccomcs effective only through the joint operation of *maniras* and the corresponding practices. The *Atharva-Veda Samhita* itself contains only the *mantras,* while its various practices are described in its many ancillary texts, particularly in its five *kalpas.* The *Atharva-Veda* is accordingly sometimes referred to as the Veda of the five *kalpas.* But mystic and esoteric verses are there in the *Atharva- Veda,* and this justifies in a way its claim to be regarded as the *Brahma-Veda,* dealing specifically with Brahman, the supreme Spirit, the other three being more or less connected with the ritual of worship.

Nine (or sometimes fifteen) *sakhas* of the *Atharva-Veda* are traditionally known , but the Samhitas of only two *Sakhas,* the Saunaka and the Paippalada, have been preserved. It was once believed that the Paippalada Sakha was restricted to Kashmir and it was therefore called, though erroneously, the Kashmirian *Atharva- Veda.* It has now been established, however, that that *Sakha* of the *Atharva- Veda* had also spread in eastern India (Orissa and south-west Bengal) and in Gujarat. The entire Paippalada recension was discovered some years ago in Orissa by the late Dr DuRiga Mohan Bhattacharyya and a small portion of it has been publishcd.

The *Saunaka Samhita* of the *Atharva-Veda* has been more commonly current. It consists of 730 *suktas* divided into twenty *kandas* (books). About five-sixths of the *suktas,* which are called *artha-suktas,* contain metrical stanzas, whereas the remaining *suktas,* which are called *parydya-suktas,* contain *avasanas* (prose-units). Unlike the *Rig-Veda Samhita,* the arrangement of the *Atharva-Veda Samhita* is not governed by any consideration either of authorship or of subject-matter. In deed, it is understandable that the historical tradition regarding authorship was not preserved in respect of this 'Veda of the masses'. Again, the *Atharva-Veda* shows considerable looseness in matters of metre, accent, and grammar, presumably because it was not subjected, as the *Rig-Veda* was, to deliberate revision and redaction.

The contents of the *Atharva-Veda* are remarkably diverse in character. There are in this Veda charms to counteract diseases and possession by evil spirits, *bhaisajyani.* The *Atharva-Veda* presents perhaps the most complete account of primitive medicine. There are also prayers for health and long life, *ayusyanv,* for happiness and prosperity, *paustikani.* There are also spells pertaining to the various kinds of relationship with women, *strikarmani.*

Another significant section of this Veda contains hymns which concern themselves with affairs involving the king, *rajakarmani,* and others which are intended for securing harmony in domestic, social, and political spheres, *sammanasydni.*

As for black magic, the *Atharva-Veda* abounds in formulas for sorocry and imprecation, for exorcism and counter-exorcism. Polarity may be said to be one of the most striking features of the *Atharva-Veda,* for side by side with the incantations for sorcery and black magic, it contains highly theosophical or philosophical speculations. These speculations, indeed, represent a significant landmark in the history of Indian thought. As has been mentioned, the *Rig-Veda* and the *Atharva-Veda* are the only two primary Samhitas, the other two Samhitas being mostly derivative in character. Again, it is to be noted in the same context that the *Sama-Veda* and the *Yajur-Veda* may be styled as Samhitas since they are, in a sense, collections of *mantras,* but in them are reflected tendencies which are not of the Samhita period but are of the Brahmana period.

2.2.2.3. The Sama-Veda Samhita

The *Sama-Veda Samhita* is a collection of *mantras* prescribed for chanting at various *soma* sacrifices by the *udgatr* (singer-priest) and his assistants,: thus this Veda serves an avowedly ritualistic purpose. Though called *Sama-Veda,* it is not strictly speaking a collection of *samans* (chants). The *Sama-Veda,* as we have said, is essentially a derivative production in the sense that most of its *mantras* are derived from the *Rig-Veda.* Three distinct stages may be inferred in the evolution of this Veda. There is a specific *mantra* taken from the *Rig-Veda* in its original form. This *mantra* is taken into the *Sama-Veda* with a view to its being made the basis of a proper *saman.* The only change that is affected in this process concerns the marking of the accents, numbers, 1, 2, and 3 now being used to indicate accents instead of the vertical and horizontal lines used in the *Rig-Veda.* In this second stage the *mantra* is called *samayoni-mantra.* The *Sama-Veda* is actually a collection of such *samayoni-mantras.* The collection is in two main parts: the *Purvardka* and the *Uttararcika.* The *Purvardka* consists of 585 single verses, of which the first 114 are addressed to Agni, the next 352 to Indra, and the last 119 to Soma. The *Uttararcika* consists of 1,225 verses grouped into 400 units of connected verses. The total number of *mantras* in the *Sama-Veda,* excluding the repeated ones, is 1,549, all of which except 78 are taken from the *Rig-Veda,* mostly from its eighth and ninth *maridaks* (books).

It is, however, not in the form in which they occur in the *Sama-Veda Samhita* that these *mantras* are employed by the *udgatr* in the *soma* ritual. The *samayommmtras* are transformed into chants or ritual melodies called *ganas.*

This is done by means of such devices as the modification, prolongation, and repetition of the syllables occurring in the *mantra* itself, and the occasional insertion of additional syllables known as *stobhas.* These *ganas,* which represent the third and final stage in the evolution of the *Sama- Veda,* are collected in four books: the *Gramageya-gana,* the *Aranya-gana,* the *Uha-gana,* and the *Uhya-gdna,* Of course, these *gdna* collections are quite distinct from the *Sama-Veda Samhita.* Normally, each *gdna* in these collections is given some technical name, for example, *Brhat, Ratkantara,* or *Gotamasya Parka.* Since one *sdmayoni-mantra* can be chanted in a variety of ways, it may give rise to several *ganas.* For instance, three *ganas, Gotamasya Paika, Kajyapasya Barhisa,* and another *Gotamasya Parka,* have evolved out of the first *mantra* in the *Sama-Veda Samhita.* Consequendy, the number of *Sama-ganas* is much laRiger than the number of *sdmayoni-mantras.*

Thirteen *sakhas* of the *Sama-Veda* are traditionally mentioned, though only three *sakhas,* the *Kauthuma,* the *Ranayaniya,* and the *Jaimini,* are well known today. Patanjali, in his *Mahabhasya,* speaks of the *Sama-Veda* having a thousand 'paths', *sahasravartma samavedah.* This characterization presumably suggests the laRige number of possible modes of *sama* chanting, rather than a thousand *Sakhas* of the *Sama-Veda,* as is construed by some. In the *Bhagavad-Gita* the *Sama-Veda* is glorified as the most excellent of the Vedas. This may be due to the great efficacy of the magical potence engendered in the Vedic ritual by the chanting of the *samans.*

2.2.2.4. The Yajur-Veda Samhita

Like the *Sama-Veda,* the *Yajur-Veda* is essentially ritualistic in character. This is clearly indicated by Yaska's derivation of the word *Yajur* from the root *yaj,* to sacrifice. But while the *Sama-Veda* concerns itself exclusively with the *soma* sacrifice, the *Yajur-Veda* treats of the entire sacrificial system. Indeed, the *Yajur- Veda* may be regarded as the first regular textbook on Vedic ritual as a whole. It deals mainly with the duties of the *adhvaryu* (fire-priest), who is responsible for the actual performance of the various sacrificial rites. Incidentally, it may be mentioned that while the *Sama-Veda* represents a very early stage in the history of Indian music, the *Yajur-Veda* marks the beginning of Sanskrit prose. Tradition speaks variously of the *Yajur-Veda* having 86 or 101 *sakhas.* But for our present purpose we may consider only its two main recensions, the *Krsna Yajur-Veda* and the *Sukla Yajur-Veda.* The difference between these two recensions lies not so much in their content as in their arrangement. In the *Krsna Yajur-Veda* the *mantras* (mostly derived from the *Rig-Veda)* and the *yajus* (sacrificial formulas in prose) and their ritualistic explanations (called the Brahmana) are mixed up together. That is

to say, in the matter of form and content, the Samhita of the *Krsna Yajur-Veda* is not particularly distinguishable from the Brahmana or the Aranyaka of that Veda. As against this, the Samhita of the *Sukla Yajur-Veda* contains the *mantras* and *yajus* only, reserving the corresponding ritualistic explanation and discussion for the *Satapatha Brahmana* which belongs to that Veda.

From among the many schools of the *Krsna Yajur-Veda* the Samhitas of only four schools are available today, either entirely or in fragments. These four schools are: the Taittiriya, the Kathaka, the Maitrayani, and the Kapisthala-katha. The Taittiriya School is traditionally divided into two branches, the Aukhya and the Khandikeya. The Khandikeya is further subdivided into five branches: the Apastamba, the Baudhayana, the Satyasadha, the Hiranyakesin, and the Bharadvaja. The Taittiriya School has preserved its literature perhaps most fully amongst all the Vedic schools, maintaining its continuity from the Samihita period, through the Brahmana, the Aranyaka, and the Upanisad periods, to the Sutra period. It is presumably on account of this fact that the Taittiriya School is often equated with the whole of the *Krsna Yajur-Veda.*

The name Taittiriya is variously explained. There is, for instance, the legend which narrates how Yajnavalkya, who had developed differences with his teacher Vaisampayana, vomited the Veda which he had learned from his teacher; how, at the instance of VaiSampayana, his other pupils, assuming the form of *tittiri* birds, consumed the vomited Veda; how, consequently, the Veda so recovered by the *tittiri* birds was called the *Taittiriya-Veda;* and how, finally, Yajnavalkya secured from the Sun-god another Veda which came to be known as the *Sukla* or bright *Yajur-Veda.* It is also suggested that, on account of the interspersion in it of the *mantras* and the *brahmana* portion, the *Krsna Yajur-Veda* appears variegated like a *tittiri* bird, and is therefore called the *Taittiriya Samhita.* However, the most satisfactory explanation of the name seems to be that an ancient sage called Tittiri was traditionally regarded as the 'seer' of this Veda.

The other Samhitas of the *Krsna Yajur-Veda* agree substantially with the *Taittiriya Samhitd* in the matter of content and arrangement, and even verbally. The nucleus of the *Kathaka Samhita* consists of three *kandas,* called *Ithimika, Madhyamika,* and *Orimika.* Two more *kandas* are added to this nucleus, presumably, by way of appendices. A comparative study of the *Krsna Yajur-Veda* and the *Sukla Yajur-Veda* shows that the *Kathaka Samhita* occupies a position intermediate between the *Taittiriya Samhita* and the *Vajasaneyi Samhita.* It may also be noted that the school of the *Kathaka* seems to have been widely current in the days of Patanjali, as is evidenced by his

statement that 'people used to talk about the *Kathaka* and the *Kalapaka* in every village'

The Samhita of the Maitrayani School (the school that is closely related to that of the *Manaras)* may be said to be more systematic in its arrangement than either the *Taittiriya Samhita* or the *Kathaka Samhita.* Its nucleus is made up of three *kandas,* but there are also a fourth *kanda,* of the nature of an appendix, *khila,* and a fifth *kanda,* which constitutes the *Matin Upanisad.* The *Kapisthalakatha Samhita* is available only in a fragmentary and more or less corrupt form. The text of this Samhita shows but little diveRigence from that of the *Kathaka Samhita.* A significant feature of the *Sukla Yajur-Veda Samhita,* which is also known as the *Vajasaneyi Samhita,* is that the entire Samhita and its Brahmana, called the *Satapatha Brahmana,* have come down in two distinct versions, the *Madhyandina* and the *Kanva.*

2.2.2.5. The Brahmanas

Many Vedic texts are traditionally called Brahmanas, but the more important among them are the *Aitareya* and the *Kausitak* belonging to the *Rig-Veda,* the *Taittiriya* belonging to the *Krsna Yajur-Veda,* the *Satapatha* belonging to the *Sukla Yajur-Veda*; the *Jaiminiya* and *Tandya* belonging to the *Sama-Veda,* and the *Gopatha* belonging to the *Atharva-Veda.* The *Aitareya Brahmana,* which naturally concerns itself mainly with the duties of the priest of the *Rig-Veda,* namely, the *hotr,* is divided into eight *pancikas* of five *adhydyas* each. Clear evidence is available of Panini's having known all the forty *adhydyas* of this Brahmana. The first twenty-four *adhydyas* of the *Aitareya Brahmana* deal with the *hautra* (the function or office of the *hotr)* of the various *soma* sacrifices; the next six with the *agnihotra* and the duties of the *hotr*s assistants; and the last ten, which show signs of being a later addition, with the *rajasuya.* The *Kausitaki Brahmana,* also known as the *Sankhayana Brahmana,* has thirty *adhyayas.* It is a better-oRiganized text and covers more or less the entire sacrificial procedure. As has been indicated already, the *Taittiriya Brahmana* is merely a continuation of the *Taittiriya Samhita.* Its three *kandas* either supplement the discussion of the ritual in the Samhita or give a more detailed treatment of some of the topics dealt with in it.

The *Satapatha Brahmana,* on the other hand, must be regarded as an independent work and it is quite remarkable in many respects. Indeed, after the *Rig-Veda* and the *Atharva-Veda,* it is perhaps the most important Vedic text in both extent and content. The *Madhyandina* version of the *Satapatha Brahmana* consists of 14 *kandas* (each with a separate name derived from its contents), 68 *prapathakas* or 100 *adhyayas* (from which the *Satapatha Brahmana* presumably gets its name as 'the Brahmana with a hundred paths

or sections'), 438 *brahmanas,* and 7,624 *kandikas.* In the *Kanva* version, the first, the fifth, and the fourteenth *kandas* are each divided into two *kandas',* thus the total number of *kandas* in that version is seventeen. Otherwise, the names of the *kandas* and their contents are generally the same.

The first nine *kandas* of the *Madhyandina-Satapatha Brahmana,* which seem to represent the older portion, fully correspond with the first eighteen *adhyayas* of the *Vajasaneyi Samhita,* and thus cover the basic sacrificial ritual. The tenth *kanda,* called *Agrdrahasya* speaks of the mystical significance of the various aspects of the sacred fires; while the eleventh, called *Astadhyayi,* recapitulates the entire sacrificial ritual. The twelfth *kanda* is called *Madhyama,* which title clearly suggests that *kandas* X-XIV constitute a separate unit added later to the original Brahmaria. This would seem to be confirmed by Patanjali's reference to this Brahmana as *Sastipatha* (sixty paths), a name presumably derived from the fact that the first nine *kandas* together consist of sixty *adhyayas.* The twelfth *kanda* concerns itself with expiation rites and the *sautramani* sacrifice. The thirteenth *kanda* deals mainly with the *abamedha* sacrifice and also, rather briefly, with the *purusamedha* and the *sarvamedha* sacrifices. The first three *adhydyas* of the last *kanda* of the *Satapatha Brahmana* are devoted to the consideration of the *praoaRigya* ceremony (introductory to the *soma* sacrifice); while the last six *adhydyas* constitute the famous *Brhaddranyaka Upanisad.* One of the important features of the *Satapatha Brahmana* is the large number of legends it contains. Among them may be mentioned: Manu and the fish; the migration of Videgha Mathava from the region of the Sarasvati to the region of the Sadanira; the rejuvenation of Cyavana; the romantic affair between Pururavas and Urvasi; and the contest between Kadru and Vinata. Another important feature is that, while some portions of this Brahmana are intimately connected with the Kuru-Pancalas, others have their provenance in Kosala-Videha. This fact clearly indicates that the *Satapatha Brahmana* is a composite work and that its composition must have extended over a wide range of time and area. In this connection it is noteworthy that the principal figure in *kandas* I-V and XI-XV is Yajnavalkya, whereas it is Sandilya in *kandas* VI-X. The *Samu-Veda* can boast of having the largest number of Brahmana texts, but only two or three of them can properly be called Brahmanas; all the others are more or less of the nature of *parimstas* (appendices). The *Jaiminiya Brahmana,* which consists of 1,252 sections and which is thus one of the bulkiest of the Vedic texts, constitutes the best source of information regarding the technique of the *samagas* (the priests who chant or recite the *Sama-Veda*). It is also a difficult text, however, since the ritual and legendary data in it are more or less isolated.

Another Brahmana which belongs to the *Sama-Veda* is the *Tandya Brahmana.* It is also known as the *Pancavirhsa Brahmana,* for, as its name implies, it consists of twenty-five books. Its chief concern is of course the *soma* sacrifice in all its varieties, but of particular interest are its detailed description of the *sattras* (sacrificial sessions) origanized on the banks of the Drsadvati and the Sarasvati, and its treatment of the *vratya-stomas* (hymns of praise). Like the *Pancavirhsa Brahmana,* the *Sama-Veda* has a *Sadvimfa Brahmana,* the last book of which deals with omens and portents; it is called the *Adbhuta Brahmana.* The *Gopatha Brahmaria,* which is the only Brahmana of the *Atharva-Veda* known to us, is perhaps the youngest of the Brahmana texts. It is also limited in extent, consisting as it does of only two books with eleven *prapathakas.* One of the *parisistas* of the *Atharva-Veda,* says, however, that the *Gopatha Brahmana* originally consisted of one hundred chapters out of which only two have survived. This is quite plausible, since many statements referred to in other texts as being derived from this Brahmana are not traceable in its extant text.

A significant point about the *Gopatha Brahmana* is that, for the most part, it contains myths, legends, and parables which illustrate and explain various ceremonies in the Vedic ritual. The Atharvanic character of this Brahmana becomes evident in several ways. For instance, it glorifies Angiras as the 'sage of sages' and emphasizes that a Vedic sacrifice performed without the help of a priest of the *Atharva-Veda* is bound to fail. In the literary history of ancient India, the Brahmanas are important for the following reasons: *(i)* they represent the earliest attempts to interpret the Vedic *mantras;* *(ii*) they mark the beginnings of Sanskrit prose; (n't) they have preserved many ancient legends; and *(iv)* they have in them the seeds of the future development of several literary forms and works, and of various branches of knowledge.

Moreover, the Brahmanas contain an exclusive and comprehensive treatment of Vedic sacrificial ritual, and thus constitute a highly authoritative source for one of the most significant periods in the religious history of India. It is, again, the Brahmanas which have prepared the background for the philosophical speculations of the Upanisads. And, finally, culture-historians can ill afford to lose sight of the various facts of socio-political history interspersed in the ritualistic lucubrations of the Brahmanas.

2.2.2.6. The Aranyakas

The Aranyakas are a kind of continuation of the Brahmanas, textually as well as conceptually. They mark the transition from the ritualism of the Brahmanas to the spiritualism of the Upanisads. While, on the one hand, most of the texts of the Aranyakas form the concluding portions of some of the Brahmanas, on the other hand, some of the Upanisadic texts are either embedded in or appended to them. The Aranyakas, which are obviously esoteric, seek to present the true mystique of the ritual by glorifying the inner, mental sacrifice as against the external, material aspect of it. The study of the Aranyakas was traditionally restricted therefore to the solitude of the forest, *aranya.* That is why they came to be called the Aranyakas. It is also not unlikely that these texts derived their name from their schematic connection with Vanaprastha *Obama* (the forest-dweller's stage). Only a few texts have come to be traditionally called the Aranyakas. The *Aitareya Aranyaka,* belonging to the *Rig-Veda,* consists of five books. The second and the third books are specifically attributed to Mahldasa Aitareya, and are generally theosophic in their tendencies. The first three sections of the second book, which are said to be intended for persons who desire liberation in gradual stages, teach the *prana-upasana* (worship of vital power). The last three sections of the second book constitute the *Aitareya Upanisad* which sets forth Vedantic doctrines.

The third book deals with the *samhita-upasana* (unified form of worship) and is meant for persons who are still attached to worldly possessions. In its other parts, this Aranyaka treats of such sacrificial ceremonies as the *Makavrata.* The *Kauntaki* or *Sankhayana Aranyaka,* which also belongs to the *Rig-Veda* consists of three books, the first two of which are ritualistic in character while the third forms the *Kausitaki Upanisad.*

As for the *Taittiriya Aranyaka,* it is, as already mentioned, a direct continuation of the Samhita and the Brahmaria of the Taittiriya School. In its first six books it supplements the treatment of Vedic ritual in the Samhita and the Brahmana by dealing with such sacrifices as the *sarvamedka,* the *pitrmedha,* and the *pravargya.* Its next three books constitute the *Taittiriya Upanisad,* while its tenth and last book is known as the *Maha-ndrayana Upanisad.* The first three *adhydyas* of the fourteenth *kanda* of the *Satapatha Brahmana* are called Aranyaka and their subject-matter is *the pravargya* sacrifice. As already mentioned, the last six *adhydyas* of this *kanda* make up the *Brhaddranyaka Upanisad.*

2.2.2.7. The Upanisads

The word *upanisad* is interpreted variously. It is made to correspond with the word *updsana* which is understood to mean either worship or profound knowledge. The word is also connected with the Pali word *upanisa* and thus made to mean something like cause or connection. In his *bhasya* (commentary) on the *Taittiriya Upanisad* Sankara interprets *upanisad* as that which destroys *(sad,* to destroy) ignorance. But the sense most commonly signified by the word *upanisad* is the esoteric teaching imparted by the teacher to the pupil who sits *(sad)*, near him *(upa)*, in a closed select *(ni)*, group. The Upanisads are also called the Vedanta, because they represent the concluding portion of the *apauruseya* Veda or Sruti, or the final stage in Vedic instruction, or the ultimate end and aim of the teachings of the Veda. The importance of the Upanisads, however, as the first recorded attempt at systematic, though not systematized, philosophizing can hardly be gainsaid. They are one of the most significant sources of the spiritual wisdom of India, and are traditionally regarded as one of the three *prasthanas* (source books) of Indian philosophy. Also, one cannot fail to be impressed by certain notable features of the Upanisads, such as: their unity of purpose in spite of the variety in their doctrines; the note of certainty or definiteness which informs them; and the various levels at which they consider and represent reality.

Much need not be said here about the Upanisads as religious literature, because they are concerned with the contemplative-realizational rather than with the ritualistic-ceremonial aspect of the spiritual life of the people. They belong to philosophy rather than to religion. There are over 200 Upanisads, including such recent works as the *Khristopanisad* and the *Allopanisad*. The *Muktikopanisad* gives a traditional list of 108 Upanisads, of which 10 belong to the *Rig-Veda*, 19 to the *Sukla Yajur-Veda*, *32* to th e *Kjsna Yajur-Veda*, 16 to the *Sama-Veda*, and 31 to the *Atharva-Veda'*, but even out of these, many texts are called Upanisads only by courtesy. Usually, thirteen Upanisads are regarded as the principal Upanisads. They are traditionally connected with one Vedic *Saha* or the other, and several of them actually form part of a laRiger literary complex.

The *Isa Upanisad* belongs to the *Sukla Yajur-Veda* and is included in the *Vajasaneyi Samhitd* as its last *adhyaya*, that is, the fortieth. This Upanisad, which derives its name from its first word, emphasizes the unity of being and becoming, but in this connection it speaks of Isa, the Lord, rather than of Brahman. It elaborates the doctrine of *vidyd* (knowledge) and *avidya* (ignorance), and sets forth the view that a fusion of both *(samuccaya)*, is a necessary precondition for the attainment of *amrtatva* (immortality). The *Kena Upanisad*, which also derives its name from its initial word, forms part of the fourth book of the *Talavakara Brahmana* of the *Sama-Veda*. It consists of four sections, of which the first two, which are in verse, deal with Brahman, *paid-vidya* (higher knowledge), and *sadyomukti* (immediate liberation); while the last two sections, which are in prose, deal with Isvara, *apara-vidyd* (lower knowledge), and *krama-mukti* (gradual liberation). This Upanisad contains the famous legend of Uma HaimavatL One of the better-known Upanisads is the *Katha* or *Kathaka Upanisad*, which belongs to the *Krsna Yajur-Veda*. It consists of two chapters which have three *vallis* (sections) each. For the background of its philosophical teaching it has the striking legend of Yama and Naciketas. A noteworthy point about this Upanisad is that it has many passages in common with the *Bhagavad-Gitd.* The *Prasna Upanisad,* the *Munda* or *Mundaka Upanisad,* and the *Mandukya Upanisad* belong to the *Atharva-Veda.* The *Praha Upanisad,* as its name suggests, deals, in its six sections, with six questions, *prasnas,* relating to such topics as the nature of the ultimate cause, the significance of *Om,* and the relation between the Supreme and the Word. The name *Munda* is suggestive of renunciation, and in its three chapters this Upanisad discusses *sannyasa* (renunciation) and *para-vidyd* as against *samsara* (the world) and *apara-vidya.* Incidentally, India's national motto *satyam eva jayate* (truth alone triumphs) is taken from this Upanisad (III. 1.6). The *Mandiikya Upanisad* is a very small text consisting of only twelve stanzas, but it has attained a significant place in the philosophical literature of India on account of the fact that Gaudapada, Sankara's predecessor, wrote a commentary on this Upanisad, his famous *Mdndukya-kdrika,* which may be said to contain the first systematic statement of the doctrine of absolute monism, later elaborated upon and given full form by Sankara. The *Taittiriya Upanisad* is a part of the laRiger literature complex of the Taittiriya school of the *Krsna Yajur-Veda.* As has been pointed out, the seventh, eighth, and ninth books of the *Taittiriya Aranyaka* constitute the *Taittiriya Upanisad,* the tenth and last being the *Mahd-narayana Upanisad.* The *Taittiriya Upanisad* is divided into three sections called *vallis:* the *Siksa-valli,* the *Brahmananda-valli* and the *BhRigu-valli.* The *Aitareya Upanisad* of the *Rig-Veda* is equivalent to the *Aitareya Aranyaka* (II. 4-6).

By far the most important of the Upanisads are the *Chandogya* and the *Brhadaianyaka.* The *Chandogya Brahmana,* belonging to the Kauthuma Sakha of the *Sama-Veda,* consists of ten chapters. The first two chapters, which comprise the *Mantra Brahmana,* deal with ritualistic subjects, while the last eight chapters constitute the *Chandogya Upanisad.* Some of the topics of particular philosophical interest in this Upanisad are the *Sandilya-vidya* (the technique taught by the sage Sandilya); the *samvaRiga-vidya* (the technique relating to the all-consuming cosmic wind), the *vaisvanara-vidya* (the technique relating to the all-consuming cosmic fire), and the teachings imparted by Prajapati to Indra, by Ghora Angirasa to Krsna Devakiputra, by Uddalaka Aruni to Svetaketu, and by Sanatkumara to Narada.

The *Brhadaranyaka Upanisad,* which belongs to the *Sukla Yajur-Veda,* is the biggest and perhaps the oldest of the Upanisads. In the Madhyandina recension this Upanisad corresponds with Chapters IV-VI1I of the fourteenth *khanda* and Chapter VI of the tenth *kanda* of the *Satapatha Brahmana* of the same recension. The *Kanva Brhadaranyaka Upanisad* (which, incidentally, Sankara chose for his commentary) is analogous to the last six chapters of the sixteenth *kanda* of the *Kanva Satapatha Brahmana.* There is, however, no material divergence between the two recensions so far as the subject-matter is concerned. The first two chapters of the *Brhadaranyaka Upanisad* constitute the *madhu-kanda,* the main purpose of which is to establish the identity of jiva and Brahman. The next two chapters, which seem to form the kernel of this Upanisad, are dominated by the personality and the teachings of the greatest of the Upanisadic philosophers, Yajnavalkya; together they make up what is known as the*yajnavalkya-kanda* or the *mum-kanda.*

Added to these ten traditionally recognized Upanisads are three others, making altogether the thirteen principal Upanisads. These three are the *Svetasvatara* and the *Maitri,* or *Maitrayani,* both of which belong to the *Krsna Yajur-Veda,* and the *Kausitaki* which belongs to the *Rig-Veda.* The *Svetasvatara Upanisad,* which has six chapters and 113 stanzas, is essentially a theistic text. It presents the supreme Brahman as Rudra, the personal God, and teaches the doctrine of *bhakti* (devotion). This Upanisad is also remarkable for its use of Samkhya terminology and its attempt to reconcile the different religious and philosophical views which were then in vogue. The *Maitri* or *Maitrayani Upanisad* has seven chapters, the last two of which are comparatively modern. It mentions the *Trimurti* concept, and, in its references to the illusory character of the world and the momentariness of phenomena, seems to betray the influence of Buddhistic thought. The *Kausitaki Upanisad,* though also called *Kausitaki Brahmana Upanisad,* is not connected with the *Kausitaki* (or *Sankhayana) Brahmana.* As we have already seen, this Upanisad is the third chaptcr of the *Sahkhayana Aianyaka.* Among other topics, it deals with the progressive definition of the Brahman, the course to *Brakmaloka* (the sphere of Brahman), and Indra as life and immortality.

Apart from these principal Upanisads there are many others, but they are essentially sectarian in character and pseudo-philosophical in content. They arc usually divided into various classes, such as Slmanya-Vedanta, Yoga, Sannyasa, Saiva, Vaisnava, and Sakta, in accordance with their main tendencies. As for the age of the principal Upanisads, they may be said to extend roughly ovcr a period from the eighth to the third century B.C., the older ones among them being decidedly pre-Buddhistic. As far as the relative chronology of the Upanisads is concerned, it is customary to speak of four classes, namely: ancient prose, early metrical, later prose, and later metrical. The Upanisads can, no doubt, be said to represent the high watermark of Vedic thought; but it also needs to be realized that certain features of their teachings, such as *Brakma-vidya* (knowledge of Brahman), were too subtle to be adequately comprehended by ordinary people. They demanded a high intellectual level and strict spiritual discipline on the part of the seeker. The Upani§ads gave the people a philosophy but not a religion.

2.2.3. Ancillary Vedic Literature

2.2.3.1. The Vedangas and the Sotras

As we have seen, the Samhitas, the Brahmanas, the Aranyakas, and the Upanisads are believed to be *apauruseya.* Not so the Vedangas, for in the reoriganization of Vedic knowledge they present an attempt to systematize various aspects of that knowledge which are necessary for understanding the Vedic texts. The six Vedangas are: *Siksa* (phonetics); *kalpa* (socio-religious practice and ritual); *vyakarana* (grammar); *nirukta* (etymology, exegesis, and mythology); *chandas* (metrics); and *jyotisa* (astronomy). Each of these six Vedangas is connected, in one way or another, with the Vedic religion, although only the Kalpa may be said to be directly religious in purpose. By the Kalpa-Sutra is usually meant a whole literary corpus comprising the Srauta-Sutra, the Grhya- Sutra, and the Dharma-Sutra; these, broadly speaking, refer respectively to the religious, the domestic, and the social aspects of the life of the people. These Sutras primarily seek to regulate and codify the practices which were already in vogue, but at the same time they also initiate new practices or modify the old ones in accordance with the times and the traditions of the school in which they originated.

There is reason to believe that each Vedic school produced its own Kalpa- Sutra though not all of them are available today. The nature of a Kalpa-Sutra will be clear from the following analysis of the contents of the Kalpa-Sutra of the Apastamba school of the Taittiriya Sakha of the *Krsna Yajur-Veda.* This Kalpa-Sutra consists of thirty *prasnas* (literally questions, chapters), the first twenty-three of which constitute the Srauta-Sutra. The twenty-fourth *praha* is called the *paribhdsa-praha* and contains the *paribhasa* (general rules and definitions) connected with the ritual. In view of its character as 'introduction', this *prasna* should have been placed at the very beginning of the Kalpa-Sutra; but, as the commentator Kapardisvamin explains, this *paribhasa* is applicable to both the Srauta-Sutra and the Grhya-Sutra and is therefore placed between the two. The *paribhasa-prasna* also comprises the *pravara* (the series of ancestors) and the *hautra* (the duties of the *hotr).* The twenty-fifth and twenty-sixth *prahas* give the *mantras* to be employed for the various *grhya* rites, while the twenty-seventh *praha* makes up the *Apastamba Grhya-Sutra* proper. The twenty-eighth and twenty-ninth *prahas* contain the Dharma-Sutra, and the thirtieth *praha* is the Sulva-Sutra. To these thirty *prahas* is sometimes added a *tknity-fsxstprabia* which constitutes the Pitrmedha-Sutra. Among such complete Kalpa-Sutras which are available today may be mentioned those belonging to the Baudhayana, the HiranyakeSin, and the Vaikhanasa schools of the Taittiriya Sakha. All these texts are called Sutras because they adopted the unique literary form which was developed during this period, namely, the *siitra* form. A *sutra* is an aphoristic statement, at once brief, unequivocal, comprehensive, generally valid, and expressive of the essential point.

2.2.3.2. The Srauta-Sutras, Grhya-Sutras, and Dharma-Sutras

As we have seen, the Srauta-Sutras contain injunctions regarding religious practices, the word 'practices' being understood in the restricted sense of ritualistic practices. Naturally, therefore, they are directly connected with the Brahmanas, particularly with the *vidhi* portions. The Srauta-Sutras, however, present the procedure of the various sacrifices in a far more complete and systematic manner. Presumably, these Sutras were composed as practical aids to the professional officiating priests. Closely related to the Srauta-Sutras are the Sulva-Sutras which deal with such matters as the construction of the sacrificial altars, the measurements of the different kinds of fire-altars, etc. The Srauta-Sutras generally treat of sacrifices in which the three sacred fires, the *ahaxianiya*, the *garhapatya*, and the *daksina* (or sometimes more) are employed. These sacrifices usually require the services of several officiating priests from among the *adhvaryu*, the *hotr*, the *brahman*, and the *udgatr*, and their assistants.

The majority of the Srauta-Sutras known today belong to the *Yajur-Veda* (particularly to the *Krsna Yajur-Veda*). This is quite understandable, for the *adhvaryu* plays the most active role in the *srauta* ritual, and the *Tajui-Yeda* is essentially the Veda for the *adhvaryu*. The *Baudhayana Srauta-Sutra* belongs to the Taittiriya Sakha of the *Krasna Yajur-Veda*; it is perhaps the oldest among the Srauta-Sutras. The *Baudhayana Srauta-Sutra* is called a *pravacana* (sacred treatise) and is written more in the style of the Brahmanas than of the Sutras.

The other Srauta-Sutras which belong to the Taittiriya Sakha, are the *Bharadvaja*, the *Apastamba*, the *Satyasadha-Hiranyakesm*, the *Vaikhanasa*, and the *Vadhula*. Of the two Srauta-Sutras belonging to the MaitrayanI Sakha, the *Manava* and the *Varaha*, the former is closely connected with the *Apastamba Srauta- Sutra*. The *Kathaka Srauta-Sutra* has become known only through references to it in other Srauta-Sutras and commentaries. The *Katyayana Srauta-Sutra* is the only Srauta- Sutra of the *Sukla Yajur-Veda*. The two Srauta-Sutras of the *Rig-Veda*, the *Asvalayana* and the *Sankhayana*, deal mainly with the *hautra*. The *Sama-Veda* has four Srauta-Sutras, the *Latyayana*, the *Drakyayana*, the *Jaiminiya*, and the *Gobhila*. The *Vaitana- Sutra* of the *Atharva-Veda* is a short text concerning the duties of the *brahman* and his assistants, and also of the sacrificer. The *Kausika-Sutra*, which also belongs to the *Atharva-Veda*, is essentially a Grhya-Sutra, but it contains several passages relating to the *srauta* ritual.

The Grhya-Sutras deal with the *grhya* (household) rites which broadly comprise the seven *paka-yajna-samsthas* and also the rites connected with the various *samskaras* (sacraments). The Grhya-Sutras have very little to do with the Brahmanas, but they are directly connected with the Samhitas since they derive their *mantras* from them. It needs to be pointed out, however, that not all the *mantras* prescribed to be employed in *grhya* rites are traceable to the Samhitas. The *grhya* rites are generally performed with the help of only one fire, and in many of them the services of officiating priests are not required. *Soma* has no place in any of them. When they form part of a corpus, the Grhya-Sutras presuppose and occur after the Srauta-Sutra. It is, however, difficult to say whether the Srauta-Sutra and the Grhya-Sutra belonging to the same school can be ascribed to the same authorship. At the same time, one does come across many verbal repetitions in the two Sutras of the same school.

Of the two Grhya-Sutras of the *Sukla Yajur-Veda,* one is the *Paraskara Grhya-Sutra,* which is also known as the *Katiya Grhya-Sutra* or the *Vajasaneya Grhya-Sutra.* The other one, the *Baijavapa Grhya-Sutra,* is known only through references to it in other works. The *Paraskara Grhya-Sutra* is connectcd with the Madhyandina Sakha. The larigest numbers of published Grhya-Sutras belong to the *Kjsna Yajur- Veda.* The *Baudhayana Grhya-Sutra* (with four *prasnas),* the *Bharadvaja Grhya- Sutra* (with three *prahas),* the *Apastamba Grhya-Sutra* (with three *prahas,* of which two give only the *mantras* for *grhya* rites while the third gives the injunctions regarding the performance of these rites), and the *Satyasadha-Hiranyakesi Grhya- Sutra* (with two *prahas)* are included in the Kalpa-Sutra corpuses of their respective Vedic schools.

Compared with Srauta-Sutras and Grhya-Sutras which are available, the Dharma-Sutras are very few. It may be pointed out, however, that besides those published, many other texts of this category have become known through quotations from them found in other works. It is also possible to presume that some of the Dharma-Sutras are now completely lost. There is another significant point about the Dharma-Sutras. This is that although the different Dharma- Sutras are traditionally believed to have been affiliated to different Vedic schools, the influence on them of those specific schools is almost negligible. It seems that while the *srauta* and *grhya* practices varied from school to school in some details at least-social practices, civil and criminal law, and polity, which constituted the principal subject-matter of the Dharma-Sutras, had in general become common to the entire Vedic-Aryan community. Understandably the connection between a Dharma-Sutra and any particular Vedic school was often tenuous. Within a Kalpa corpus the Dharma-Sutra usually follows the Grhya-Sutra. It may also be noted that many topics, such as the *asrama-dharmas* (special duties of each period of life), are common to the Grhya- Sutra and the Dharma-Sutra. The arrangement of the subject-matter in the Dharma-Sutras is not at all orderly. In the light of the classification of topics in some of the later metrical Smrtis, however, it is possible to classify the topics of the Dharma-Sutras under three main heads: *acara* (conduct), *vyavahara* (dealings), including *rajadharma* (a king's duty), and *prayaicitta* (expiation). As for the literary form of the Dharma-Sutras, they contain *sutras* interspersed with metrical passages; two exceptions to this are the *Gautama Dharma-Sutra* and the *Vaikhanasa Dharma-Sutra.*

2.2.3.3. Dharma-Sutras and Dharma-Sastras

Broadly speaking, the Dharma-sastras or metrical Smrtis represent a later stage than the Dharma-Sutras in the evolution of the literature on Dharma- Sastra. But it cannot be assumed on this account that every Smrti had as its basis a Dharma-Sutra, or that every Dharma-Sutra developed in course of time into a metrical Smrti. This point has special relevance in connection with the problem relating to the *Manu Smrti* and the *Manava Dharma-Sutra.* It was suggested that the extant *Manu Smrti* was a metrical redaction of the *Manava Dharma-Sutra* which belonged to the Maitrayani Sakha of the *Kfsna Yajur-Veda.*

But no *Manava Dharma-Sutra* has become available so far, nor is it even mentioned in any other work. Various arguments have been advanced to prove that the *Manava Dhavma-Sutra* had once existed but was lost; there have also been counter-arguments to disprove the existence of this Sutra. Neither of these claims is conclusive, and the question has to remain open. By and laRige, the entire Vedic literature, both *apauruseya* and *pauruseya,* may be said to be dircctly religious in character. As against this, in the post-Vedic Sanskrit literature, which is by no means homogeneous either in form or content, religion is but one of the many fields covered. One may, nonetheless, hasten to add that there is hardly any ancient or medieval Sanskrit text, even of an avowedly secular type, which is not religion-oriented in one sense or other.

2.2.4. The Post-Vedic literature: A Survey

The logical and chronological sequence which characterizes the Vedic periods is absent in the post-Vedic Sanskrit literary periods. We have therefore to consider the post-Vedic Sanskrit religious texts not chronologically but in groups formed in accordance with their contents and tendencies. The end of the period of the major *Upanisads* saw the gradual dwindling of the influence of the Vedic tradition. Four cultural movements emerged during this interregnum. Firstly, heterodox religions like Buddhism and Jainism began to assert themselves. Secondly, as a natural reaction to this challenge to orthodox Brahmanism, attempts were made to consolidate the Vedic way of life and thought by reoRiganizing and systematizing all Vedic knowledge and Vedic practice. The Sutra-Vedanga literature was the outcome of these attempts. Thirdly, for the purpose of counteracting the cult of renunciation generally encouraged by the Upanisads, there grew what may be called secular and materialistic tendencies best manifested in a work like the *Artha tastra* of Kautilya. And, finally, there emerged a form of Hinduism which steered clear of the heterodoxy of Buddhism and Jainism on the one hand and the revivalism of the Sutra-Vedanga movement on the other. It was a federation of tribal religious cults, most of which were originally non-Vedic in provenance and which tended to converge in the course of historical development-this federation being held together by the running thread of formal allegiance to the Vedas.

The literature relating to the second movement, the Sutra-Vedanga literature has been already dealt with in the previous section on the Vedic literature. Now we are concerned with the literature of the fourth movement which proved to be of the greatest consequence in the history of

India, namely, Hinduism. The main characteristics of this new religious movement may broadly be set forth as follows:

(i) The indigenous popular gods, such as Siva and Visnu and His various incarnations, superseded the Vedic gods, such as Indra and Varuna;

(ii) The doctrine of *bhakti* or devotion to a personal God began to prevail, and the different religious practices associated with it, such as *puja* (worship), replaced the Vedic sacrificial ritual;

(iii) The ideal of *lokasaiigraha* (social solidarity) acquired as much importance as the Upanisadic ideal of *atma-jnana* (Self-realization). Consequently, Karma-yoga came to be encouraged as against Sannyasa;

(iv) The response of Hinduism to external and internal challenges was one of gradual assimilation and adaptation rather than of opposition and isolation, and the tendency to synthesize various religious practices and philosophical doctrines into a single harmonious way of life and thought became prominent; (a) A new polity

and statecraft was sponsored. The influence of some of these trends in Hinduism becomes evident even in the ancillary texts of the different Vedic schools, such as the *pariiistas,* the *prayogas,* and the *paddkatis,* all of which, of course, belong to a fairly late date. The *Vaikhanasa-Sutras,* for instance, which claim to belong to a school of the *Yajur-Veda,* are actually related to a Vaisnava school in South India. Similarly, the *Baudhayana Grhya-paritista-sutra* deals with some aspects of *Visnu-puja.* Such texts, though ostensibly Vedic, have taken over many non-Vedic beliefs and practices.

2.2.5. The Bhagavad-Gita and the Epics

The characteristics of Hinduism, as just set forth, are best reflected in the *Bhagavad-Gita* which may, indeed, be regarded as the principal scripture of this new religious ideology. They are also reflected in the character of Krsna, its enunciator, as portrayed in the great epic, the *Mahabharata,* which is in many ways a unique literary phenomenon. It is by far the biggest single literary work known to man. Its vastness is aptly matched by the encyclopaedic nature of its contents and the universality of its appeal. The claim is traditionally made, and fully justified, that in matters pertaining to *dharma* (religion and ethics), *artha* (material progress and prosperity), *kama* (enjoyment of the pleasures of personal and social life), and *moksa* (spiritual emancipation), whatever is found in this epic may be found elsewhere; but what is not found in it will be impossible to find anywhere else.

The *Mahabharata,* as we know it today, is the outcome of a long process of addition, assimilation, expansion, revision, and redaction. Presumably, it originated as a bardic-historical poem called *Jaya,* which had the eventful Bharata war as its central theme. In the course of time, a larige amount of material belonging to the literary tradition of the *sutas* (bards), which had been developing side by side with the *mantra* tradition embodied in the Vedic literature, was added to the historical poem, thereby transforming it into the epic *Bharata.* This transformation of *Jaya* into *Bharata* received added momentum from another and, from our point of view, more significant factor, the rise of Krsnite Hinduism. The protagonists of this religion realized that the bardic poem, which enjoyed wide currency, would serve as the most efficient vehicle for the propagation of their ideology. So they redacted the poem in such a way that the *Bhagavad-Gita* became the corner-stone of the new epic superstructure, with Krsna as its central character. Thus we find that this new literary product, *Bharata,* had derived its bardic-historical elements from the ancient *suta* tradition and its religio-ethical elements from

Krsnite Hinduism, and upon this was gradually superimposed elements derived from Brahmanic learning and culture and from other elements of Hinduism. The result was that *Bharata* became the *Mahabharata.* Indeed, it is on account of the contributions of Krsnaism, Brahmanism, and Hinduism that the *Mahabharata* became a veritable treasure-house of religious beliefs and practices.

The *Mahabharata,* which must have assumed its present form in the first centuries before and after Christ, is traditionally believed to consist of 100,000 stanzas divided into eighteen *parvans.* Some typical religious sections are: the *Surya-namasta-sataka (Aranyakaparvan),* the *Sanat-sujatiya* (*Udyogaparvan*), the *Bhagavad-Gita* and the *Vasudeva-stuti* (*Bhismaparvan*), the *Satarudriya (Dronaparvan),* the *Japakopakhyana,* the *Narayaniya,* and the *Unchavrttyupakhyana* (*Santiparoan),* the *Siva-sahasranama-stotra,* the *Ganga-stava,* and the *Visnusahasranama-stotra* (*Anusasanaparvan),* the *Isvara-stuti* and the *Anu-Gita (Asvamedhikaparvan).* There is also the *Harivamsa* which is traditionally regarded as a *khilaparvan* of the great epic. If the *Mahabharata* (with the *Harivamsa)* glorifies the Krsna incarnation, the other epic, the *Ramayana,* gives an account of the Rama incarnation. This incarnation is traditionally believed to have been earlier than the Krsna incarnation; composition of the *Ramayana,* however, which is laRigely the work of a single poet named Valmiki, seems to have begun after that of the *Mahabharata,* but ended before the *Mahabharata* assumed its final form. The Ayodhya episode in the *Ramayana* probably has some historical basis; but with the exile of Rama, the theme of the poem is enlaRiged to epic proportions, and the prince of Ayodhya becomes transformed into an incarnation of the highest God. Cleverly interwoven with these two strands is a third, that of an agricultural myth. Compared with the *Mahabharata,* the *Ramayana* presents a more unitary structure; it is not too overloaded with extraneous *sautic* (bardic) material and is disti nguished by several features of classical Sanskrit poetry. It has seven *kandas*-the entire seventh *kanda* evidently is a later interpolation. It contains several sections of religious significance, such as the *Surya-stava* (which is also called *Aditya-hrdaya- stotra)* by Agastya and the *Rama-stuti* by Brahma (both in the *Yuddha-kanda).* Its principal religious appeal, however, springs from the idealized domestic and social virtues which its characters embody. Indeed, this appeal has, through the centuries, proved to be direct and sustained.

The *Ramayana* and the *Mahabharata* represent the ethos of ancient India. The *Ramayana,* according to tradition, owes its origin to an extraordinary circumstance. A fowler's arrow killed one of a pair of curlews. Moved to pity at this tragic incident, the sage Valmlki cursed the fowler, but he did so in a verse which came out spontaneously from his lips. This poetical expression of profound grief is said to have been the first verse composed (in the epic period); and the sage, who became the author of the *Ramayana,* is called the *adikavi,* the first poet of the classical period of Sanskrit literature. Anandavardhana (ninth century a .d .), the famous rhetorician, analysing Valmlki's state of mind as he reacted to the pathetic sight of the bird being killed, is of the opinion that the experience had not only culminated in the utterance of the first verse, but also gave rise to the idea of *rasa1* in poetry. The origin of the *Mahabharata,* according to tradition, is that it was penned by the elephant-headed deity Ganesa and dictated by sage Vyasa. The cpics had come into existence long before the art of writing was known. Dawn the ccnturies they were transmitted orally through, mainly, two classes of people: the *sutas* (bards in the royal courts); and the *kusilavas* (travelling singers). Before they were committed to writing, the epic stories gathered many accretions; and even after they were written down, additions and alterations continued. The diverse nature of the changes made explains the great popularity of the epics throughout the length and breadth of India. Though the epic stories are very old and some of them hark back to Vedic times, their present forms are of a much later date. It is generally believed that the *Mahabharata* had attained its present form by about the fourth century A.D. The *Ramayana* probably assumed its present shape a century or two earlier.

2.2.5.1. The Ramayana

Tradition places the *Ramayana* earlier than the *Mahabharata.* The nucleus of the *Mahabharata* may have been older than that of the *Ramayana,* but in their present forms the *Ramayana* appears to be the earlier work. The *Ramayana* is more ornate than the *Mahabharata,* more refined and sophisticated; the ballad style of the *Mahabharata* is not present here. The *Ramayana* is more or less a unified work. Much shorter than the *Mahabharata,* it does not show the jumble of diverse matters that is found there.

The main story of the *Ramayana* is briefly this: Dasaratha, king of Ayodhya, is about to install his eldest son, Rama, on the throne. Kaikeyi, Rama's step-mother, wants her own son Bharata to be crowned king, and Rama to be sent into exile for fourteen years. The old and infirm king, though reluctant, has to agree. Rama goes to live in the forest, accompanied by his consort, Sita, and his brother, Laksmana. The demon-king of Lanka, Ravana, abducts Sita. Rama, determined to rescue Sita, wages a dour war against Ravana who is ultimately vanquished and killed. Rama comcs back to Ayodhya and assumes his position as king, with Slta as queen. The story of the genuine portion of the epic ends here. In the last Book, which is suspected by many modern scholars to be spurious, it is narrated that the people of Ayodhya speak ill of Rama for taking back Sita from Ravana's custody and Rama banishes her in deference to public opinion.

Some historian believed that the Homeric story of Helen and the Trojan War exercised a deep influence on the *Ramayana* is not substantiated by reliable evidence. Some scholars, think that the epic was based on an ancient Buddhist legend of Rama, the *Dasaratha Jataka*. But it is possible that the tranquillity and mildness of Rama's character may have been, to some extent, due to the influence of Buddhism, which was extremely popular. As Sita can be traced to the *Taittiriya Brahmana*, the *Rig-Veda*, the *Atharva-Veda*, and some of the Grhya-Sutras, some zealous mythologists regard these as bearing the first germs of the story of the *Ramayana*.

2.2.5.1.1. Literary Characteristics

In the *Ramayana*, as compared with the *Mahabharata*, the art of poetry appears to have made great progress. To a great extent it appears to develop consciously, for content is no longer the sole concern of the poet; he is not a little concerned with form too. The poet is an adept in characterization, and this is displayed in a series of unparalleled portraits: Rama's supreme sacrifice for the sake of his father; Laksmana's obedience to his elder brother, at whose command he acts even against his conscience; the self-abnegation of Bharata in abjuring royal comforts during the absence of Rama; and the unflinching loyalty of Hanuman to his master at the cost of his personal comfort and even at the risk of life. Across the sea, in Lanka, we find Ravana, of tremendous physical and mental vigour, falling a victim to the frailties fleh is heir to. Among the women, Sita is the glowing example of chastity and highmindedness, the paragon of all domestic virtues. She spurns the pleasures of the royal palace in order to follow her husband and be with him in his perilous forest-life.

Amidst the various temptations held out to her by Ravana, who seeks her love, her fidelity to her husband is unshaken. King Rama banishes her for no fault on her part; and, instead of accusing her husband, she accepts him decree without a word of protest, taking it as a decree of her own destiny Kaikeyi, the typically designing and jealous queen, prevails upon Dasaratha, her husband, to banish Rama and install Bharata on the throne. She gains her objective, but loses the respect of her noble son. The author of the *Ramayana* has thus presented a magnificent life-gallery throbbing with profound human appeal, and in the centre of this gallery the character of Rami shines and shines almost like the Pole Star. He is a model son, husband, brother, king, warrior, and man. Though occasionally dazzled by flashes from his superhuman nature, we are not 'blinded or bewildered' by them.

The use of simile and imagery in the *Ramayana* is superb. King Dasaratha, overwhelmed with grief, is compared to the sun under eclipse, to fire covered by ashes, to a lake the water of which has dried up and so on. In the Asoka grove, Hanuman catches a glimpse of the emaciated Slta. She looks, he thinks, like the thin line of the crescent, the flame enveloped in smoke, a lotus destroyed by the frost. The white moon moving in the sky is like a swan swimming in the blue waters. Held in the clutches of the dreaded Ravana, Sita warns him that temporarily he may overpower her, but he cannot subdue her just as a fly can swallow clarified butter but cannot assimilate it. The employment of other figures of speech too has been done with a masterly skill and effortless ease.The poet's description of nature is also masterly.

The *Ramayana,* unlike the *Mahabharata,* brings out the close relationship between external nature and internal nature expressed in the minds and moods of people. There is, moreover, suggestiveness in the picture of nature drawn by the author of the *Ramayana.* In the *Mahabharata,* descriptions are merely objective, but here the poet brings personal experience or his own interpretation to bear upon his depiction of nature. Unlike the other epic, the *Ramayana* creates an idyll out of nature and produces a lyrical effect. The sad prospect of Rama's going into exile casts a shadow of gloom not only on the minds of the people, but also on nature all around.

Various sentiments have been introduced, into the epic, but the main sentiment is the heroic. At the same time, pathetic scenes are described with - masterly skill. Dasaratha broken down by the separation from his dearest son, Rama; the city of Ayodhya bereft of Rama; Rama separated from his beloved; Sita pining in alien surroundings-these scenes are so poignantly described that the appreciative reader has to shed tears. The author's capacity to delineate the fierce and the cruel is shown in his description of a grim battle, or of Bharata's awful dream.

Although ornate, the style of the epic is racy, and not pedantic. In form and content it is a very near approach to the *mahakavya,* as defined in poetics. It is thus a precursor of the vast and varied classical *kavya* literature in Sanskrit. The epic is a *kavya* of the romantic type, the element of romance being most marked in the *Sundara-kanda.* The language is simple, and yet dignified, and does not indicate that straining after literary exercise which characterizes some later poetical works, especially those of the decadent age. The author of the epic appears to have been the first poet to adapt *anustubh,* the Vedic metre, to later Sanskrit literature, although with certain modifications. Valmiki thus may aptly be described as the father of classical Sanskrit poetry. Some other scholars consider the Rama story to be allegorical. Rama, they hold, symbolizes Aryan culture, and his expedition against Ravana represents the cultural domination of the southern regions by the Aryans.

2.2.5.1.2. Artistic Merit

In the view of some Western critics, the *Ramayana* as a piece of literary art suffers from some defects, such as diffuseness, frequent use of hyperboles, and exaggerations. Besides, verbiage, hyperbole, exaggeration, diffuseness, etc. are natural in most poetical literature. The *Ramayana,* therefore, could not be an exception. In fact, most of the artistic drawbacks of the *Ramayana* are attributable to the later versifiers who added to, and altered the original production by Valmlki. The *Ramayana,* indeed, is a marvellous piece of art which India can legitimately be proud of. In the whole range of Sanskrit literature, there axe very few poems more charming than this one by the *adikavi.* 'The classical purity, clearness, and simplicity of its style, the exquisite touches of true poetic feeling with which it abounds, its graphic descriptions of heroic incidents and nature's grandest scenes, the deep acquaintance it displays with the conflicting workings and most refined emotions of the human heart, all entitle it to rank among the most beautiful compositions that have appeared at any period or in any country.

2.2.5.2. The Mahabharata

The kernel of the *Mahabharata* story is briefly this: The Pandavas, headed by Yudhisthira, and the Kauravas, headed by Duryodhana, descended from common ancestors. Duryodhana becomes jealous and, coveting the crown invites Yudhisthira to a game of dice. As the result of a rash wager, Yudhisthira loses his kingdom to Duryodhana and is then forced to go into exile, together with his brothers and DraupadJ, the common consort of the Pandavas, for twelve years, followed by one year during which they must live incognito. But even when the stipulated period is over, Duryodhana refuses to give even a fraction of his territory to Yudhisthira, the rightful owner. A grim battle ensues. The Kauravas are routed and ruined, and the Pandavas regain their lost kingdom.

2.2.5.2.1. Literary Characteristics

The *Mahabharata* has been characterized as a 'whole literature', a 'repertory of the whole of the old bard poetry of ancient India'. The nucleus of the epic, as we have seen, is simple, but around this nucleus has gathered a diverse mass of material dealing with innumerable topics-legendary, didactic, ethical, heroic, aesthetic, philosophical, political, and so on. Of the legends, some are edifying and testify to the great literary skill of the author. This may be seen, for example, in the legends of Nala and Damayanti, of

Savitrl and Satyavan, of Dusyanta and Sakuntala. Even a casual reader is struck by the wealth of characters in the epic, and the way they have been so beautifully portrayed. The composer is obviously a keen observer of human nature, and he can depict a character with masterly skill. He knows the value of contrast, for he shows how a good character shines brighter against a bad one. Each of the five Pandava brothers has his own distinct traits of character. Yudhisthira, the eldest, never departs from the age-old path of virtue, however great his privation or humiliation, and however grave the provocation may be. Unflinching in his devotion to *dharma,* he has an unshaken faith that *Dharma* must ultimately triumph. Arjuna is the warrior *par excellence.* Bhima, of tremendous physical vigour, is rather blunt and impatient; nevertheless, he is obedient to his eldest brother when he counsels patience and restraint. Nakula and Sahadeva are extremely loyal to their brothers and skilled in sword-exercise. Duryodhana is a designing and ambitious person. But he is well-versed in politics and statecraft and also in the art of warfare. Materialistic in outlook, he is concerned mainly with *artha* (wealth) and *kama* (desire), and does not bother himself about *dharma.* He thus serves as an excellent foil to Yudhisthira. Karna, the faithful friend of Duryodhana, is a self-made man. Though contemptuously referred to as the 'son of a charioteer', he is a master of his craft, and in the art of warfare he can be matched only with Arjuna. His fidelity to the Kauravas, even after he learned of his close kinship with the Pandavas, is ideal. His charity even at tremendous personal sacrifice is proverbial. The suffering caused by their enemies rouses the righteousness of Draupadi, the wife of the five Pandavas. Her speech to spur the quid Yudhisthira to action is fiery and imbued with the high Ksatriya spirit.Gandhari, the mother of the Kauravas and wife of the blind Dhrtarastra, is similarly forthright. She condemns Dhrtarastra as the one who is fully responsible for the rout and ruin of the Kauravas, thus clearly showing that she is not blinded by attachment to her husband or by affection for her sons. Her judgment is impartial and sound. Damayanti and Savitri are models of chastity, ever solicitous of the welfare of their husbands for whose well-being no sacrifice is too great for them.

The dominant sentiment in the *Mahabharata* is the heroic, but here too the pathetic sentiment is equally noteworthy. The battlefield is littered with corpses, some of them mutilated, others changed beyond recognition; the air is rent by the frantic wails of the bereaved women, in particular, of the aged queen-mother Gandhari, and the heart-rending laments of Dhrtarastra. Fate has afflicted him with blindness, and now, a forlorn father, he is doubly helpless. Such scenes cannot but draw forth the tears of the reader. The lament of Gandhari, is in fact a masterpiece of elegiac poetry.

The epic reveals the poet's mastery of the art of description. The battlescenes appear most vividly before our inward eye. The accounts of the forest life led by the Pandavas, the penances performed by Aijuna, the *svayamvara,* self-choice, of Draupadi and many other such scenes are all equally graphic. The description of Dvaitavana with its wealth of flowers and foliage, birds and beasts, and its hermitages, reveals the poet's eye for colour and his ear for music, and before the mind's eye of the reader it presents an unforgettable idyll. The poet of the epic is, however, as aware of the violent aspects of nature as of the pleasant. A most realistic picture is presented of the devastating storm that confronted the Pandavas on their way to Mount Gandhamadana: the reader vividly sees the ravages caused by the storm as the rivers swell with the heavy rain.

In general, the style is effortless. Unlike the writers of Sanskrit poems of the post-Kalidasa period, particularly of the decadent period, the composer of the epic is concerned more with matter than with manner. The long compounds, the difficult words, and the recondite allusions which disfigure the poetry of the age of decadence, are absent here. The epic shows spontaneous use of figures of speech. The flowing ballad style of the epic conjuresup the age of simplicity and reflects its popular character. Interest is also created by a mass of legends and the occasional inclusion of supernatural elements, such as the appearance of gods and their direct intervention in human affairs. The epic contains beautiful imagery too. The mighty tree entwined by clusters of flowering creepers under which Yudhisthira with his brothers gathered, immediately reminds the poet of a huge mountain surrounded by leviathan elephants. Even in the philosophical *Bhagavad-Gita* there are flashes of good imagery. Krsna's mouth is wide agape, and as the people enter into it, they are fancied as insects jumping into a burning flame to meet with certain doom. Again, the heroes of the world rushing into his flaming jaws are seen as so many currents of rivers flowing to merge into the occan. The effulgence of *Visvarupa* (the Lord's universal form) assumed by Krsna standing before the perplexed Arjuna, is conceived as the brilliant radiance of a thousand suns rising simultaneously. The description of the ocean in the *Adipatoan* is a marvellously picturesque one. It is rich in detail, in colour, and in vividness. The imaginative touch also is very captivating.

Some scholars have tried to find an allegory in the *Mahabharata.* One has suggested that the Pandavas symbolize the seasons, and Draupadi (Krsna) the dark earth possessed by five successive seasons. At times the seasons lose their wealth of lustre, as in the disastrous game of dice with Duryodhana when Krsna is left with only a single garment, that is, the earth becomes denuded in winter. Another critic finds in Pandu (literally pale or white) the name of a royal family of a white race that migrated into India from the north and was afterwards known as Arjuna (literally white). According to yet another scholar, the epic story is an account of the relationship and the conflict among the different systems of Hindu philosophy and religion. The epic has been a veritable fount at which the people of India, and indeed, of all climes and times, have drunk deep in seeking to quench their insatiable thirst for the truth. The key to the universal popularity of the epic seems to lie in the fact that it has invaluable treasure to offer on three planes: the mundane, the ethical, and the metaphysical. On the mundane plane, it is a work of great art, transporting the reader to a new world vivified by intense imagination and masterly delineation. On the ethical plane, we find in it the eternal conflict between *dharma* and *adharma,* with, *dharma* having temporary reverses but with the ultimate and inevitable triumph of good over evil. The *Bhagavad-Gita,* the quintessence of the ethical teaching of the epic, teaches the philosophy of disinterested action, a philosophy highly prized by the wise of all ages and all lands. It also teaches us to practise *samatva* (equipoise) which, indeed, is the essence of *Toga.* On the metaphysical plane, the epic demonstrates the ultimate Truth. And yet, in between all this, we find simple incidents which declare that the secret of the universal popularity of the epic is its tremendous human appeal-the actions of such noble characters as Yudhisthira and Karna, the exhortation of the hero-mother Vidula to her cowardly son Sanjaya to act like a true Ksatriya, or the sage counsel of Vidura to face the challenges of life with aplomb and dignity.

2.2.5.2.2. Artistic Merit

The *Mahabharata* is not a homogeneous and unified work of art. It is as a whole, a literary monster containing so many and so multifarious things. It has also been characterized as a 'jungle of poetry'. All this is true, yet it is a fact that the epic is 'more suited than any other book to afford us an insight into the deepest depths of the soul of the Indian people. The Brahmanas utilized this popular epic as a medium for the propagation of their ideas among the people, ideas that were religious, philosophical, moral and ethical, political and economic. In doing this, they incorporated a mass of material, including legends and myths, into the corpus of the epic. Thus from the earliest times the epic literature did not emeRige as an entity distinct from philosophy and moral and religious teaching. This accounts for the fact that, like the *Rig-Veda* and the Upanisads, the *Mahabharata* contains beautiful poetry juxtaposed with philosophical or other topics which are, perhaps, to the ordinary reader, insipid and jejune. In the course of time, when the Buddhists assumed political power, they seized upon the popular *Mahabharata* as a convenient tool for the dissemination of their doctrines and moral principles. The Jains, too, did not lose the opportunity to spread their doctrines among the masses through the framework of this popular epic. The epic thus underwent changes which have made it a medley of miscellaneous matters. It is not, however, amorphous, nor is it meaningless. It has the single purpose of upholding the glory of *dharma* and proclaiming the eternal value of peace and tranquillity in society.

While parts of the *Mahabharata* contain profound wisdom and at the same time testify to the artistic skill of the composer, there are other portions which, as pieces of literature, are pedestrian. This phenomenon prompted Winternitz- to say that if one has to believe that the epic is by one and the same hand, then it must be presumed that the author was at once a sage and an idiot, a finished writer and a wretched scribbler. But modem research has proved that the *Mahabharata* is not one single poetic production at all; it is a literary complex. So the presence of portions of varying merits in one and the same work is not surprising. It is not fair to say that the *Mahabharata* began as a simple epic but ended in 'monstrous chaos'.

2.2.5.3. Conclusion

Both the epics are essentially didactic and ethical in spirit. Hence they arc regarded as Dharma-sastras and Niti-sastras. They provide detailed guidelines for rulers, for statesmen, for law-givers, and for persons belonging to the four castes and stages of life. Both have tried to propagate the same message: It is virtue not vice, truth not false hood, that ultimately wins and prevails. The pictures drawn in the epics of happiness, harmony, and understanding in the domestic and social spheres are ideal. Affection of the parents, loyalty of the brothers, love of the wives, obedience of the children, and so on, have an irresistible effect on the minds of the reader. 'Indeed,' observes Monier Williams, 'in depicting scenes of domestic affection, and expressing those universal feelings and emotions which belong to human nature in all time and in all places, Sanskrit epic poetry is unrivalled even by Greek Epos. Verily, the epics reflect the national character of ancient India, her wisdom, her beauty, and her power. They are, therefore, aptly called India's 'national epics', India's 'pride and treasure'. Keeping in view the two other great epics of the world, the *Iliad* and the *Odyssey,* it can be said that as monuments of the human mind and as documents of human life and manners in ancient times, the Indian epics are no less interesting than their European counterparts. The life and literature of the Indian people beginning from the remote antiquity down to the modern times, have been larigely influenced by these two great epics. In fact, the story of Rama and many of the episodes of the *Mahabharata* are stock-subjects, which appear over and over again in the later literature. Many paintings, and architectural and sculptural pieces have also been designed after the *Ramayana* and the *Mahabharata* motifs. On epigraphs and coins also the influence of the epics is considerable. They became so popular and famous that they travelled far beyond the limits of India, to the countries in the west, north, south and south-east, and to a great extent moulded their art and literature.

2.2.6. The Puranas

The Puranas are a very important branch, of the Hindu sacred literature. They enable us to know the true import of the ethos, philosophy, and religion of the Vedas. They clothe with flesh and blood the bony framework of the Dharma-Sutras and the Dharma-Sastras.The Puranas relate to the whole of India so far as the historical portion therein is concerned and to the whole world so far as their ethical, philosophical, and religious portions are concerned.

H. H. Wilson's view that the Puranas were 'pious frauds written for temporary purposes in subservience to sectarian imposture' is as patently incorrect as it is blatantly unjust. Nor is it right to say that they are the expressions of a later and perverted Hinduism. These and other deprecatory opinions are based on insufficient knowledge and inadequate understanding and are as much opposed to truth as to tradition.

2.2.6.1. Meaning and Characteristics

The term *purana* means that which lives from of old, or that which is always new though it is old. Works like *Satapatha Brahmana* and the *Chandogya Upanisad* refer to *itihasa* and *purana.* But probably these two terms relate to the stories and parables contained in the Vedas themselves. The references in the Dharma-Sutras, the *Ramayana,* the *Mahabharata,* and Kautilya's *Artha-Sastra* are, however, to the Puranas proper. The tradition is that sage Vyasa compiled the Puranas and taught them to Lomaharsana who was a *suta,* a professional bard and story-teller, and that Lomaharsana taught them to his six disciples. It is also said that the *suta* is a person who is a non-Brahmin, the son of a Ksatriya father and a Brahmin mother. The Puranas were written with the object of popularizing the truths taught in the Vedas by presenting them in relation to specific personages and to the events of their lives. Modern scholars, however, say that the Puranas must be the work of many minds of diverse times and that the name Vyasa indicates a mere arranger and compiler.

This postulation seems to have been justified by several of the Puranas themselves. For example, the *Matsya Purana* says that Vyasa arises in every *dvaparayuga* to re-arrange the Puranas and give them to the world. Some scholars find something tangible and important in the statement made in some of the Puranas (e.g. *Brahmanda Purana*) that the Puranas were heard by Brahma even before the Vedas issued out of his four mouths. From this they infer that the Puranas were regarded as earlier productions than the Vedas. They forget that some affirmations are there only by way of praise. The statements were merely meant to extol the value of the Puranas and not to deride or decry the eternal, self-existent, and self-proved nature of the Vedas. The real function of the Puranas is to explain, illustrate, and amplify the Vedas.

In the *Amarakosa* it is said that a Purana should have five characteristics: *sarga* (primary creation), *pratisarga* (dissolution), *vamsa* (genealogies of gods, demons, patriarchs, sages, and kings), *manvantaras* (periods of different Manus), and *vamsanucarita* (histories of royal dynasties). This is affirmed in the *Kurma Purana* also. It seems that this description refers to the special and specific topics contained in the Puranas and does not in any way affect the truth that the main value of the Puranas consists in amplifying, enforcing, and illustrating the spiritual truths stated in the Vedas in the form of injunctions and commands. The teaching of the Vedas has been likened to masterly commands *(prabhu-sammita)* and that of the Puranas to friendly counsel, and this is amply confirmed by the contents and delivery of these two classes of Brahmanic literature. The five *laksanas* (characteristics) are found fully in the *Visnu Purana,* and fully or partly in the other Puranas. It may be mentioned here that these five *laksanas* or characteristics are amplified in the *Bhagavata* and the *Brahmavaivarta Puranas* into ten. But the classification into five *laksanas* by Amarasimha is the most usual, widespread, and important.

The Puranas then proceed to describe the historic evolution of the human destiny in the course of unfoldment of time. The four *Jugas* (ages of the world), viz. *krta (satya), treta, dvapara* and *kali;* the *mahayugas* or the *manvantaras;* and the *kalpas* are described to illustrate the eternal cycle of the creation, destruction, and re-creation of the world, which constitutes a fundamental concept in all the Puranas.

Much has been made of the sectarian and contradictory character of the Puranas and consequently an impression of rivalry and even of enmity has been adumbrated between Brahma, Visnu, and Siva. In the Vedas no such rivalry is stated at all. As the Puranas merely illustrate and amplify the Vedic truths, they could not have asserted any gradation among the *Trimurti* (the Trinity). The Trinity is really and essentially one divinity with three divine forms associated with the three cosmic functions, viz. creation, preservation, and destruction. A careful study of the different Puranas, however, enables us to deduce that they had no real pugnacity in them. The fact is that each Purana has preferences, but no exclusions, in regard to the gods. Whether we call a Purana a Saiva Purana or a Vaisnava Purana, we find references to the *lilas* (exploits) of various gods in each of them. For the purpose of intensifying devotion to one god, he is described as the supreme, but this does not mean a denial of godhood to the other gods. In the *Brahma Purana,* Visnu teaches Markandeya that he is identical with Siva. The *Padma Purana* says in express terms: 'Brahma, Visnu, and Mahesvara, though three in form, are one entity. There is no difference among the three except that of attributes. The *Vayu Purana* says that he who affirms superiority and inferiority among the gods is an ignorant fellow and that he who realizes their oneness is a man of true knowledge. We find it stated in the *Visnu Purana* that 'The Bhagavan Visnu, though one, assumes the three forms of Hiranyagarbha (Brahma), Hari (Visnu), and Sankara (Siva) for creation, preservation, and destruction of the world respectively. Again in the same Purana the identity of Visnu and Laksmi with Siva and Gauri is affirmed.

The fact is that each of the functions of creation, preservation and destruction implies the others and contains the others in a latent form. The Vedas and the Puranas affirm only one God; call him by any name you like. Some Puranas affirm the origin of Visnu and Brahma from Siva. Others affirm the *causa causans* to Visnu. We can easily see the significance of this apparent variation.

The one God conceived in His pre-tripartite state is described as the parent of Himself in His tripartite capacity.

2.2.6.2. Contents

The principal (*Maha*) Puranas are eighteen in number, viz. *Brahma, Padma, Visnu, Vayu, Bhagavata, Naradiya, Markandeya, Agni, Bhavisya, Brahmavaivarta, Linga, Varaha, Skanda, Vamana, Kurrna, Matsya, Garuda* and *Brahmaiida.* Some times *Vayu Purana* is substituted for *Siva Purana* in the list. There are also eighteen secondary (*Upa*) Puranas but their names vary in different accounts. It is, however, not possible to give here a resume of the contents of all the Puranas. These contain about 4, 00,000 verses on the whole and relate to a vast variety of topics. It may be mentioned for the benefit of those who wish to know briefly the contents of the Puranas, that the *Matsya Purana* gives a short summary of them. A brief summary of six different Puranas is given here to show how they really speak with one voice and help us understand the true import of the Vedas and how they show that they are the basis on which the fabric of modern Hinduism rests.

In the *Brahma Purana* we find at the beginning a description of creation. It is stated to be caused by Visnu, who is described as being one with Brahma and Siva. The Purana then describes the oldest Manu (Svayambhuva Manu), his wife Satarupa and the Prajapatis or patriarchs. The successive *manvantaras* are also described. The Puraria then speaks of the various continents of the earth and also the nether regions (*patala*) and the upper regions *(svarga).* It next deals with the sacred places of India, especially Utkala (Orissa) and the worship of the Sun there, as well as the Ekamra forest which is the favourite abode of Siva. We have got also a detailed account of Daksa's sacrifice and the passing away of Sati and the birth and marriage of Uma. There is also a description of Puri of Jagannath. The Purana then proceeds to describe Visnu's teaching to Markandeya that he is one with Siva and that he pervades all things. It then tells of Sri Krsna's life and doings. Then follow the *yugas* (ages) and the *pralaya* (dissolution) jof the world, the nature of Yoga and Samkhya (systems of philosophy), and *mukti* (liberation) by attaining oneness with Vasudeva. The Purana has also an *uttara-khanda* or supplementary portion, describing the stories connected with Brahma including his propitiation of Siva.

The *Padma Purana* has five parts. The first part, i.e. *srsti-khanda* tells how Brahma was born in the *padma* (lotus). It then describes creation according to the Samkhya terminology. Its speciality is that Brahma is given a prominence which is absent in the other Puranas. It also extols the supremacy of Visnu. After treating the divisions of time from an instant to the life span of Brahma, it speaks of the Prajapatis, Rudras, and Manus. It states the importance of *sraddhas,* especially at Gaya. It describes the lunar dynasty more elaborately than the solar. This part also dwells upon various *vratas* or observances of vows at length. The second part or *bhumi-khanda* describes the lives of Prahlada and Vrtrasura as also of Vena and Prthu. It then proceeds to enumerate the human embodiments of holiness (*jangama Urthas,* i.e. the parents and the *gurus) and* the sacred shrines (*sthavara tirthas,* i.e. places of piligrimage) at Mahakala, Prabhasa, Kuruksetra, etc. The third or *svarga-khanda* tells of the upper spheres inhabited by the gods, in the coursc of King Bharata's ascent to *Vaikuntha* (abode of Visnu) beyond *Dhiuva-mandala* (the sphere of the Pole Star). It then describes the four *varnas* (castes) and the four *asramas* (stages of life) and their duties as well as *karma-yoga* and *jnana-yoga.* The fourth or *patala-khanda* speaks of the nether regions. It also narrates in detail the exploits of the kings of the solar dynasty. The *Bhagavata* is extolled in this part as the last and the best of the Puranas. The last part of the Purana is the *uttara-khanda,* which deals with the story of Jalandhara. It praises the *mantra* (hymn), *'Om Laksmi -natayatiabhjam namah* as the greatest of all *mantras,* and says that it can be taught to all classes including the Sudras and women after *diksa* (initiation). It describes also the *para, vyuha,* and *vibhatia* aspects of Visnu, and emphasizes the special sanctity of the month of *kartika* and of *ekadasi*. It also discusses *kriya-joga*, which deals with practical devotion as distinct from *dhyana-yoga* or the path of contemplation.

The *Visnu Purana* was narrated by Parasara to his pupil Maitreya. It is divided into six parts, each of which is subdivided into many chapters. The first part gives an account of creation, which is attributed to Purusa and Prakrti. Visnu, who is Paramatman, desired to create the universe so that the souls might perform their *kaima* (work) and attain *moksa* (salvation) by means of God-realization. Creation is due to His mercy *(krpa)* and is His sport *[krida)*. Then follow accounts of the *avatara* (incarnation) of Lord Visnu as *varaha* (boar), of the *Svayambhuva-manvantara*, of the Prajapatis (lords of creation), of the churning of the ocean which yielded nectar (*amrta*), and of the life of Dhruva who, by his devotion to Visnu, was lifted to the supreme height of the *Dhruva-mandala*. Dhruva's descendants are then described. The power of faith in Visnu, however, finds its most magnificent expression in the legend of Prahlada. The second part describes the earth and the nether worlds, and the courses of the planets. The third speaks of the Manus, the Indras, the gods, the sages and the Vyasas (compilers). The fourth deals with the genealogies of the kings of the solar and the lunar dynasty, and brings them up to the *kaliyuga*, among whom are included the Magadha and Andhra kings and even later ones. The fifth part describes the life of Krsna. The last part is philosophical and teaches how devotion to Lord Visnu is the means to the attainment of beatitude.

The *Brahmavaivarta Purana* in four parts gives a detailed description of Sri Krsna and Radha whose supreme abode is in *Goloka*. Sri Krsna is stated to be the supreme divine Principle from whom have come Prakrti, Brahma, Visnu, and Siva. The first part *(Brahma-khanda)* presents an account of Narayana (Visnu) and Siva emerging from the right and left sides of Krsna and Brahma from His navel. Radha emerges from the left side of the Lord. The *gopas* and *gopi* come from Krsna and Radha respectively. Brahma then proceeds to create the ordinary universe. The second part or *Prakrti-khanda* describes the evolution of Prakrti according to the Samkhya school of thought, but affirms that it is under the control of Isvara and is his *sakti* (power). *Sakti* has five aspects: Radha, Durga, Laksmi, Sarasvati, and Savitri. She has innumerable minor aspects as well. The third part or *Ganesa-khanda* is devoted to the birth and exploits of Ganesa. The last part or *Sri Krsna-janma-khanda* deals with the life of Sri Krsna. The meeting of Krsna and Radha and their union form the theme of a most remarkable and picturesque poetic description in this part.

The *Vayu Purana* largely emphasizes the worship of Siva It has been mentioned earlier that in some of the lists of the main Puranas the place of *Vayu Purana* is sometimes taken by the *Siva Purana.* The two works, as now extant, are separate. The *Vayu Purana* is divided into two *khandas* (parts) and four *padas* (quarters), and gives the story of creation, the history of the kings of the solar and the lunar dynasty, the description of the four *yugas* and fourteen *manvantaras,* and so on. It is worthy of note that this Purana also contains accounts of the actions of Visnu for the good of the world. Expositions of the Advaita system of thought are also to be found in this Purana.

In the *Agni Purana,* the emphasis is on the glory of Siva, but descriptions of the glories of Visnu also occur. It contains, in addition, a detailed account of political science, law, judicature, medicine, and rhetoric. The foregoing survey of the six important and typical Puranas shows their method of treatment and their aim and content. It is seen that their main object, their very life, is to amplify the Vedic injunctions about morality and spirituality. They form in a way the kindeRigarten of the uprising soul which grows into fulfilment by means of *Brahma-vidya* (knowledge of the supreme Spirit). They give us lessons in pure *pravrtti* (enjoyment) and *nivrtti* (renunciation) and make us fit for the ascent towards, and realization of, the highest spiritual truths taught in the Vedas and the Upanisads.

2.2.6.3. Assessment

It has been shown that the Puranas are viewed by early Indian tradition frpm two standpoints. One is the *upabrahmana* theory of Manu: they illustrate and amplify the Vedic truths. The other is the *panca-laksana* theory of Amarasimha: they deal with the five topics stated earlier. Manu's view stresses the real essence of the Puranas, whereas Amarasimha's view relates to their external aspects. The description of creation and its dissolution is only to affirm and declare the glory of God, while the account of the lives of divine incarnations, sages, and kings is only to illustrate and inculcate moral and religious principles.

Whatever may be the appioach, it is clear that the Puranas aie a vital poition of the scriptures of the Hindus. They are primarily au extension, amplification, and illustration in a popular manner of the spiritual truths declaied in the Vedas. The Puranas have, in fact, beerrdescribed by the Upanisads as the fifth Veda and by the Smrtis as the very exposition of what the Vedic seers realized. Outsiders may call them legends like the works of fiction current today. Some Indians too may regard them in a similar way. But the bulk of the Hindus and the main body of traditional opinion attribute to the Puranas a double character, namely: their illustrative value and impressive actuality. They reflect in meticulous details contemporary life and thought and have laRigely moulded public life, belief, conduct, and ideal in India for centuries and have contributed a great deal in bringing about religious harmony and understanding amongst the diverse sections of the Hindu society. As a Western scholar has observed, 'the Puranas afford us far greater insight into all aspects and phases of Hinduism-its mythology, its idol-worship, its superstitions, its festivals and ceremonies and its ethics, than any other works. It will not be fair to regard the Puranas as a meie mass of legends and the characters depicted in them as just creations of the poet's imagination. Rama and Krsna, for instance, are still believed by millions of Hindus as actual human beings who walked the earth veiling their supreme glory and this faith is a part and parcel of their very existence.

The Puranas, by modem standards, may not be considered technically very happy as literary productions. But it must be remembered, while assessing their literary merit, that they are primarily of a didactic and lituRigical character and have, therefore, a greater religious interest than literary. Besides, they have undergone numerous editions, transcriptions, and revisions in different periods of history. Lack of thematic and structural homogeneity, and of concentration and proportion, versification of a mixed character, weak vocabulary, fantastic details, etc. have, therefore, been some of the inevitable results. Yet, there are many passages in the Puranas which contain profound thought and wisdom and delineate moments of supreme human emotion. There are also instances of rare mastery in descriptive art.

Stotras or devotional hymns abound in the Puranas. From the stylistic and metrical points of view, they will be found interesting even to a modem reader. Most of these hymns are rich in philosophical or ritualistic contents. At the same time, 'the intensity of devout feeling', and 'the elevated mood of prayer and worship' expressed in them very often lift them 'to the level of charming poetic utterance. Mention may be made here of *Pradosa-stotrastaka* in the *Skanda Purana,* the hymns addressed to Siva by Asita and Himalaya in the *Brahmavaivarta Purana,* and so on.

The Puranas have exercised a powerful influence on the subsequent literary productions. The later poets and dramatists repeatedly turned to them for theme and even for style. Historians have discovered in them a chronicle of prehistoric ages; commentators have considered them as an inexhaustible treasurehouse; and law-givers have referred to them as works of dependable authority. Thus, the Puranas are immensely helpful in tracing the evolution of ancient Indian thought and culture in all their aspects.

As texts, the Puranas are chronologically of a much later date than the two epics; for, their final redaction was accomplished in the age of the Guptas. Conceptually, however, they belong to the ancient literary tradition of the *sutas,* which is also known as the *itihasa-purana* tradition. It is customary to divide the *itihasa-purana* literature into three broad classes: *itihasa* or epic history, represented by the *Mahabharata; kavya* or epic poetry, represented by the *Ramayana;* and *purana* or epic legends, represented by the Puranas. *Purana* is traditionally defined as comprising five main topics: *sarga* (creation), *pratisarga* (dissolution and recreation), *vamsa* (divine genealogies), *manvantara* (ages of Manus), and vasmanuchari (genealogies of kings). This definition clearly indicates that the Puranas, in their original form, had very little to do with religious beliefs and practices. But none of the Puranas, as we know them today, strictly adhere to the five topics mentioned in the definition, the *panca-laksana.* Nor do they adhere even to the five additional topics, altogether forming the *dasa-laksana* (ten topics). The five additional topics are: *vrtti* (means of livelihood), *raksa* (incarnations of gods), *mukti* (final emancipation), *hetu* (living beings), and *apakaya* (Brahman). In the course of the growth of the Puranas many more subjects came to be incorporated into them, and these dealt with religious instruction, sectarian cults, and rituals. Some of the topics thus included were: *dana* (gift), *vratas* (vows), *tirtha* (place of pilgrimage), *sraddha, bhakti,* and *avatara* (incarnation of God). It is these subjects which have given the Puranas their religious character, thus confirming their claim to be the Veda of the common people.

Tradition speaks of eighteen Mahapuranas. These are: the *Brahma,* the *Padma,* the *Visnu,* the *Vayu,* the *Bhagavata,* the *Naradiya,* the *Markandeya,* the *Agni,* the *Bhavisya,* the *Brahma-vaivarta,* the *Varaha,* the *Linga,* the *Skanda,* the *Vamana,* the *Kurma,* the *Matsya,* the *Garuda,* and the *Brahmanda Puranas.* They are classified either as *sattvika, tamasa,* and *raj as a* (as in the *Padma Purana*), or in accordance with the divinity (such as Visnu, Siva, Brahma, Devi) which they glorify (as in the *Skanda Purana).* Tradition also speaks of eighteen Upapuranas, *upa* meaning 'secondary'. These are: the *Sanatkumara,* the *Narasimha,* the *Nanda,* the *Sivadharma,* the *Durvasas,* the *Naradiya,* the *Kapila,* the *Vamana,* the *Usanas,* the *Manava,* the *Varun,* the *Kali,* the *Mahesvara,* the *Samba,* the *Saura,* the *Parasara,* the *Marica,* and the *Bhargava Puranas.* The Upapuranas are obviously of a later date than the Mahapuranas and are more emphatically sectarian. Originally their number may have been much larger.

The *Bhagavata Purana,* which is of special interest, appears to have been produced in the Tamil country some time between the tenth and eleventh centuries. It is intensely religious in character and has wielded very great influence over the succeeding periods of the history of Vaisnavism. Among other significant works may be mentioned the *Brhat Samhita* of Varahamihira (A.D.550). Though it is a work on astronomy and astrology, it is almost encyclopaedic in scope and contains much material of a religious character, such as details of private and public worship, works of charity, iconography, and temple architecture. The *Adhyatma Ramayana* (fifteenth century), which is part of the *Brahmanda Purana,* is usually treated as an independent work. It is an attempt to superimpose monistic Vedanta on the doctrine of devotion to Rama. Among the manuals dealing with *bhakti* are: the *Bhakti- Sutras* of Narada (tenth century); the *Bhakti-Sutras* of Sandilya (earlier than the tenth century); the *Bhakti-ratnavali* (a .d . 1400), an anthology compiled by Visnu Purana containing passages relating to *bhakti* taken from the *Bhagavata Purana;* and Vallabha's *Bhakti-vardhini.* Several imitations of the *Bhagavad-Gita* were attempted. Among them the better known ones are the *Isvara-Gita* which occurs in the *Kurma Purana* and is itself a *Pampata* (Saivite) redaction of a Vaisnava work, and the *Avadhita-Gita* which is regarded as one of the *Sannyasa Upanisads.*

2.2.7. The Dharma-Sastras

The Dharma-sastras, or Smrtis, are religious in character and are more or less similar to the Dharma-Sutras. They have preserved the traditional rules governing personal, domestic, and social behavior. The best-known work among them is the *Manu Smrti.* This work, which is also called *the Bhrgu Samhita,* seems to belong to the period when the *Mahabharata* was undergoing its final redaction. Consisting of twelve chapters, it begins with a statement regarding the process of creation, and then proceeds to lay down, in the next five chapters, rules of conduct for persons belonging to the different *varnas* and to the different *abamas.* It then goes on to discuss the duties of kings, the administration of justice and, at some length, and eighteen sections of law. The final sections mention some *prayafcittas* and include a desultory discussion of a few philosophical topics such as *karma* and the *gunas* (qualities). The other Smrtis mostly follow the pattern of the *varnasrama-dharma* as laid down in the *Manu Smrti.* It is only in the matter of *vyavahara* (civil and criminal law) that these law books appear to differ from one another. For instance, the *Yajnavalkya Smrti,* which belongs to the fourth-fifth centuries A.D. is divided into three clear-cut sections: religious law; civil and criminal law; and expiation. It puts greater stress upon private law than upon criminal law, and shows great advance over the *Manu Smiti* in the law of inheritance. An interesting work, of the nature of a 'digest of law', is the *Caturvarga-cintamam* by Hemadri (1260-1309). He deals especially with various topics of religious significance such as *vratas, danas, srdddhas,* pilgrimages, and ritual.

In ancient and medieval India, religion and philosophy, generally speaking, were not sharply demarcated. The literature relating to the various systems of philosophy developed almost independently of religion. This literature, which divides into three principal classes, the Sutras, the expository works on the Sutras, and independent treatises, is quite extensive. We shall not deal with it, however, in this survey of religious literature. The ethico-didatic literature in Sanskrit (and not a little of the poetical and dramatic literature) may be characterized as religious so far as theme and ultimate purpose are concerned. However, for obvious reasons, this literature too cannot be dealt with here. Thus we now come to two types of distinctively religious literature in Sanskrit, the Tantras and the *Stotras.*

2.2.8. The Stotras

Stotra literature in Sanskrit is very vast, for *stotras* are prayers or hymns. Indeed, one wonders whether any proper count has ever been made, or can be made, of the works belonging to this class. This literature enjoyed the widest currency among the people. The tradition of prayers and hymns is quite ancicnt and may be traced back to the *Rig-Veda. Stotras* have been included in the epics, the Puranas, and the Tantras; and some epic poems contain fine specimens of hymnal poetry. Among these are the hymn to Visnu (Kalidasa, *Raghuvamsa*); the hymn to Brahma (Kalidasa, *Kumarasambhava*); the hymn to Mahadeva (Bharavi, *Kiratarjuniya* closing canto); the hymn to Krsna (Magha, *Stiupalavadha*); and the hymn to Candi (Ratnakara, *Haravijaya*). In a sense, the *rtandi* verses (invocations) in Sanskrit dramas may also be regarded as religious lyrics. But the larger part of the *stotra* literature originated independently. Apart from single works of more or less definite authorship, there are many collections of *stotras* available in print which includc many anonymous *stotras.* Among these collections arc: *Brhat-stotra-muktahara,* the two *Brhat-stotra-ratnakaras,* the *Brhat-stava-kavaea-mala,* and some of the *gucchakas* of the *Kavya-mala.*

The major *stotras* usually relate to one of the five divinities: Ganapati, Surya, Siva, Sakti, and Visnu, most of the prayers being addressed to Siva who also receives most of the praise. Then there are *staves* addressed to the ten incarnations of Visnu, either individually or collectively. Again, a substantial number of *stotras* are addressed to what may be called localized divinities, such as Venkateta of Tirupati, Minaksi of Madurai, Visvanatha of Varanasi, and Snranganatha of Srirangam. Minor divinities like Sasthi, Sitala, and Manasa, rivers, and holy places also have their share of *stotras. Stotras* have a twofold appeal, religious and literary. Actually, however, the majority of *stotras,* with a few noteworthy exceptions, are known for their religious appeal rather than for their lyricism. And even this spiritual appeal is characterized by conventionalized idiom rather than by an effusion of religious emotion. An early *stotra,* attributed to Bana (seventh century), is the *Candishtaka.* It is in praise of *Mahisasura-mardini* (the goddess who slew the buffalo demon) and has one hundred and two verses. The *Surya-Sataka* by Bana's contemporary and close relative Mayura has, however, received greater approbation from literary critics. The great Sankaracarya is traditionally said to have composed nearly two hundred *stotras.* Among those which seem to be genuinely his work we may mention the *Ananda-lahari,* the *Saundarya-lahari* in praise of Sakti, the *Mohamadgara* which is also known as the *Dvadasa-manjarika;* the *Bhaja-govindam* which is also known as the *Carpata-manjari;* and the *Sivaparadha-ksamapana.*

In most of these, devotional fervour is well-matched by poetic elegance, and deep mysticism by musical rhythm. The *Pancaiati* describes the physical charms of Kamaksi, the Mother Goddess, in erotic terms, and is ascribed to the poet Muka who is believed to be a contemporary of Sankaracarya. The *Sivamahimnah-stotra,* which is ascribed to Puspadanta (ninth century), is perhaps more philosophical than religious in tenor, and it has over twenty commentaries. To about the same period belong the *Devi-Jataka* of Anandavardhana (A.D. 850); it seems to have been planned more as an essay in *alamkara* than as a religious hymn. The hymnal literature produced by the Kashmiri poets includes: the *Stava-cintamani* of Bhatta Narayana (ninth century); the *Swa-stotravali* of Utpaladeva (tenth century); the *Bhavomahlra* of Cakrapaninatha (eleventh century); and the *Ardhananharastotra* of Kalhana (twelfth century). The *Samba-pancasika,* which is a hymn to the Sun-god, and which is traditionally attributed to Krsna's son Samba, is also probably the work of a Kashmiri poet.

Coming from Kashmir to Kerala, we may mention the *Mukunda-mdld* of Kulasekhara (A.D. 700). It has only about thirty verses (the number varies in different versions), but it is remarkable for its devotional earnestness and the author's sense of style. *Narayaniya* by Narayaria Bhatta of Kerala (A.D. 1585), on the other hand, is an extensive poem of one thousand verses and is labored in both form and content. It glorifies Krsria of Guruvayur, who is said to have cured the author of his asthma. Among *stotra* texts belonging to the Visistadvaita school are the *Stotra-ratna* of Yamunacarya (eleventh century), the *Gadyatraya* of Ramanuja (eleventh-twelfth century), and *Nyasa-dasaka* and *Astabhujastaka* by Vedanta Depika. Jagannatha Pandita (seventeenth century) wrote five *laharis* (books of verse) which present a pleasing combination of sincere devotion, deep learning, and great poetic ability. They are: *Amrta, Sudha, Ganga,* and *Laksmi laharis.* Nilakantha Diksita of about the same period wrote a hymn to Minaksi, called *Ananda-sagara-stava;* while his pupil Ramabhadra wrote three poems in praise of Rama's various weapons, and the *Varnamala-stotra* which is an alphabetically arranged eulogy of Rama. Hymnal literature was also produced in connection with the Caitanya movement, such as the *Siksastaka* by Caitanya himself (fifteenth century), the *Stava-mala* of Rupa Gosvamin, and the *Stavavali* of Raghunathadasa.

2.2.9. Other Sanskrit Literature

We also have a large body of books dealing with various sciences, law, medicine and grammar. Kautilya's *Arthashastra* is an important treatise of the Mauryan times. It reflects the state of society and economy at that time and provides rich material for the study of ancient Indian polity and economy. The works of Bhasa, Shudraka, Kalidasa and Banabhatta provided us with glimpses of the social and cultural life of northern and central India in times of the Guptas and Harsha. The Gupta period also saw the development of Sanskrit grammar based on the works of Panini and Patanjali.

The Kushana kings patronised Sanskrit scholars. Ashvaghosha wrote the *Buddhacharitra* which is the biography of the Buddha. He also wrote *Saundarananda,* which is a fine example of Sanskrit poetry.

Besides such prayers and hymns, Sanskrit is rich in religious poetry which is very artistic. The inspiration for this kind of poetry is derived mainly from the *Bhagavata Purana.* The *Kisna-karnamrta* is a striking collection of devotional lyrics in which the sentiment of *bhakti* for the youthful Krsna is expressed through religio-erotic idiom and imagery. The *Gitagovinda* by Jayadeva (twelfth century) is a unique work in many respects. It presents a series of what may be called musical monologues by three characters, Krsna, Radha, and Radha's companion. The action takes place in Vrndavana in the background of the *rasakrida* (the sportive dance of Krsna and the *gopis,* milkmaids). Its central theme is that *rasa,* the realization of blissful personal communion with the Lord, is the final goal of all religious activity. This theme is vivified by Jayadeva through his masterly exploitation of the media of poetry, music, and *abhinaya* (gcsture-dance). The *Gitagovinda* is variously described as a lyric drama, a pastoral, an opera, a melodrama, and a *yatra* (a popular dramatic entertainment).

It has twelve cantos, and cach canto contains *padabalis* (songs) set to different *ragas* (melody patterns). These songs are introduced by one or two metrical stanzas which seem intended to be sung in chorus. The great popularity of the *Gitagovinda* is vouched for by its several imitations. In some of these, Rama and Sita or Siva and Parvati take the place of Krsna and Radha. But the truly glorious period of Sanskrit religious poetry-or, for that matter, of Sanskrit poetry in general must be said to have ended in the twelfth century with Jayadeva himself.

India produced great literary works on subjects like Maths, Astronomy, Astrology, Agriculture and Geography etc. Books on medicine were written by Charak and on surgery by Sushruta. Madhava wrote a book on pathology. Books written on astronomy by Varahamihira and Aryabhatta and on astrology by Lagdhacharya had all achieved prominence. There is none that can compete with Varahamihiras Bhrihatsamhita, Aryabhatia and Vedanga Jyotisha. The post-medieval period in northern India saw the rise of Sanskrit literature in Kashmir. Somadeva's *Katha-sarit-sagar* and Kalhan's *Rajatarangini* are of historical importance. It gives a vivid account of the Kings of Kashmir. The Sanskrit literary tradition also has a vast corpus of numerous works on different aspects of art and architecture, sculpture, iconography and related fields.

2.2.10. Summary

- Ever since human beings have invented scripts, writing has reflected the culture, lifestyle, society and the polity of contemporary society.
- Sanskrit is the most ancient language of our country. It is one of the twenty-two languages listed in the Indian Constitution. The literature in Sanskrit is vast, beginning with the most ancient thought embodied in the Rig Veda, the oldest literary heritage of mankind.
- Sanskrit is perhaps the only language that transcended the barriers of regions and boundaries.
- The Vedas are the earliest known literature in India. The Vedas were written in Sanskrit and were handed down orally from one generation to the other. The preservation

of the Vedas till today is one of our most remarkable achievements.

- There are four Vedas, namely, the- Rig Veda, Yajur Veda, Sama Veda and Atharva Veda. Each Veda consists of the Brahmanas, the Upanishads and the Aranyakas.
- The word *upanisad* is interpreted variously. It is made to correspond with the word *updsana* which is understood to mean either worship or profound knowledge.
- The Upanisads are also called the Vedanta, because they represent the concluding portion of the *apauruseya* Veda or Sruti, or the final stage in Vedic instruction, or the ultimate end and aim of the teachings of the Veda.
- Vedangas, present an attempt to systematize various aspects of that knowledge which are necessary for understanding the Vedic texts.
- The *Ramayana* and the *Mahabharata* represent the ethos of ancient India. Tradition places the *Ramayana* earlier than the *Mahabharata.* The nucleus of the *Mahabharata* may have been older than that of the *Ramayana,* but in their present forms the *Ramayana* appears to be the earlier work.
- The Puranas are a very important branch, of the Hindu sacred literature. They enable us to know the true import of the ethos, philosophy, and religion of the Vedas. They clothe with flesh and blood the bony framework of the Dharma-Sutras and the Dharma-Sastras.
- The Puranas relate to the whole of India so far as the historical portion therein is concerned and to the whole world so far as their ethical, philosophical, and religious portions are concerned.
- We also have a large body of books dealing with various sciences, law, medicine and grammar. Kautilya's *Arthashastra* is an important treatise of the Mauryan times. It reflects the state of society and economy at that

time and provides rich material for the study of ancient Indian polity and economy.

- The works of Bhasa, Shudraka, Kalidasa and Banabhatta provided us with glimpses of the social and cultural life of northern and central India in times of the Guptas and Harsha. The Gupta period also saw the development of Sanskrit grammar based on the works of Panini and Patanjali.

2.2.11. Exercise

1. Write shorts notes on: Rig Veda, Upanishds, Mahabharat, Dharmasastra.

2. Write an essay on the vedic literature.

3. What is upansihad? How they are helpful in growth of Sanskrit literature.? Discuss.

4. Write an account on the literary characteristics of Indian Epics.

5. What is Purana? Enumerate the religious and historical importantce iof Purana in India.

2.2.12. Further Reading

- Basham , A . L., *Studies in Indian History and Culture.* Sambodhi Publications Pvt. Ltd., Calcutta, 1964
- Basham , A . L., *The Wonder That Was India.* Sidgwick and Jackson, London, 1954
- Dimock, E. C. (Jr.), and Others , *The Literatures of India.* Chicago University Press, Chicago, 1974
- Durant, W., *Our Oriental Heritage* (Being the first volume of the series *The Story of Civilization*). Simon and Schuster, New York, 1935
- Kabir, H, *The Indian Heritage.* 3rd Edn. Asia Publishing House, Bombay, 1955
- Luniya, B.N., *Evolution of Indian Culture.* 4th Edn. Lakshmi Narain Agarwal, Agra, 1967
- Majumdar, A. K., and Prajnanananda , Swam i (Eds.), *The Bases of Indian Culture.* Ramakrishna Vedanta Math, Calcutta, 1971

CHAPTER-III
HISTORY OF BUDDHIST AND JAIN LITERATURE

PALI, PRAKRIT AND SANSKRIT, SANGAMA LITERATURE & ODIA LITERATURE

Structure

2.3.0. Objectives

In this lesson, students investigate the growth of a vast corpus of literarature under the Buddhism and Jainism. Throughout the chapter, an emphasis will be on the growth and importance of Pali, Prakrit and Sanskrit language in ancient India. After completing this chapter, you will be able to:

- *understand the growth of canonical literature of Jainism and Buddhism;*
- *discuss the development of Prakrit and Pali literature in ancient India.*
- *describe the origin and growth of Sangam literature.*
- *identify the various other texts of Buddhism and Jainism beside the canonical one;and*
- *trace a brief history of Odia literature through ages.*

2.3.1. Introduction

The religious books of the Jains and the Buddhists refer to historical persons or incidents. The earliest Buddhist works were written in Pali, which was spoken in Magadha and South Bihar. The Buddhist works can be divided into the canonical and the non-canonical. The canonical literature is best represented by the "Tripitakas", that is, three baskets - Vinaya Pitaka, Sutta Pitaka and Abhidhamma Pitaka. Vinaya Pitaka deals with rules and regulations of daily life. Sutta Pitaka contains dialogues and discourses on morality and deals with Dharma while Abhidhamma Pitaka deals with philosophy and metaphysics. It includes discourses on various subjects such as ethics, psychology, theories of knowledge and mataphysical problems.

The non-canonical literature is best represented by the Jatakas. Jatakas are the most interesting stories on the previous births of the Buddha. It was believed that before he was finally born as Gautama, the Buddha practising Dharma passed through more than 550 births, in many cases even in the form of animals. Each birth story is called a Jataka. The Jatakas throw invaluable light on the social and economic conditions ranging from the sixth century BC to the second century BC. They also make incidental reference to political events in the age of the Buddha.

The Jain texts were written in Prakrit and were finally compiled in the sixth century AD in Valabhi in Gujarat. The important works are known as Angas, Upangas, Prakirnas, Chhedab Sutras and Malasutras. Among the important Jain scholars, reference may be made to Haribhadra Suri, (eighth century AD) and Hemchandra Suri, (twelfth century AD). Jainism helped in the growth of a rich literature comprising poetry, philosophy and grammar. These works contain many passages which help us to reconstruct the political history of eastern Uttar Pradesh and Bihar. The Jain texts refer repeatedly to trade and traders.

2.3.2. Literature of Jainism

Jaina literature begins with the last of the Tirthankaras1, Mahavlr, who reorganized the old Nirgrantha sect and revitalized its moral and religious zeal and activities. He preached his faith of *ahimsa* (non-violence or harmlessness) and self-purification to the people in their own language which was not Sanskrit, but Prakrit. The form of Prakrit which he is said to have used was Ardha-Magadhi, by which was meant a language that was not pure Magadhi but partook of its nature.

2.3.2.1. Twelve Angas

Mahavira's teachings were arranged in twelve Angas (parts) by his disciples. These Angas formed the earliest literature on Jainism, *Acaranga* laid down rules of discipline for the monks, *Sutrakrtanga* contained further injunctions for the monks regarding what was suitable or unsuitable for them and how they should safeguard their vows. It also gave an exposition of the tenets and dogmas of other faiths, *Sthananga* listed in numerical order, categories of knowledge pertaining to the realities of nature, *Samavayanga* classified objects in accordance with similarities of time, place, number, and so on, *Vyakhya-prajnapti* or *Bkagavat* explained the realities of life and nature in the form of a catechism, *Jnatrdhamakatha* contained hints regarding religious preaching as well as stories and anecdotes calculated to carry moral conviction, *Upasakadhyayana* or *Upasaka-dasaka* was meant to serve as a religious code for householders, *Antakrddasaka* gave accounts of ten saints who attained salvation after immense suffering, *Anuttaraupapatika* contained accounts of ten saints who had gone to the highest heaven after enduring intense persecution, *Prsnna-vyakarana* contained accounts and episodes for the refutation of opposite views, establishment of one's own faith, promotion of holy deeds, and prevention of evil, *Vipaka-Sutra* explained how virtue was rewarded and evil punished and finally the *Drstivada* included the five sections namely *Parikarmani* contained tracts describing the moon, the sun, Jambudvipa, other islands and seas, as well as living beings and nonliving matter, *Sutra* gave an account of various tenets and philosophies numbering no less than 363, *Prathamanuyoga* recounted ancient history and narrated the lives of great kings and saints. *Purvagata* dealt with the problems of birth, death, and continuity.

2.3.2.2. The Digambara Tradition

This comprehensive collection of practically the whole knowledge of the imes, secular as well as religious, could not survive long in its original form. According to the Digambara Jains, the whole canon was preserved for only 62 years after Mahavira that is up to the eighth successor, Bhadrabahu. After hat, portions gradually began to be lost. So, after 683 years from the *nirvana* of Mahavira, what was known to the *Acaryas* (teachers) was only fragmentary. It was only the knowledge of a few portions of the *Purvagata* or *Parvas* that was imparted at Girinagara in Kathiawar by Dharasena to his pupils Puspadanta md Bhutabali who, on the basis of it, wrote the *Satkhandagama* in the *sutra* form during the first or second century A.D. The *Satkhandagamas*, therefore is the earliest available religious literature amongst the Digambaras. It is for them the supreme authority for the teachings of Mahavira.

2.3.2.3. The Svetambara Tradition

The literary tradition of the Svetambara Jains is, however, different. They agree with the Digambara view so far as the continuity of the whole canon up to Bhadrabahu is concerned. The Svetambaras say that after Bhadrabahu had migrated with a host of his adherents to the South on account of a famine, the monks who remained in Magadha met in a Council at Pataliputra, under the leadership of Sthulabhadra. There a compilation was made of the eleven Angas together with the remnants of the twelfth. This was the first attempt to systematize the Jaina Agama. But in the course of time, the canon became disorderly. Therefore, the monks met once again at Valabhi in Gujarat under the presidentship of Devarddhi Ksamasramana in the middle of the fifth century A.D. All the sacred texts available today were collected, systematized, redacted and committed to writing by this Council.

They are as follows: The eleven Angas named above, twelve Upangas, Ten Prakirnas, Six Cheda-Sutras, two Culika-Sutras, and four Mula-Sutras.

It is therefore evident that books written up to the time of the Valabhi Conference were included in the canon. Perhaps some later works were also included in the Agama as is shown by the enlargement of the list up to fifty. But there is no doubt about a good deal of the material in the Agama texts being genuinely old as is proved by the absence of any reference to Greek astronomy and the presence of statements which are not altogether favourable to the Svetambara creed, such as Mahavira1 s emphasis on nakedness.

2.3.2.4. The Jaina Canon: An Estimate

The language of these texts is called *arsa* by which is meant Ardha-Magadhi. But it is not uniform in all the texts. The language of the Angas and a few other texts, such as thc *Uttaradhyayana,* is evidently older and amongst them the *Acaranga* shows still more archaic forms. The language of the verses generally shows tendencies of an earlier age also. On the whole, the language of this Agama does not conform fully to the characteristics of any of the Prakrits described by the grammarians; but it shares something with cach of them. Though the contents are quite varied and cover a wide range of human knowledge conceived in those days, the subject-matter of this canonical literature is mainly the ascetic practices of the followers of Mahavira. As such, it is essentially didactic, dominated by the supreme ethical principle of *ahimsa.* But, subject to that, there is a good deal of poetry and philosophy as well as valuable information about contemporary thought and social history including biographical details of Parsvanatha, Mahavira, and their contemporaries. Many narrative pieces, such as those found in the *Uttaradhyayana,* are interesting and instructive and remind one of the personalities and events in the Upanisads and the Pali texts. From the historical point of view, the life of Mahavira in the *Acaranga,* information about his predecessors and contemporaries in the *Vyakhyaprajnapti* or *Bhagavati* and the *Upasakardasaka,* about his successors in the *Kalpa- Sutra,* and about monachism practised in the days of Mahavira in eastern India in *Dasa-vaikalika* are all very valuable.

2.3.2.5. The Commentaries on the Jaina Canon

A vast literature of commentaries has grown round the Agamas themselves. The earliest of these works are the *niryuktis,* attributed to Bhadrabahu. They explain the topics systematically in Prakrit verse, and elaborate them by narrating legends and episodes. Ten of these works are available.

Then, there are the *bhasyas* similarly composed in Prakrit verse. These, in some cases, have been so intermingled with the *niryuktis* that it is now difficult to separate them. The *bhasyas* carry the systematization and elaboration further. These texts, of which there are eleven available, are mostly anonymous. The elaborate *bhasya* on the *Avasyaka-niryukti* is, however, attributed to Jinabhadra Ksamasramana and that on the *Kalpa-Sutra* to Sanghadasagani.

The *curnis,* of which twenty texts are available, are prose glosses with a curious admixture of Prakrit and Sanskrit. Some of them contain valuable historical information as well. The *Avasyaka-curni,* for example, makes mention of a flood in Sravasti, thirteen years after Mahavira's enlightenment. The *Nisitha-curni* contains a reference to Kalakacarya who invited a foreigner to invade Ujjjain. All the *curnis* are indiscriminately ascribed to Jinadasagani.

The last strata of the commentary literature consist of *tikas* which carry the expository and illustrative process to its logical conclusion. They are written in Sanskrit retaining, in many cases, the Prakrit narratives in their original form. The well-known *tika* writers are Haribhadra, Silanka, fSanti Suri, Devendra alias Nemicandra, Abhayadeva, Dronacarya, Maladharin Hemacandra, Malayagiri, Ksemakirti, Vijayavimala, Santicandra, and Samayasundara. Their activities were spread over a period of 1,100 years between the sixth and seventeenth centuries. A number of other forms of commentaries called *dipikas, vrttis,* and *aoaciirnis* are also extant.

2.3.2.6. Jaina literature in Sanskrit

The language of Jaina literature was primarily the Prakrits which were prevalent amongst the people at one time or the other in different parts of the country. But Sanskrit was not altogether shunned. Amongst the Jains, the earliest work in Sanskrit devoted to religious writing is the *Tattvarthadhigama- Sutra* of Umasvamin which epitomizes the whole Jaina creed in about 375 *sutras* arranged in ten chapters. The work occupies a unique position in Jaina literature as it is recognized as authoritative equally by the Digambaras and the Svetambaras with a few variations in the readings, and is very widely studied by both. It has been commented upon by the most eminent authors of both the sects.

The next commentary on it is *Tattvartha-raja-varttika* of Akalanka (eighth century) which offers more detailed explanations of the *sutras,* as well as of the important statements of Pujyapada. The *Tattvartha-sloka-varttika* of Vidyanandin (ninth century) gives expositions in verse and makes valuable clarifications. For yogic practices, the *Jnanarnava* of Subhacandra and the *Yogasastra* of Hemacandra are valuable guides, while the *Ratna-karanda-*

sravakacara is more popular amongst the laity. Jaina Sanskrit literature is considerably enriched by a series of works on Nyaya (logic) begun by Samantabhadra and Siddhasena Divakara and followed up by Akalanka, Vidyanandin, Prabhacandra, Manikyanandin, Hemacamha, and many others.

2.3.2.7. Jaina Nerrative Literature in Sanskrit and Prikrit

The narrative literature of Jainism has mostly as its subject-matter the life of one or more of its sixty-three great men. These are the twenty-four Tirthankaras, twelve Cakravartins, nine Baladevas, nine Narayanas, and nine Prati-Narayanas. In the lives of the Tirthankaras the five auspicious events *(kalyanaka)* namely, conception, birth, renunciation, enlightenment, and salvation, receive special attention from the poets. The conquest of the six sub-divisions of Bharata-khanda is the main achievement of the Cakravartins. The Baladevas are charged with the special responsibility of getting rid of the tyrants of their times, the Prati-Narayanas, with the assistance of the Narayanas. They form triples. Rama, Laksmana, and Ravana form one triple while Balarama, Krsna, and Jarasandha form another, these two triples being the last of these nine triples; it is they who, next to the Tirthankaras, have inspired most of the narrative poetry. Descriptions of the universe and of the past lives of the persons under discussion, the introduction of numerous subsidiary stories to illustrate one point or another and occasional discourses on religious topics are some of the other features of this Puranic literature. The narration as a rule begins in the saintly assembly of Lord Mahavira with a query from Srenika, the king of Magadha, and the reply is given by the chief disciple of the Tirthankara, namely, Gautama. A rich literature of this kind is found, written in Prakrit and Sanskrit as well as in Apabhramsa.

The earliest epic available is the *Paumacariya* of Vimala Suri, which gives the Jaina version of the *Ramayana.* It has marked differences from the work of Valmiki which was, no doubt, known to the author. The language is chaste Maharastri Prakrit and the style is fluent and occasionally ornate. Just as Valmiki is the *adikabi* of Sanskrit, Vimala Suri may be called the pioneer of Prakrit *kavya* (poetry). According to the author's own statement, the work was produced 530 years after Mahavira's *nirvana* (that is, at the beginning of the first century A.D). The *Padma-carita* of Ravisena (seventh century) in Sanskrit follows closely Vimala Suri's work, and the same epic is beautifully rendered in Apabhramsa by Svayambhu (eighth century), and later on by Raidhu. The linguistic interest and poetic charm of the Apabhramsa works are remarkable as they set the model for the earliest epics of Jayasi and Tulasidasa in Hindi.

Jinasena's *HarivamSSa Purana* (eighth century) is the earliest Jaina epic on the subject of the *Mahabharata,* the chief heroes being the twenty-second Tirthankara Neminatha and his cousin Krsna Narayana. The Apabhramsa version of it is beautified by the genius of Svayambhu and his later followers, Dhavala and Yasahkirti.

The most comprehensive work, and again the earliest of its kind, is the *Mahapurana* of Jinasena and Gunabhadra (ninth century). The first part of it, called the *Adipurana,* ends with the *nirvana* of the first Tirthankara, Adinatha or Rsabhadeva, while the second part, called *Uttarapurana,* narrates the lives of the rest of the Tirthankaras, and the remaining *salaka-purusas.* The work of Jinasena may be called the Jaina encyclopaedia. It enlightens its readers on almost every topic regarding religion, philosophy, morals, and rituals. The philosophical knowledge of the author is demonstrated by his commentary, the *Jayadhavala,* and his poetic ability is evinced by his *Parsvabhyudaya-kavya* in which he has transformed the lyrical poem *Meghaduta* by Kalidasa into an equally charming epic on the life of the twenty-third Tirthankara. This whole *Mahapurana* has been rendered into Apabhramsa with commensurate skill and in charming style by Puspadanta in his *Tisatthi-mahapurisa-gunalankdra* (tenth century). Another Sanskrit- version of it is found in the *Trisasti-Mahapurusa-carita* of Hemacandra which again has a charm of its own. Its historical value is enhanced by the additional section called the *Parsistaparvan* or *Sthaviravali-carita* which gives valuable information about the Jaina community after Mahavira's *nirvana.*

2.3.2.8. Biographies of Sages and Saints in Sanskrit and Prakrit

A large number of works have been written on the lives of individual Tirthankaras, and other personages of the hierarchy, in Sanskrit, Prakrit, and Apabhramsa. The more important of these are:

In Sanskrit: Life of the twelfth Tirthankara, Vasupujya, by Vardhamana Suri; life of the thirteenth Tirthankara, Vimala, by Krsnadeva; life of the fifteenth Tirthankara, Dharmanatha, by Haricandra; lives of the sixteenth Tirthankara, Santinatha, by Deva Suri, Manikyanandin, and Sakalakirti; lives of the twenty-second Tirthankara, Neminatha, by Vagbhatta and Suracarya; and lives of the twenty-third Tirthankara, Parsvanatha, by Jinasena, Vadiraja (eleventh century), Bhavadeva, and Manikyacandra.

In Prakrit: *Adinathacarita* of Vardhamana (eleventh century), *Sumatinathacaria* of Somaprabha (twelfth century), *Supasanahacana* of Laksmanagani, and *Mahaviracarita* of Gunacandra and also of Devendra.

In Apabhramsa: The *Mehesaracariu* of Raidhu (fifteenth century) on the life of the first Tirthankara; the *Candappahacariu* of Yasahklrti (fifteenth century); the *Santindhacariu* of Mahlcandra (sixteenth century); the *Nemindhacanu* of Haribhadra (eighth century), of Damodara (thirteenth century), and of Lakhmadeva (sixteenth century), the *Pasanahacariu* of Padmaklrti (tenth century), of Sridhara (twelfth century), of Asavala (fifteenth century), and of Raidhu; and the *Vaddhamanacariu* of Sridhara and of Jayamitra.

There is also a very vast literature in all the three languages concerning the lives of persons who attained fame for their religious zeal and sacrifice. The *Yasastilaka-campu* of Somadeva (tenth century), the *Tilakamanjari* of Dhanapala (tenth century), the *Jivandhara-campu* of Vadibhasimha and of Haricandra are some of the Sanskrit works which belong to this category. The foregoing works are also noteworthy for their style which admits of an admixture of prose and verse, as well as for their diction which vies with the best prose style of the Sanskrit *kathas*.

A very large number of Jaina works are still lying in store in various places, and new works of considerable antiquity are coming to light every day. This literature has a beauty and grandeur of its own in form, matter, and spirit. The Jains never showed partiality for one language, like the Brahmanas for Sanskrit and the Buddhists for Pali. Instead, they cultivated all the languages of their time and place, devoting almost equal attention to each. Even the Dravidian languages of the South were not neglected, and the earliest literature in Tamil and Kannada is found to have been developed and enriched by Jaina contributions. This literature was not meant as a pastime or as mere pedantry, but for the cultivation of those virtues without which man, through his so-called progress, may be led to his doom. Signs of this danger are not wanting in the present set-up of world forces and the trend of events. If humanity is to fulfil its role of establishing peace on earth and goodwill amongst mankind, it must extricate itself from greed and selfishness. In the task of realizing human destiny, Jaina literature, with its lessons of nobility and the virtue of tolerance, and with its message of non-violence, love for humanity, and supremacy of the spiritual over the material gain, has much to offer to mankind.

2.3.3. Prakrit language and literature

Broadly speaking, Indo-Aryan speech has flowed in two streams: Samskrta and Prakrta (which will be spelt hereafter as Sanskrit and Prakrit) and, at various stages, these two streams have constantly influenced each other. Prakrit, which means 'natural or 'common', primarily indicates the uncultivated popular dialects which existed side by side with Sanskrit, the 'accurately made', 'polished', and 'refined' speech.

The Prakrits, then, are the dialects of the unlettered masses, which they used for secular communication in their day-to-day life, while Sanskrit is the language of the intellectual aristocrat, the priest, pundit, or prince, who used it for religious and learned purposes. Yet the language of every-day conversation even of these people must have been nearer to the popular Prakrits than to literary Sanskrit. The former was a natural acquisition; while the latter, the principal literary form of speech, required training in grammatical and phonetic niceties.

Side by side with the Vedic language, which was an artistic spccch employed by the priest in religious songs, there existed popular dialects which probably owed their origin to tribal groups, and developed through use of the Aryan speech by indigenous people. Vedic literature gives some glimpses of popular speeches, the primary Prakrits; but no literature in them has come down to us.

Classical Sanskrit, as standardized by Panini and his commentators, respectfully shelved all that was obsolete in the Vedic speech and studiously eschewed all that belonged to the popular tongue; the use of such a rigorously standardized language was a task for a selective group. Whenever a preacher or a prince wanted to address the wider public, not from the monopolized temple or sacrificial enclosure but from the popular pulpit, the tendency to employ a popular dialect of the day was but natural. Thus, in the sixth century B.C., Mahavira and Buddha preferred to preach in the local Prakrits of eastern India; and the great emperor Afoka (third century B.C) and, a century later, King Kharavela addressed their subjects in Prakrit.

Practically all over India, Prakrits were freely used for inscriptions almost up to the Gupta age, and the earlier inscriptions, up to about the first century A.D., were all in Prakrit. Dialectal distinctions are fairly clear, though the problems of localization are not so easily solved. The Asokan inscriptions do show, to a certain extent, dialectal differences according to regions; and they are not altogether without some correspondence with the known literary dialects.

It is held by some scholars that the early secular literature comprising drama, epics, lyrical poetry, and so on, was originally in Prakrit; and that some time in the second century A.D. through the initiative of the Saka Satraps of western India, Sanskrit gradually entered the field of secular composition. The epic idiom shows contamination with Prakritism which the bards must have contracted from the Prakrits they used in day-to-day conversation, in fine, from their vernaculars. The so-called *gatha* literature of the Buddhists is a good specimen of queer admixture of Sanskrit and

Prakrit. In drama, different characters spoke different languages in the same play; the earliest known plays of Asvaghosa (c. a .d . 100) bear evidence to the antiquity of this practice. There can hardly be any doubt that when these dialects were first employed in drama they were contemporary local vernaculars; but later on they became stereotyped, and their usage was a matter of conventional fixing. Kings and courtiers spoke Sanskrit; ladies of rank spoke SaurasenI; and the lower characters spoke Magadhi.

The Prakrit grammarians give a sketchy description of various Prakrit dialects: Maharastrl, Sauraseni, Magadhi, Paisaci, and Apabhramsa. Pali and Ardha-Magadhi are also Prakrits and are used in the Buddhist and Jaina canons. From the point of view of the evolution of language, the inscriptional Prakrits, Pali and Paisaci, form an earlier group; Sauraseni and Magadhi come next, one a central and the other an eastern dialect. Ardha-Magadhi is close to Pali with regard to its vocabulary, syntax, and style, but is phonologically later in age. Maharastri has provcd to be an elastic medium for learned epics and lyrical poetry on popular subjects. Some of these were raised to literary status from a regional footing; but they gradually became stereotyped, with scant deference to their local colour from the grammarians. By that time the popular dialects had already advanced, and the gap between the literary Prakrits and contemporary popular speech went on increasing. Popular elements, stray forms from a popular vernacular, even percolated now and then into some of the earlier Prakrit works.

By about the fifth century AD. Sanskrit and Prakrit were equally stereotyped as literary forms'of expression. Their cleavage from the current vernaculars was felt more and more; and once again an effort was made to raise the then popular speech to a literary stage, an effort represented by Apabhramsa which, as a literary language, is to be distinguished from Sanskrit and Prakrit. Like Sanskrit and Prakrit, Apabhramsa no longer remained local. The standard literary Apabhramsa looks very much like a forerunner of Old Rajasthani and Old Gujarati, but it appears to have been used on a wider scale even outside the expected area. It is heavily indebted to literary Prakrits for its vocabulary, while its other elements, such as nominal and verbal terminations, pronouns, adverbs, and particlcs, arc drawn from the popular speech-stratum, in a few cases, possibly, with some foreign influence. The metrical dressing was peculiaily popular and novel, and to a certain extent this influenced its phonetic shaping. In its turn, Apabhramsa also reachcd a fixed form like Sanskrit and the Prakrits; and side by side came into being what we call today the 'modern Indian languages. The Prakrits and Apabhramsa represent the Middle Indo-Aryan stage. Maharastri and Apabhramsa appear to have been developed first by the common people for their songs and couplets; and it was through these channels that they obtained recognition from the learned as well and were admitted into literature. Sudraka admitted Maharastri verses in the *Mrcchakatika*; Kalidasa (*c.* A.D. 400) employed Apabhramsa songs in his *Vikramorvasiya*; and Vidyapati (A.D. 1400) used Maithili verses in his Sanskrit-Prakrit dramas. As literary languages to be written after a close study of grammar and literature, Sanskrit, the Prakrits, and Apabhramsa were cultivated simultaneously for a considerable length of time, even after the Modem Indo-Aryan stage was actually reached in the popular language of day-to-day conversation.

Judging from its abiding values, especially the thoughts it contains and the way in which they are expressed against a background of human experience and natural and social environments, Prakrit literature is many-sided and remarkable. It records the noble thoughts of one of the greatest kings of the world; and it embodies the ideology of a religion which is realistic in philosophy, ascetic in morals, and humanitarian in outlook. It presents a valuable, though complicated, picture of linguistic and metrical evolution in the last two thousand years or more.

The society depicted in Prakrit literature is more popular than aristocratic. Eminent monks and outstanding poets have earnestly contributed to its treasures. Some of these authors are quite frank about personal details, and the chronological data afforded by them have special significance in reconstructing the history of Indian literature. Indian linguistics would certainly be poorer in the absence of Prakrit literature, for on its lap have grown the modem Indian languages. Prakrit literature goes a long way in helping to add important and significant details to our picture of Indian culture and civilization.

2.3.4. Buddhist Literature

Gautama Buddha's speeches, sayings, discourses, and conversations were handed down orally through a succession of teachers. Proper attention was not, therefore, paid for preserving Buddha's actual words. Recitation and memorization were then the means for the preservation of records. Such practice had been in vogue in India since the earliest Vedic period. From the *Mahaparinibbana-Suttanta* we learn that Buddha anticipated that his sayings might be misrepresented and so he advised his disciples to verify his words in four ways. His prophesy came true after his *mahaparinibbana.*

Subhadda who entered the Order (Sangha) in his old age felt happy at Buddha's *mahaparinibbana.* He thought that there would be none to take the monks to task for non-observance of the Vinaya rules thenceforth. They would be able to do what they would like.The elder monks (*theras*) were highly annoyed at this and felt it necessary to avoid the dangerous effects of his disparaging utterances in the Sangha. They convened a Council headed by Mahakassapa Thera to settle all controversial points in regard to Subhadda's sayings. This Council was known as the First Buddhist Council in the history of Buddhism. It was at this Council that a full collection of Buddha's teachings was made and that the Dhamma (Doctrine) and Vinaya (Discipline) were settled. The Abhidhamma had no separate existence then. It formed part of the Dhamma. In other words, Dhamma and Vinaya were the two principal divisions under which the traditional teachings of Buddha were collected. A hundred years later another Council called the Second Buddhist Council was held in which the rules of morality were discussed. The violation of the Vinaya rules enjoined on the monks was the subject of discussion at this Council. We, however, find no mention of the Abhidhamma as having been discussed at this Council. There was another Buddhist Council known as the Third Buddhist Council held more than two hundred years after the *mahaparinibbana* of Buddha. The texts of the Sutta and Vinaya were rehearsed and settled and the Abhidhamma was recognized as a part of the canon. Dhamma and Vinaya which were then two divisions of the Buddhist scriptures were divided into three parts in the Council-Sutta, Vinaya and Abhidhamma. Dhamma was thus divided into two parts-the Sutta Pitaka and the Abhidhamma Pitaka. This Council thus witnessed the appearance of the whole of the Buddhist canonical literature in three divisions, viz. Vinaya Pitaka, Sutta Pitaka and Abhidhamma Pitaka. This is technically called Tipitaka. It should be mentioned here that the term *pitaka* literally means basket. But here it is used in the sense of tradition, i.e. ca long line of teachers and pupils handing on, in these three sacred Pitakas or Baskets, from ancient times down to today, the treasures of the Dhamma (of the Norm).

The Buddhist literature, both HInayana and Mahayana, is preserved mainly in Pali, Buddhist Sanskrit, and Pure Sanskrit. The originals of some of these texts are lost. But fortunately they are preserved in Tibetan and Chinese translations. The Buddhist texts were also rendered into the language of the countries to which Buddhism spread. Of all the languages, Pali is the earliest. In other words, Pali Tipitaka represents the earliest and most complete collection of the Buddhist literature.

2.3.4.1. Pali and its origin

Pali means 'row' (*pankti*), 'text', 'sacred texts, and 'reading'. *Pali* always signifies the text of the Buddhist scriptures. In the *Mahavamsa* we find that 'only the text has been brought here not the commentaries'. It also means that which preserves the import of words. Pali belongs to the early Middle

Indo-Aryan period. Opinions as to its origin, however, differ among the Indologists, both oriental and occidental. According to some scholars, Pali was Magadhi Prakrit or Magadhi-bhasa which was held out to be the *mulabhasa,* 'the primary speech of all men'. Buddha spent most of his time in Magadha and preached his doctrine there in the dialect of that region. It is but natural that the early Buddhist scriptures were composed in Magadhi in which Buddha himself spoke. According to others, Pali has a close relationship with Paisaci Prakrit spoken at that time in the Vindhya region. Some scholars further hold that Pali was the language of Kalinga (South Orissa and East Telugu country) whence Buddhism was introduced into Ceylon (modern Sri Lanka). There are again others who think that Pali was an old form of Sauraseni Prakrit as the phonetics and morphology of Pali are mostly identical with it.

It is said that Emperor Asoka sent his son Mahindra to preach the Saddhamma (Buddhism) in Ceylon. Some scholars maintain that he carried with him the text of the Tipitaka, while according to others, he went to Ceylon after memorizing the whole of the Tipitaka. Through the patronage of the king, Buddhism was, however, well established there. The Tipitaka was committed to writing during the reign of Vattagamani Abhaya in the first century B.C. According to Ceylonese monks, this Tipitaka and the Tipitaka which was compiled in the Third Buddhist Council, however, was the one and the same. Some scholars do not subscribe to this view. They hold that this Tipitaka was not the same as that compiled in the Third Council-it is but a revised edition. The Tipitaka composed in Pali and Buddhist Sanskrit was derived from the old Tipitaka which was written in Magadhi. It is striking to note here that before the compilation of the Tipitaka, the Buddhist literature was divided into nine *angas* or parts. This ninefold division is not the ninefold classification of the literature. It points out but specimens of nine types of composition in the literature. For instance, they are extant in the *Anguttara Nikaya.* It is said that these diverse forms existed in the Buddhist literature even at the time of the compilation of the Buddhist scriptures. Let us now turn to the Pali Tipitaka and give a brief survey of the texts constituting it.

2.3.4.2. The Vinaya Pitaka

The Vinaya Pitaka contains rules of discipline. It deals with the rules and regulations for the guidance of the Buddhist Sangha and precepts for the daily life of the *bhikkhus* (monks) and *bhikkhunis* (nuns). These rules and regulations were promulgated by Buddha himself during the early period as the occasion arose. The Vinaya Pitaka thus contains mainly moral instructions. It relates all that belongs to moral practices. *Sila* (code of morality) is the principal subject-matter. The Buddhist tradition records that Vinaya is the life of Buddha's teachings. And as long as Vinaya lasts, his teachings also last. It is the main gateway to *nibbana.* The Vinaya Pitaka comprises the following texts: *(i)* the *Suttavibhanga,* *(ii)* the *Khandhakas,* and *(Hi)* the *Parivara* or the *Parivarapatha.*

The *Suttavibhanga,* i.e. the explanation of the *suttas,* tells in a sort of historical introduction how, when, and why the particular rule in question came to be laid down. The words of the rule are given in full, followed by a very ancient word-for-word commentary, which in its turn is succeeded by further explanation and discussion on doubtful points. It comprises *(a) Mahavibhanga* which has eight chapters dealing with eight classes of transgressions against discipline, and *(b) Bhikkhunivibhanga,* a shorter work, a commentary on the code for the nuns. It should be noted that *Patimokkha,* the oldest text, which is included in the *Suttavibhanga,* is the nucleus of the Vinaya Pitaka. It deals with the ecclesiastical offences requiring confession and expiation. In other words, it contains a set of rules to be observed by the members of the Sangha

The *Khandhakas* contain various rules and regulations for the guidance of the Sangha and the entire code of conduct for the daily life of the *bhikkhus* and *bhikkhunis.* They give us a coherent picture of the life in the Sangha. They form a sort of continuation and supplement to the *Suttavibhanga.* They are divided into two parts-the *Mahavagga* and the *Cullavagga.*

(a) The *Mahavagga* furnishing the story of the formation of the Sangha and the rules for admission into the Order, the observance of the *uposatha* ceremony, the mode of life during the rains, observance of the *pavarana* and the *kathina* ceremonies, food, clothing, seats, conveyances, medicaments, dress, and the like. It also furnishes us with many moral tales as also the everyday life of India. It further contains ample information on the social and urban life of the then India. In short, the *Mahavagga* is replete with various kinds of invaluable materials for reconstructing the ancient history of India.

(b) The *Cullavagga* deals with the rules of conduct of the *bhikkhus* and *bhikkhunis* and with atonement and penances. It also deals with the dwellings, furniture, and lodgings as also the duties of monks and the exclusion from the *patimokkha* ceremony. It furnishes us with an account of the formation of the *Bhikkhuni Sangha* (Order of nuns). It further gives us an account of the first two Councils held at Sattapanniguha of Rajagraha and Valukarama of Vesali.

The *Parivdra* or the *Parivarapatha* is the concluding text of the Vinaya Pitaka and was composed much later than the *Suttavibhanga* and the *Khandhakas.* It was probably composed in Ceylon, and not in India, by a monk named Dipa. It is an appendix to the Vinaya and contains nineteen chapters. It is the only key which unlocks the subjects of the *Suttavibhanga* and the *Khandhakas.* Its first chapter gives us a list of *vinayadharas* (masters of discipline). The list is indeed invaluable in the history of the Buddhist Sanghas of India and Ceylon.

2.3.4.3. The Sutta Pitaka

The Sutta Pitaka is a collection of the doctrinal expositions, large and small. The *suttas* are usually in prose, occasionally interspersed with verses. They are the most important literary products of the Buddhist literature. The Sutta Pitaka is thus the primary source for the doctrine of Buddha and his earliest disciples. It consists of five *Nikayas* or collections, viz. *Digha Nikaya, Majjhima Nikaya, Samyutta Nikaya, Anguttara Nikaya,* and *Khuddaka Nikaya* which, however, comprises fifteen independent treatises.

The *Digha Nikaya* is the collection of longer discourses on various points of Buddhism. It contains thirty-four *suttas.* These *suttas* are mostly longer in extent than the general *suttas.* The *Brahmajala-Sutta* provides us with sixty-two doctrinal and philosophical speculations current in the then India. The *Mahaparinibbana- Suttanta,* which is by far the best *sutta* of the *Digha Nikaya,* contains a realistic account of Buddha's last days, peregrination and his last speeches and sayings. It throws much light on the extent of the spread of Buddhism as also on our geographical knowledge of ancient India. The *Mahagovinda-Sutta* is particularly important from the points of view of the ancient Indian history and geography.

The *Majjhima Nikaya* is a collection of one hundred and fifty-two *suttas* of medium length. Most of these *suttas* are devoted to the refutation of the views of others. Like the *Digha Nikaya,* the *Majjhima Nikaya* also throws ample light on the *sila, samadhi,* and *panna,* the three corner-stones of Buddhism. The most famous is the *Mulapariyaya-Sutta* which strikes the keynote of the entire doctrine of Buddha *(sabbadhammamulapariyaya).* A few *suttas,* however, enumerate different kinds of offences-burglary, robbery, adultery and the like and the consequent punishment thereof. It thus reveals the penal laws of the country.

The *Samyutta Nikaya* contains fifty-six groups *(samyutta).* The *Mara* and the *Bhikkhuni samyuttas* which are ballads in mixed prose and verse are of great poetical merit. They are regarded as sacred ballads, counterparts of the *akhyanas* with which the epic poetry of India began. In short, the *Samyutta Nikaya* contains subjects dealing with ethical, moral and philosophical matters.

The *Anguttara Nikaya* is a collection of *suttas* arranged serially in an ascending order. Some of the *suttas* deal with women. There are others which acquaint us with the methods of punishment and the criminal law of the then India. This *Nikaya* contains a variety of subjects which may be regarded as its distinguishing features. It, however, gives much emphasis on the doctrinal points. The *Anguttara Nikaya* is only a forerunner of the Abhidhamma Pitaka, for the text of which it probably formed the foundation.

The *Khuddaka Nikaya,* consists of fifteen independent treatises. It is also called 'collection of miscellanies'. There is not yet a consensus of opinion among the scholars as to its canonical dignity. Some scholars believe that the texts constituting the *Khuddaka Nikaya* were composed a few years after the appearance of the four *Nikayas.* Judged from the standpoints of the subject-matter, there is no resemblance among the different texts-they are all independent texts. Most of the texts are composed in verse. They are of great value for the *kavya* literature.

2.3.4.4. Abhidhamma Pitaka

The Abhidhamma Pitaka is the third division of the Tipitaka. According to the Pali tradition, it is said that Buddha first preached the Abhidhamma to the *tavatimsa* gods, while living among them on the Pandukambala rock at the foot of the Paricchattaka tree in the *tavatimsa* heaven during his visit to his mother there. Subsequendy, he preached it to Sariputta who used to meet Buddha when he came down to the Manasasarovara for meals. Then Sariputta handed it down to Bhaddaji and through a succession of disciples it reached Revata and others, and took its final form in the Third Council held during the reign of King Asoka.

As far as the contents of the Abhidhamma are concerned they do not form a systematic philosophy, but are a special treatment of the Dhamma as found in the Sutta Pitaka. Most of the matter is psychological and logical; the fundamental doctrines mentioned or discussed are those already propounded in the *suttas* and therefore, taken for granted. The Abhidhamma Pitaka consists of seven books, usually known as the *Sattapakaranas,* which are *Dhammasangani, Vibhanga, Kathavatthu, Puggalapannatti, Dhatukatha, Yamaha* and *Patthana.*

The *Dhammasangani* (the title of the text indicates its subject-matter) literally means the enumeration of the Dhamma, i.e. the psychical conditions and phenomena belonging both to *laukika* (mundane) and *lokottara* (supramundane) realms. All phenomena belonging to the internal and external worlds have been classified and examined carefulkly. It is a learned work and has been held in great esteem in Ceylon.

The *Vibhanga* deals generally with the different categories and formulae given in the *Dhammasangani.* Different methods of treatment have, however, been employed therein. The *Dhammasangani* analyses the psychical conditions and phenomena while the *Vibhanga* synthesizes them. Thus the *Dhammasangani* lays much emphasis on their analysis while the *Vibhanga* on their synthesis.

The *Kathavatthu* is the only work of the Tipitaka ascribed to a definite author. It was composed by Moggaliputta Tissa Thera, President of the Third Buddhist Council held at Pataliputta under the patronage of King Asoka. It comprises twenty-three chapters containing discussion and refutation of the heretical views of various sects. It is important from the point of view of the history of Buddhism as it throws sufficient light on the development of Buddhist doctrine of the ages after Buddha.

The *Puggalapannatti* is a short work deals with the nature of the personality according to the stages along the spiritual path. The main purpose of this text is to examine the various types of individuals and not the study of the various *dhammas.* It is significant to note that the *Puggalapannatti,* one of the earliest parts of the Abhidhamma Pitaka, is nothing but a collection of portions selected from the *Anguttara Nikaya.*

The *Dhatukatha* is a discussion on the mental elements and their relations to other categories. The *Khandhavibhanga,* the *Dhatuvibhanga* and the *Ayatana-vibhanga*-the three chapters of the *Dhammasangani* form the foundation of the *Dhatukatha.* There are fourteen chapters in this book. All these chapters discuss *khandhas, dhatus* and *ayatanas* from different points of view in the form of questions and answers. The *Yamaka* is a book on psychological subjects and their analysis is arranged as pairs of questions. It is so called because of its method of treatment. Throughout the work all the questions are presented and answered in two ways. It contains ten chapters. Each of the chapters is complete in itself and capablc of being regarded as an independent one.

The *Patthana* is the most notable and voluminous book of the Abhidhamma Pitaka. It is devoted to the discussion on causation and mutual relationship of phenomena. It is also called the *Mahapakarana.* The *Patthana* is nothing but a detailed exposition of the *paHcca-samuppada.* The twelve links of the *paticca-samuppada* have been explained very lucidly in the *Patthana* in the form of twenty-four *paccayas.*

2.3.4.5. Post-canonical Pali literature

Apart from the canonical literature in Pali, there are also a large number of post-canonical Pali works. Most of them are the works of the monks of Ceylon. They comprise mostly *tikas* and *tippanis,* i.e. exegetical literature and grammatical treatises. For the convenience of our treatment we propose to classify them into the extracanonical works first, next the commentaries, then the chronicles, manuals, poetical works, grammars, and works on rhetoric and metrics, and lastly, the lexicons.

Extra-canonical works : Let us take up the works composed in between the closing of the Pali canon and the writing of the Pali commentaries by Buddhadatta, Buddhaghosa and Dhammapala. The works belonging to this period may rightly be called the extra-canonical works. Among them the *Milindapanha,* the *Netti-pakarana,* the *Petakopadesa* deserve our special attention as they originated in India.

The *Milindapanha* is the oldest and most famous work of the non-canonical Pali literature. The original text was not composed in Pali. It was composed in northern India in Sanskrit or in some North Indian Prakrit. The original text is lost, and the present work is a Pali translation of the original made in Ceylon. It contains a learned dialogue between King Milinda and venerable monk Nagasena on a good number of problems and disputed points of Buddhism. It is of immense value from the points of View of the Buddhist literature and philosophy. It occupies a unique position in the post-canonical Pali literature.

The *Netti-pakarana* is contemporaneous with the *Milindapanha.* It is ascribed to Mahakaccana, a great disciple of Buddha. It is a work on the textual and exegetical methodology. It is the earliest text which gives us a connected treatment of Buddha's teachings. It is the text which refers first to the science of logic.

Commentaries: The commentaries have made Buddha's abstruse teachings intelligible to the common people, thereby making them popular. Among the Pali commentators the three most illustrious names stand out-Buddhadatta, Buddhaghosa and Dhammapala. Of them Buddhaghosa was the most celebrated. Buddhadatta wrote a number of commentaries on the Vinaya and Abhidhamma treatises. Of them *Vinayavinicchaya, Uttaravinicchaya, Abhidhammavatara* and *Ruparupavibhaga* are the most important. The *Vinayavinicchaya* and the *Uttaravinicchaya* are the two commentaries on the Vinaya Pitaka. They contain rules of discipline for the monks and the nuns of the Sangha. The *Uttaravinicchaya* is a supplement to the *Vinayavinicchaya.* The *Abhidhammavatdra* contains twenty-four chapters.

It is composed in verse and prose. It deals with *citta, cetasika, drammana* (support), *vipaka-citta* (resultant consciousness), *rupa, nibbana,* and the like. The principal objective of this text is to analyse the *dhammas* contained in the Abhidhamma. It forms an introduction to the study of the Abhidhamma, and stands out foremost among Buddhadatta's works. The *Ruparupavibhaga* is composed in verse. *Rupa, citta, cetasika,* and the like form the subject-matter of this treatise. It deals mainly with *nama* and *rupa.*

Buddhaghosa, whose name stands out pre-eminent as one of the greatest commentators and exegetists, wrote a number of commentaries on the texts of the Tipitaka. Apart from his commentaries, he wrote two other works, the *Nanodayaya* and the *Visuddhimagga.* The *Visuddhimagga* is Buddhaghosa's first work which was composed in Ceylon. It contains something of almost everything of the early Buddhist literature. It is a digest of the whole of the Tipitaka texts. It is indeed an encyclopaedia of Buddha's teachings.

The *Kankhavitarani* is a commentary on the *Patimokkha* of the Vinaya Pitaka. Apart from commenting on the rules of the *Patimokkha,* it throws much light on the later development of the Buddhist monastic life. It is remarkable for the restraint and matured judgment that characterize Buddhaghosa's style. The *Sumangalavilasim* is a commentary on the *Digha Nikaya.* It furnishes us with valuable information on the social, political, philosophical, and religious history of India during the time of Buddha. It also gives us interesting geographical information.

Lastly, we come to Dhammapala and his works. He wrote a commentary known as the *Paramatthadipani* on the *Cariyapitaka, Thera-Therigathas, Petavatthu, Vimanavatthu, Itivuttaka* and *Udana* included in the *Khuddaka Nikaya.* He also wrote a commentary called the *Paramatthamanjusa* on Buddhaghosa's *Visuddhimagga.* He also composed a commentary on the *Netti-pakarana.* Dhammapala's commentaries throw much light on the religious condition of South India and Ceylon.

Chronicles: Here is given a brief survey of a few of the important Pali chronicles. The *Dipavamsa* and the *Mahavarhsa* are the two great Pali chronicles of Ceylon. They were composed on the basis of the Pali *atthakathas.* The author of the *Dipavamsa* is not known; Mahanama, who lived towards the later part of the fifth century A.D. was the author of the *Mahavamsa.* The two works bear close resemblance in respect of subject-matter and composition. We find hardly any difference even in their language and style. The two works give us the life-history of Gautama Buddha. They trace the genealogy of the old royal families of India and Ceylon as also gives us a brief account of the first three Buddhist Councils. They also relate the propagation of Buddhism in Ceylon by Mahinda and Sanghamitta. The works are of great value for a comprehensive account of the spread of Buddhism not only in Ceylon but in India too.

The *Mahabodhivamsa* or the *Bodhivamsa* was composed by monk Upatissa at the beginning of the eleventh century A.D. It provides us with an account of the attainment of enlightenment of Gautama Buddha, his *mahaparinibbana* and first three Buddhist Councils. It also furnishes us with the history of the comingof the Bodhi tree in Ceylon. It is written mostly in prose.

The *Dathavamsa* or the *Dantadhatuoarhsa* was written by the distinguished monk, Dhammakitti, who was well versed in Sanskrit, Magadhi, and *vyakarana* (grammar). It contains five chapters. It is written not in pure Pali but in Sanskritized Pali. It gives us an account of the tooth-relic of Buddha brought to Ceylon by Dantakumara, prince of Kalinga. From the point of view of the history of Buddhist literature it is indeed an important contribution to Pali literature. The work further shows us Pali as a medium of epic poetry.

The *Thupavamsa* was written by Vacissara in the thirteenth century A.D. It exists in both the Sinhalese and Pali languages. The work may conveniently be divided into three principal chapters. The first chapter is devoted to the previous existences of Buddha and the *thupas* (topes) erected over his relics. The second chapter provides us with the life of Buddha from his birth to his attainment of the *mahaparinibbana* as also the distribution of his relics. The third chapter gives us a later account of the relics.

The *Gandhavamsa* was also written in Burma by a monk named Nandapanna. It contains five chapters written mostly in prose. It provides us with the history of the Pali canon and further gives us an account of more modem Pali works written in Burma and Ceylon. In short, it is a brief and interesting outline of the history of Pali books. It is thus of immense value from the point of view of the history of Pali literature.

The *Camadevivamsa* is another important chronicle for the study of Siamese (Thai) Buddhism written by the Bodhiramsi. It is written in prose and verse and divided into fourteen sections. It describes Buddha's visit to northern Siam, the story of the foundation of the city of Haripunja, Camadevis accession to the throne, the establishment of Buddhism and reigns of several kings after Camadevi.

Manuals: The manuals present their subject-matter systematically in a terse and concise form. The *Saccasankhepa* was written by Culla Dhammapala. It is a short treatise containing five chapters on Abhidhamma materials; it deals with the *rupa, vedana* (feeling), *cittappavatti* (thought), *pakinnakasangha,* and *nibbana.*

The *Abhidhammattha-sangaha* was written about twelfth century A.D. by Anuruddhchariya, an Indian monk of Kancipuram or Kanjivaram. It is a manual of the psycho-ethical philosophy of the Theravada school. The work deals with the four ultimate categories, viz. *citta, cetasika, rupa,* and *nibbana.* It is not a systematic digest of the entire Abhidhamma Pitaka. But it gives us in outline the form which the teaching of the Dhamma took, when for the Buddhists, it became Abhidhamma.

Poetical works: There is no lack of poetical works in Pali literature. Most of the works were written about tenth-fifteenth centuries A.D in Ceylon. Some of the important works includes; The *Anagatavamsa* was composed by Kassapa, a native of the Cola country. It is composed in verse. It is an account of the life and career of Maitreya, the future Buddha. The *Jinacarita* was composed by Vanaratana Medhankara. It is a poem of more than four hundred and seventy stanzas composed in different metres. It deals with the life of Buddha on the basis of the material found in the *Midanakatha.* The *Telakatahagatha* is a poem in ninety-eight stanzas supposed to have been uttered by Kalyaniya Thera who was cast into a cauldron of boiling oil by Kalyani Tissa on suspicion of his carrying on an intrigue with his queen. It deals with the vanity of human life and the good religion of Buddha. The *Saddhammopayana* was composed by Buddhasamapiya. It dealing with the fundamentals of Buddhism in general and the ethical doctrines in particular. The *Pancagatidipana* is a poem enumerates the deeds performed in this world by body, word, and mind, for which human beings are reborn in one or other of the five conditions of life- as human beings, animals, ghosts, gods or hell creatures.

Grammars : There is no dearth of Pali grammars in the Pali literature. All the grammatical works were written in Ceylon and Burma. Of the grammarians, three deserve special mention. They were Kaccayana, Moggallana and Aggavamsa. Kaccayana wrote the first Pali grammar named *Susandhikappa.* Many *suttas* of this work agree closely with those of the Sanskrit *Katantravyakarana.* The *Maharupasiddhi, Balavatara,* and the like were composed on the basis of Kaccayana's *suttas.* The *Payogasiddhi, Padasadhana,* and others were composed on the system of Moggallana's grammar. The famous *Cullasaddaniti* was composed on the system of the famous *Saddaniti* of Aggavamsa. There were, besides, many grammars written by eminent teachers later on.

Works on Rhetoric and Metrics : The number of works on this subject is very small. The few that we have were written on the model of Sanskrit works. They do not, however, exhibit any originality or profound knowledge of the authors concerned. Some of the important such treatises available at present are includes; the *Subodhalankara* is the only noteworthy work on rhetoric. It was written by the distinguished *Acariya,* Sangharakkhita of Ceylon, on the pattern of Dandin's *Kavyadarsa.* The life of Buddha has been illustrated by the figures of speech herein. The *Vuttodaya* is the most notable work on metrics. It was also written by Sangharakkhita in imitation of the Sanskrit works dealing with metrics. The *Kamaṇdaki, Chandoviciti, Kavisara-pakarana,* and *Kavisara-tikanissaya* are other works on this subject.

Lexicons: In Pali literature we have also lexicographical works, written on the pattern of Sanskrit lexicons. We are told that the Vevacanahara of the *Netti-pakarana* containing synonyms may be regarded as the early model of the Pali lexicon. The two most well-known lexicons are the *Abhidhanappadipika* and the *Ekakkhara-kosa.*

The *Abhidhanappa-dipika* was written by the distinguished monk, Moggallana of Ceylon, in the twelfth century A.D. It is divided into three parts. The *Ekakkhara-kosa* was composed by Saddhammakitti, a student of Ariyavamsa in the sixteenth century A.D. It was also modelled on the Sanskrit works of the similar type.

The Pali literature is, indeed, vast and rich in varied compositions. But unfortunately it is deficient in drama or novel, strictly so-called. There are, however, some *suttas* like the *Brahmajala-Sutta, Samanaphala-Sutta, Sakkapanha- Sutta* and the *Mahaparinirbana-Suttanta* which exhibit vividly dramatic settings. As to novel, the historical narratives contained in the *Mahaparinibbana-Suttanta,* the *Milindapanha,* the *Udanavatthu,* and the *Visakhavatthu* are of special literary merit.

It is worth noting that the contribution of Pali towards Indian history and culture is unique and unparalleled. As a literary language, Pali shows some remarkable points of agreement with the Jaina Ardha-Magadhi and with the languages of the inscriptions of Aioka. Modem Indian languages, such as Bengali, Odia, Assamese, Hindi, Marathi, Maithili, and the like as well as the languages of the neighbouring countries of India, e.g. Burmese, Ceylonese, Siamese, and others, contain ample material traceable directly or indirectly to Pali.

2.3.4.6. Buddhist Sanskrit Literature

Like the Pali Tipitaka, there is also the Tripitaka in Buddhist Sanskrit consisting of Agama, Vinaya, and Abhidharma. But a complete set of the Tripitaka is still a desideratum. Some of them exist in fragments of manuscripts and others are lost beyond recall. Fortunately, some fragments of manuscripts of the Tripitaka of the Sarvastivada school, one of the main branches of Hinayana Buddhism, composed in Buddhist Sanskrit have been discovered in Central Asia and Gilgit (now in Pakistan).

As regards the characteristics of Buddhist Sanskrit, it may be observed here that there was a class of Buddhist writers of Sanskrit who paid more attention to meanings than to correct forms. In other words, they cared more for sense than for forms. And the consequence was that their writings abounded in grammatical and other irregularities.

2.3.4.7. Hinayana Buddhist Sanskrit texts

The Agama as mentioned above is divided into four books entitled *Dirghagama, Madhyamagama, Samyuktagama* and *Ekottaragama,* corresponding to the four Pali *Nikayas,* viz. *Digha Nikaya, Majjhima Nikaya, Samyutta Nikaya* and *Anguttara Nikaya.* The *Dirghagama* consists of thirty *sutras* only as against thirty-four in Pali. Among the *sutras,* the fragments of the *Sangiti* and *Atanatiya Sutras* have been discovered in Central Asia. The *Madhyamagama* contains two hundred and twenty *sutras* as against one hundred and fifty of the Pali text. The manuscript fragments of the *Upali* and *Suka Sutras* have only been discovered. The *Samyuktagama* is divided into fifty chapters. It contains a larger number of *sutras* than those of the Pali text. The manuscript fragments of the *Pravarana, Candropama* and *Sakti Sutras* have been discovered in Central Asia. The *Ekottaragama* contains fifty-two chapters, while the Pali text contains eleven *nipatas (ekadafakanipata)* consisting of one hundred and sixty-nine chapters. The manuscript fragments of the *Pankadha,* the *Purnika* and other *sutras* have been discovered in Central Asia. The manuscript fragments of the *Ksudrakagama* of this school corresponding to the Pali *Khuddaka Nikaya* have not yet been discovered. Fortunately, a complete copy of the *Dhammapada* as also a few fragments of the *Sthaviragatha* has been discovered.

The Vinaya Pitaka contains four divisions- *Vinayavibhanga, Vinayavastu, Vinaya-ksudrakavastu* and *Vinaya-uttaragrantha.* The *Vinayavibhanga* corresponds to the *Suttavibhanga,* the *Vinayavastu* to the *Khandhakas,* i.e. the *Mahavagga* and portions of the *Cullavagga,* the *Vinaya-ksudrakavastu* and the *Vinaya uttaragrantha* to the *Cullavagga* and *Parivarapatha* respectively. The *Vinayavastu* is further divided into seventeen chapters. The *Vinaya-ksudrakavastu* and the *Vinaya-uttaragrantha* contain various minor rules of the Vinaya. Of the Tripitaka texts of the Sarvastivada School a large number of manuscript fragments of the Vinaya Pitaka only have been discovered in Central Asia and Gilgit.

The Abhidharma Pitaka of the Sarvastivada School has seven treatises like the Theravadins. The *Jnana-prasthana* by Aryakatyayanlputra, the *Sangitiparyaya* by Mahakausthila, the *Prakaranapada* by Sthavira Vasumitra, the *Vijnanakaya* by Sthavira Devaiarma, the *Dhatukaya* by Purnia, the *Dharmaskandha* by Arya Sariputra, the *Prajnaptisastra* by Arya Maudgalyayana. These seven Abhidharma texts have nothing in common with the seven Pali Abhidhamma texts, except as to their total number.

The *Mahavastu* is one of the most important works belonging to the school of Hinayana. It is undoubtedly an encyclopaedia of Buddhist legends and doctrines. It claims to be the first book of the Vinaya Pitaka of the Lokottara vada, a branch of the Mahasanghika School. It agrees with the Pali *Nidanakatha* in that it treats the life of Buddha in three sections. It also corresponds to that part of the Vinaya Pitaka which recounts the history of the rise of the Sangha. The doctrines and stories found in it breathe the spirit of the Puranas testifying to the interrelation existing between the Buddhist and Brahmanical schools of thought. Though largely written in Buddhist Sanskrit, its language is not uniform. It, however, preserves many old traditions and old versions of texts which appear in the Pali canon. Its language and style of composition seem to suggest that the work must have been written as early as the first or second century B.C., even though it was enlarged in the third or fourth century A.D.

Apart from those mentioned above, this school has to its credit a large number of works under the caption Avadana literature which comprises the *Jatakamala,* the *Avadansataka,* the *Divyavadana,* the *Avadana-kalpalata,* etc. Another important treatise, the *Abhidharma-kosa-vyakhya,* a commentary on the *Abhidharma-kosa,* belongs to this school.

2.3.4.8. Mahayana Buddhist Sanskrit texts

The Mahayana school's contribution to Indian thought is indeed unique. It had an extensive literature of its own. Of the numerous Mahayana works, nine books, 'so-called nine Dharmas', which are held in great reverence, deserve to be specially noted in as much as they trace the origin and development of Mahayana as also point out its fundamental teachings. They are: *Astasahasrika Prajnaparamita, Saddharmapundarika-Sutra, Lalitavistara, Lankavatara, Suvarnaprabhasa, Gandavyuha, Tathagata-guhyaka, Samadhiraja* and *Dasabhumisvara.* They are also known as *Vaipulya-Sutras.*

The *Prajmparamitas* belong to the earliest Mahayana *sutras* and are considered to be the most holy and the most valuable of all Mahayana works. They are further of great importance from the point of view of religion. Of the different recensions of the *Prajmparamitas,* the *Astasahasrika Prajnaparamita* is probably the earliest. The *Saddharmapundarika Sutra* is the most important Mahayana *sutra* and as a work of literature it stands foremost. It deals with the characteristic peculiarities of Mahayana and is more devotional. It is the main scripture of a few sects in China and Japan. The *Lalitavistara* is a biography of Buddha, more superman than man. In twenty-seven chapters, the text gives us an account of the Buddha legend up to the sermon of Varanasi, embodying in it all the germs of an epic. It exhibits all the remarkable features of Mahayana. From the points of view of the history of religion and literature, it is of immense value to us. The *Lankavatara,* which is one of the latest books of this group, presents us with valuable material for the study of the early Yogacara system. It teaches Vijnanavada. According to it, nothing exists but thought.

The *Suvarnaprabhasa-Sutra* is also one of the later Mahayana works. A few fragments of this work have been discovered in Central Asia. It is both philosophical and ethical. Tantric rituals are further referred to herein. It is very popular in Mahayana Buddhist countries. The *Gandavyuha* corresponds to the Chinese translation of the *Avatamsaka* which comes just after the *Satasahasrika Prajnaparamita* and *Astasahasrika Prajnaparamita.* It depicts the wanderings of the youth Sudhana who attained the highest knowledge through the advice of Bodhisattva Samantabhadra. It is quoted several times in the *Siksa-samuccaya.* At the end of the *Gandavyuha,* there are a few verses which are used even at the present day for purposes of worship in all the Mahayana Buddhist countries. The *Tathagata-guhyaka,* which probably belonged to the seventh century A.D., contains Mahayana teachings mingled with elements of Tantricism. It is regarded as one of the authoritative works on the earliest Tantras. The *Samadhiraja-Sutra* which is also one of the works of later Mahayana *sutras* lays the greatest emphasis on meditation for the attainment of perfect knowledge. It also enumerates the practices necessary for developing the mental state. The *Dasabhumisvara* contains an exposition of the ten stages of spiritual progress essential for the attainment of Buddhahood (enlightenment).

2.3.4.9. Pure Sanskrit texts

The Buddhist literature was further enriched by a galaxy of eminent scholars. Prominent among them were Asvaghosa, Nagarjuna, Aryadeva, Asanga, Vasubandhu, Sthiramati, Dinnaga, Vasumitra, Dharmapala, Dharmakirti, Santideva and Santaraksita. Their works were composed in pure Sanskrit and mainly on Buddhist philosophy and logic. Some of them are available in Sanskrit and others are preserved in Tibetan and Chinese translations.

The *Buddha-carita* and the *Saundarananda* are the two important poetical works composed by Asvaghosa. The former is a *mahakavya* gives us an account of the life and work of Buddha from his days in the royal palace till the conversions in Varanasi. It is for the first time that the life and teachings of Buddha have been depicted by a real poet in a true *kdvya* style. The mythological traditions and the pre-Buddhist philosophical system of the then India are also mentioned herein. The latter is also connected with Buddha's life-story, but actually it narrates the love-story of Nanda, Buddha's half-brother, who was ordained as a monk by Buddhas and his beautiful wife Sundari. The *Sariputra-prakarana,* a drama in nine acts, is the oldest dramatic work extant in Sanskrit literature.

The *Madhyamika-sastra,* popularly known as the *Madkyamika-karika,* can certainly be called Nagarjuna's masterpiece. It presents in a systematic manner, in twenty-seven chapters, the philosophy of the Madhyamika School. It teaches *Sunyata* (the indescribable absolute) to be the sole reality. This work alone is enough to show what a mastermind Nagarjuna was and how he shines in solitary splendour among the intellectuals of this country, past and present.

Catuhsataka of Aryadeva, which is available in Sanskrit at present, is next in importance to Nagarjuna's *Madhyamika-karika.* It contains four hundred *karikas* (verses) and is one of the principal works of the Madhyamika philosophy.

The *Yogacara-bhumi-Sastra* by Asanga in its original Sanskrit form has been discovered by Rahul Sankrityayana. It is divided into seventeen *bhumis* (chapters) and describes in detail the path of discipline according to the Yogacara School.

The *Vimsika* and the *Trimsika* of Vasubandhu, containing twenty and thirty *karikas* respectively, are the basic works of the Vijnanavada system of thought. Both repudiate all belief in the reality of the objective world, maintaining that *citta* (*cittamatra*) or *vijnana* (*vijnanamatra)* is the only reality.

The *Nyayapravesa* of Dinnaga, the father of Indian logic, is a monumental work on logic. It deals with different types of terms, viz. *paksa, sadhya, drstantas* (examples), etc. for demonstration and refutation of fallacies. Perception and inference have also been discussed herein for self-understanding.

The *Nyayabindu* by Dharmakirti is regarded as one of the important works on logic. It is divided into three chapters: *Pratyaksa* (perception), *Svarthanumana* (inference for one's own self), and *Pararthanumana* (inference for the sake of others).

The *Siksa-samuccaya* is a work of Santideva. It is a compendium of Buddhist doctrines. It consists mainly of quotations and extracts from various Buddhist sacred works. It is a manual of Mahayana Buddhism consisting of nineteen chapters. It deals with the following subjects: faith, restraint, avoidance of evil, sacrifice of the body, application of merit, duty of self-preservation, the snare of Mara, the Buddhist Satan, truthfulness, rules of decency, evil of talkativeness, contemplation of thought, good conduct, and so on. The *Bodhicaryavatara,* another work of Santideva, is an important and popular religious-cum-philosophical work of Mahayana Buddhism. According to this text, the perfect charity *(dana-paramita)* is not an actual deliverance of the world from poverty, but an intention for such deliverance. It is a grace of the spirit. Poverty here means misery due to worldly desire. The purity of will is the greatest of all virtues and the foundation of all. The perfect conduct (*sila-paramita*) consists essentially in the will not to hurt any living being.

The *Tattva-sangraha* of Santaraksita is an important philosophical work. It criticizes various other philosophical systems of his time-Buddhist and non-Buddhist.

2.3.4.10. Tantric Buddhism

In the course of time, Mahayana Buddhism underwent profound changes yielding place to a new form of Mahayana, commonly known as the Mantrayana or Tantric Buddhism. *Mantras, dharanis, mudras* and *mandalas* and other Tantric rites gradually crept in to this new system. Later, there appeared Vajrayana, Sahajayana and Kalacakrayana from this system. A vast literature on Tantricism also grew up. It is still popular and exerts a great influence over the spiritual life of the people of some parts of Asia including India. Most of these works are extant in Tibetan translations. A few of them that are available are discussed below.

The *Jnanasiddhi,* a work on Vajrayana, points out that *bodhicitta* (thought of enlightenment) is really the *vajra* (invincible). When it would attain the nature of *vajra* (diamond), a meditating monk would then attain enlightenment *(bodhi).* The *Dohakosa* and *Caryagiti* (in Old Bengali) give us a fair idea about the meditational practices of the Sahajayana system. The *Laghukalacakra-tantraraja-tika* furnishes us with the doctrinal views of the Kalacakra system. The language used in these Tantric texts is technically known as the *sandhya-bhasa* having two meanings-esoteric and exoteric. As it has been indicated, Tibetan has an enormous mass of Buddhist literature, Buddhist Sanskrit and Pure Sanskrit, originals of which are lost. The study of Tibetan is, therefore, a necessity for a proper understanding of our glorious heritage.

The Chinese canon, another vast store of Buddhist literature, preserves in translation many works of the various schools of Buddhist thought. The works embedded in the Chinese canon are of course of a very varying nature. Although it consists of works of very unequal merits and translated at different periods, its value as a storehouse of Buddhism cannot be doubted. An idea of the number of texts contained in the canon can be had from the catalogues of Nanjio and Hobogirin. It is apparent from the foregoing discussion that Buddhist literature is the mainstream of Buddhist thought and culture. It contains works chiefly of religious nature. Considered from the point of view of antiquity, these works of Buddhist literature stand unparalleled for their sublime thought, super-intellectual treatment and unique literary excellences. They may easily be compared with the best productions of European literature.

2.3.5. Sangam Literature

In ancient times the association or academy of the most learned men of the Tamil land was called 'Sangam' (or 'Cankam'), whose chief function was promotion of literature. Later Tamil writers mention the existence of three literary academies (Sangams) at different periods. The last academy is credited with the corpus of literature now known as 'Sangam Works'. It is, however, almost certain that some noteworthy literature existed even before the Sangam era. Dr K. K. Pillai, a renowned Tamil historian, is of the view that academies of the type of the Sangam must have flowered under an earlier designation like Avai or Kudal. Naturalism and romanticism were the salient features of the poems of the Sangam bards. Excepting *Tolkappiyam,* the earliest work *on* Tamil grammar and poetic techniques, no other works attributed to the first two Sangams have come down to us in their entirety. However, from the titles of the awritings traditionally traced to these Sangams, it is evident that they dealt with music and the art of dancing.

Tolkappiyam, the name signifying the ancient book or 'the preserver of ancient institutions', was written by Tolkappiyanar and is the oldest extant Tamil grammar dating back to 500 B.C. It lays down rules for different kinds of poetical compositions drawn from the examples furnished by the best works then extant. *Iyal* is elucidated clearly and systematically in *Tolkappiyam.* Containing about 1,610 *suttirams* (aphorisms), it is in three parts-*ezhuttu* (orthography), *Sol* (etymology), and *porul* (literary conventions and usages)-each with nine sections. While the first two parts are interesting from both linguistic and philological points of view, the third, *poruladhikdram,* is most valuable as it gives a glimpse of the political, social, and religious life of the people during the period when the author of this treatise lived.

The principal works of the third Sangam have come down to us in the shape of anthologies of poems. The two compilations forming the corpus of the poetry of the third Sangam are *Ettuttogai* (eight anthologies) and *Pattuppattu* (ten idylls), They exhibit a consistency in the use of words and forms which is lacking in later literature. There were about 473 poets during this period; the writers of 102 poems are, however, unidentified. Of the identified poets, about thirty are women, the famous poetess Auvaiyar being one of them. The anthologies of the third Sangam consist of poems divided into two broad categories-*aham* or interior and *puram* or exterior. The former concerns all phases of love between men and women. An allegory of the different stages through which the soul of man passes from its manifestation in the body to its final unification with the Supreme Being is seen in *aham*. The *puram* covers varieties of distinctive poems, mostly relating to man's social behaviour. Analogous to five major regions of Tamil Nadu, these poems describe five types of tracts with their distinctive features. These are: *kurinci* (mountainous region), *mullai* (forest region), *marutam* (agricultural region), *neytal* (coastal region), and *palm* (desert region). True love, which is either *karpu* (wedded) or *kalavu* (furtive), is considered under five aspects, namely, *punartal* (union), *pirital* (separation), *irutal* (patience in separation), *irangal* (bewailing), and *udal* (sulking), and these are made to correlate with *tinai*, the fivefold physiographical divisions.

Ettuttogai consists of *Narrinai, Kuruntogai, Ainkurunuru, Padirruppattu, Paripadal, Kalittogai, Ahananuru,* and *Purananuru.* A collection of 400 verses in *ahaval* metre, *Narrinai* deals with the five *tinais* on the theme of love. These poems were compiled at the instance of the Pandya king Maran Vazhudi. *Kuruntogai,* literally meaning 'a collection of short lyrics' on love, by about two hundred poets, was compiled under the patronage of a chieftain called Purikko. *Ainkurunuru*, which means 'the short five hundred', is divided into five parts, each devoted to one of the five aspects of love and consisting of a hundred verses in *ahaval* metre. Orambogiyar, Ammuvanar, Kapilar, Odalandaiyar, and Peyanar are said to be the respective authors of rnndred verses each on *marutam, neytal, kurinci, palai,* and *mullai tinais.* Kudalur Kizhar is the compiler of this work. *Padirruppattu* or 'ten-tens' consists of rroups of ten poems, each by one of ten poets. It contains 'a museum of obsolete vords and expressions, archaic grammatical forms and terminations, and obscure customs and manners of the early western Tamil people who were the ancestors of the modem Malayalis. This work is a storehouse of historical acts about the Chera kings. A true picture of the political conditions of the Tamil and about two thousand years ago is beautifully portrayed in it. The first and last series of poems of this work are lost.

Paripadal (lit. 'Stanzas of strophic metres') contained originally seventy long poems of which twenty-four only have survived. Love is the general theme of hese verses. Some of them, however, relate to gods, the river Vaigai, and the hillock Tirupparankunram (one of the six houses of Lord Muruga). A commentary on it by Parimelazhagar is available. A collection of one hundred and fifty exquisite lyrics in *kali* metre, *Kalittogai* dwells on the theme of love; it also contains many moral maxims. Perunkadungo, Kapilar, Marudan Ilanaganar, Cola Nalluttiran, and Nallanduvanar are the poets of this anthology; it is the general belief that one of these five poets, Nallanduvanar, was the ompiler. It has a gloss written by Naccinarkkiniyar. *Ahananuru* or *Neduntogai* s a collection of 400 poems on love and is divided into three sections: *kalirriyatai- nirai* (array of male elephants), *manimidaipavalam* (string of corals interspersed with gems), and *nittilakkovai* (necklace of pearls). Containing contributions of is many as 145 poets, this work was compiled by Uruttirasanmanar under the patronage of the Paridya king Ukkirapperu Vazhudi. *Purananuru* is a very popular and valuable anthology of 400 verses of the *puram* type dealing with the diifferent facets of ancient Tamil culture, war, and State matters. It is the counterpart of *Ahananuru* which treats of love. The contributors to this collecion, about 150 in number, were loyal advisers and faithful friends of the monarchs. Through their poems they even averted war.

Pattuppattu contains the following ten idylls by eight different authors: *Tirumuruganuppadai, Porunararruppadai, Cirupamrruppadai, Perumpanarruppadai,Mullaippattu,Maduraikkanci,Nedunalvadai,Kurincippattu, Pattinappalai,* and *Malaipadukadam.* These idylls are short poems describing mostly pastoral scenes or events. *Tirumurugarruppadai* by Nakkirar is in praise of Muruga and the various shrines in which he is worshipped. The life of ancient Tamils is also depicted therein. Naccinarkkiniyar has commented upon this idyll. *Porunararruppadai* by Mutattamakkanniyar is in praise of the wisdom and martial glory of the Cola king Karikalan. Sung by Nattattanar, *Cimpanarmppadai* extols the chieftain Nalliyakkodan. Descriptions of cities and villages and of the life led by the people there abound in this poem. *Penmpamrruppadai* by Uruttirankananar is a poem similar to *Cirupanarruppadai.* It glorifies Tondaiman Ilantiraiyan, king of Kanchi. Shortest of the idylls (103 lines), *Mullaippattu* portrays the feelings of an ideal wife awaiting her husband's return from a military expedition. It is sung by a gold merchant Napputanar and generally supposed to have been composed in praise of the Pandya king Neduncezhiyan.

Maduraikkanci, written by Mangudi Marudanar, is the longest of the idylls consisting of 782 lines. It gives a vivid picture of the ancient city of Madurai and celebrates the great Pandya king Neduncezhiyan, hero of the Talaiyankanam battle. *Nedanalvadai* by Nakklrar, written in praise of the same Pandya king Neduncezhiyan, has a fine description of winter. The title is very apt, meaning 'the tedious but favourable cold north wind'. *Kurincippattu* by Kapilar contains a beautiful portrayal of the mountain scenery. It brings out the social conditions of the Tamil land in prominent relief. This idyll is said to have been composed to acquaint the Aryan king Pirahattan with the charms of the Tamil language and literature. That the qualities of modesty and chastity alone adorn women is emphasized in this poem. *Pattinappalai,* literally meaning 'a port and separation', is a song of love. It was composed by UruttiranKannanar, author of *Perumpdnarruppadai,* to glorify the Cola king Karikalan. Torn between love and the call of the battle drum, the hero finally decides to remain with his beloved. It gives a very graphic picture of Puhar or Kavirippumpattinam, great port-capital of the Cola kingdom, and has valuable information regarding trade relations of the Tamil land with foreign countries. *Malaipadukadam,* last of the idylls, is a long poem of 600 lines. It means literally 'the secretion oozing from a mountain and figuratively 'the echo or rut of a mountain'. Sung by Perunkausikanar, it extols the chieftain Nannan and his court. The poem gives a beautiful description of Nature and presents a critical account of the art of dancing as well as the details of musical instruments along with the artists' way of life.

The delineation of the early Tamil society in these poems is remarkably clear and a great deal of light is thrown on the civilization of the Tamils. The rugged virility in the songs of these early bards is not found in the more polished compositions of later ages. Sangam works provide us with valuable information regarding religion, social life, government, commerce, arts, music, dance, courtship, manners and customs, and the daily life of the Tamils. In those days heroism was exalted to the position of religion. From the equanimity of the Sangam poets came the sermons of equality. The concept of unity in existence was preached through their poems. The poetry they bequeathed to posterity is not a mere dream woven out of an idle fancy, but it is the record of human struggles and achievements, both in the field of action and in the realm of thought. What this ancient race felt and thought, throughout the long centuries of its existence, lies indelibly recorded in the pages of its literature. The configuration of the land has changed, the hills and rivers familiar to the ancient Tamilians have sunk beneath the ocean-bed, the waters of the Indian Ocean roll over the spots where proud Tamilian cities flourished, yet the songs of the bards of ancient Tamil land, passing down through the centuries, fall on our ears and awake in our hearts the selfsame rapture which they roused in the hearts of those who first listened to them.

2.3.5.1. Tirukkural

There is a collection of eighteen 'minor works' known as *Padinen-kizhk-kanakku* which deals mainly with moral virtues. Some of these works are assigned to the third Sangam, while the others belong to a much later period. They are, however, grouped together in Tamil literature and called *kizhkkanakku* which denotes a literary piece short in length. But these 'minor works' are not less important than other poems from the literary point of view. Among them, the most notable is Tiruvalluvar's '(*c.* first century B.C.) *Tirukkural* or *Kural,* which is in the form of couplets and deals with the three aims of life-*aram* (righteousness), *porul* (wealth), and *inbam* or *kamam* (pleasure). It consists of 133 chapters each containing ten couplets. Conveying noble thoughts couched in terse language, each couplet is a gem by itself. The first part of *Kural (arattuppal)* gives the essentials of Yoga philosophy. Besides, it deals with the happy household life as well as the excdlence of the path of renunciation. The thoughts of *Kural* in its second part *(porutpal)* centre on polity and administration, including citizenship and social relations, in an admirable way. The third part *(inbattuppal* or *kamattuppal),* consisting of couplets in dramatic monologues, treats of the concept of love. It is difficult to find similar delineation of emotion even in Sangam poetry. In *Tirukkural* one can see a life spiritual that is yet secular, a life secular that is yet spiritual to the core. Tiruvalluvar's philosophy of life hinges on his conception of Godhead, for to him God is the *summum bonum* of life.

2.3.5.2. Post-Sangam period: The Epics

The five major epics-*Silappadikaram, Manimekalai, Jivaka-cintamani, Valaiyapati,* and *Kundalakesi*-are the outstanding contributions of the post-Sangam period. *Silappadikaram,* earliest extant Tamil work in the nature of drama, gives a vivid picture of Tamil society after its contact with Aryan culture. As it contains all the three aspects of Tamil literature, viz. *iyal, isai,* and *natakam,* it has been designated as a *muttamizhk-kappiyam.* It is, therefore, invaluable as a source-book of ancient Tamil dance and classical music-both vocal and instrumental. The Aryan concept of Karma is embedded in the story and stated explicitly through the female protagonist, Kannagi. The author of this work is the ascetic-poet Ilanko Adikal, younger brother of the Cera king Cenkuttuvan (latter half of the second century A.D.). *Silappadikaram* gives a vivid description of the stage, the actor, the singer, the drummer, the fluteplayer, and *the yazh* (a typical vina). It contains beautiful specimens of *vari, kuravai, ammanai, kandukam, vallai,* and other classes of musical plays. *Manimekalai,* a direct sequel to *Silappadikaram,* is also a great source of information on ancient Tamil society. Written by Cittalai Cattanar, this epic marks a new development in Tamil literature by presenting philosophical and religious debates in mellifluous style.

The other major epics, although grouped together, do not fall within this period. Jaina ascetic Tiruttakka Devar is the author of *Jivaka-cintamani (c.* tenth century A.D.). It is also called *Mudi-porul-todar-nilai-seyyul,* suggesting that it deals with the fourfold object of life, namely, virtue, wealth, pleasure, and bliss. This work is commendable for its chaste diction and sublime sentiment. Apart from establishing certain conventions and setting the pace, this epic introduces Sanskrit prosody for the first time in Tamil poetry. Its verses are 'distinguished by an immense expressional wealth, brilliant style, and prosodical variegation. Even in this respect it is an indicator of further development of Tamil epical poetry'. Only fragments of the last two epics, Valaiyapati and Kundalakesi, are available. Besides these major epics, there are five other minor works probably by Jaina authors. They are: *Culamani, Perunkathai, Nilakesi, Yasodara-kaviyam, and Nagakumara-kaviyam*. Among this *Culamani and Perunkathai* deserve special mention, since they are notable specimens of literary elegance. The influence of Sanskrit is clearly noticeable in them. An adaptation of *Brhatkatha, Perunkathai or Udayanan-kathai* is composed by 'Konkuvelir'. Portrayal of ideal characters, description of Nature, and stress on renunciation are some of the important features of these two epics.

2.3.6. Odia Literauture

Odia is the official language of the State of Orissa which forms a part of the Indian Union. In ancient days Orissa was known variously as Utkala, Kalinga, and Odradesa. There is ample historical evidence to show that the people of Utkala, excelled in every branch of the arts, and the Odia literature was one of the earliest to flourish in the Indian Sub-continent. Recognized in the Indian Constitution as one of the major languages, Odia is spoken by people residing in Orissa and in the contiguous areas of the neighbouring States. The language was derived from Magadhi Prakrit and influenced by the local pre-Aryan and other Middle Indo-Aryan or Prakrit dialects used by the Aryan-speaking people who had settled in Orissa from the Ardha-Magadhi and Sauraseni areas. Odia as a New or Modem Indo-Aryan language came into being about the tenth century A.D. It can be looked upon as the immediate sister of Bengali and Assamese, and first cousin of Maithili. For convenience, the history of the Odia language and literature may be classified broadly into three main periods, namely, the Old (up to A.D. 1500), the Middle (A.D. 1500-1800), and the New or Modem (after A.D. 1800). In the course of evolution through the periods mentioned, the language and literature of the land have assumed distinct traits as a result of various political, social, and cultural movements, culminating in the present form.

2.3.6.1. Old Odia literature

Orissa, the land of Lord Jagannatha, has absorbed almost all the religions of India, and this is reflected not only in its art and architecture, but also in its literature. The Hathigumpha inscription of King Kharavela (first century

B.C.) in Prakrit may be taken to be the earliest indigenous literary expression in the land. The language of this inscription, having a definite artistic flair, is much closer to Modem Odia. 'It is almost an Ode on military conquest and imperial grandeur, written in a befitting grand manner'. The Chinese traveler Hiuen Tsang's (seventh century A.D.) reference to the language of this region as somewhat differing from the speech of midlle-India definitely indicates that Odia, which took its modem regular shape by the thirteenth century, had developed as a distinct speech by that time.

The first major literary specimens of ancient Odia literature may be traced in the Buddhist *caryapadas* and *dohas* of the seventh-ninth centuries. These poems are the natural outcome of the influence of Buddhism which was prevalent in Orissa for over a millennium. Arguments claiming these compositions as their own have, however, been advanced on behalf of other literatures (viz. Bengali, Assamese, Hindi, and Maithili) also. After Buddhism, Saivism spread in Orissa and influenced its literature; Saktism came closely after. *Cautisas* (poetic compositions in thirtyfour stanzas, each successive stanza beginning serially-with a consonant of the Odia alphabet) were composed in this age depicting in most cases the divine relationship of Siva and Parvati. Vatsa Dasa's *Kalasa-cautisa,* Avadhuta Narayana Svami's *Rudra-sudhdnidhi* (both belonging to the thirteenth-fourteenth centuries), and a few anonymous votive tales in prose, *vratakathas*, such as *Somanatha-vratakatha* and *Nagala-caturthi-katha* bear testimony to the spread of Saivism in Orissa. Vatsa Dasa's *Kalasa-cautisa* is a noteworthy specimen of lyric poetry which exhibits the finesse of a pure Odia style of the romantic order. Avadhuta Narayana Svami's *Rudra-sudhdnidhi* is accepted as one of the finest examples of poetic prose in Odia and is claimed as unparalleled in the prose literature of the whole of India during the thirteenth and fourteenth centuries. It is again the earliest complete prose work in Odia. The language of *Rudra-Sudhanidhi* is chaste and forceful. With contents of Yogic, Tantric, and Vedantic philosophies, the work is as charming as Banabhatta's *Kadambari.*

The influence of Saktism centring round the worship of Female Energy (Sakti) is clearly seen in the epic poetry of Sarala Dasa (fourteenth-fifteenth centuries) which comprises the *Mahabharata, Vilanka Ramayana,* and *Candi Purana* . Saraja Dasa's *Mahabharata,* his masterpiece, is a high watermark in the realm of epic poetry in Odia. By giving this brief version of the *Mahabharata* (in 700 verses), Sarala Dasa brought the theme of the great epic within the reach of the common man at a period when Sanskrit had become inaccessible and almost unknown to the ordinary people. Sarala Dasa's *Vilanka Ramayana* has as its theme the killing of the thousand-headed

Ravana by Sita, when Rama and his brother Laksmana as well as Hanuman failed in their attempt to encounter him in battle. His third work, *Candi Purana,* glorifies Goddess Durga. This work is the first of its kind in Odia. Sarala Dasa was the most modern of all the poets in Old Odia literature and a feminist in the true modern sense.

Markanda Dasa's lyrical ballad *Kesava-koili* is a famous work of the fourteenth century. It depicts the grief of Yasoda when Krsna, her foster child, departed from Vrndavana to Mathura. It combines both *cautisa* and *koili* patterns in it. Under the influence of Sarala Dasa, Arjuna Dasa (fifteenth century) composed an episodic poem, *Rama-bibha.* This marked the beginnings of the *kavyas* in Odia literature, which swept the whole land a couple of centuries later. Among other poets of the fifteenth century, Nilambara Dasa's name deserves mention. He translated the *Jaimini Mahabharata* and the *Padma Purana* into Odia.

2.3.6.2. Middle Odia literature

The Middle period in Odia literature witnessed the spread of Vaisnavism, the last and the most fruitful religious influence that left a far-reaching impact on the literature and people of the land. Five outstanding poets, known as the *panca sakhas* or 'five friends' of Caitanya (1485-1533), flourished during the first quarter of the sixteenth century and left behind them an enormous mass of religious literature in Odia, which is still read and enjoyed by hundreds. These poets are Balarama Dasa, Jagannatha Dasa, Ananta Dasa, Yasovanta Dasa, and Acyutananda Dasa. These *panca sakhas* advocated Vaisnavism, and their literature chiefly dealt with man's quest of God for the attainment of salvation. Their works, particularly the adaptations of the epics and Puranas, solved the problem of illiteracy in Orissa to a great extent. Among the *panca sakhas,* Balarama Dasa wrote the first Odia *Ramayana* (A.D. 1500). He has to his credit a large number of smaller works also, of which *Bhavasamudra* deserves special mention. Jagannatha Dasa's *Bhagavata* Pushkalavati and Sagala (apparently the largest of such residences) would house a number of dynasties in their times.

During the two centuries of their rule, the Indo-Greek kings combined the Greek and Indian languages and symbols, as seen on their coins, and blended ancient Greek, Hindu and Buddhist religious practices, as seen in the archaeological remains of their cities and in the indications of their support of Buddhism. The Indo-Greek kings seem to have achieved a level of cultural syncretism with no equivalent in history, the consequences of which are still felt today, particularly through the diffusion and influence of Greco-Buddhist art.

According to Indian sources, Greek ("*Yavana*") troops seem to have assisted Chandragupta Maurya in toppling the Nanda Dynasty and founding the Mauryan Empire. By around 312 BC Chandragupta had established his rule in large parts of the north-western Indian territories as well. In 303 BC, Seleucus I led an army to the Indus, where he encountered Chandragupta. Chandragupta and Seleucus finally concluded an alliance. Seleucus gave him his daughter in marriage, ceded the territories of Arachosia (modern Kandahar), Herat, Kabul and Makran. He in turn received from Chandragupta 500 war elephant which he used decisively at the Battle of Ipsus. The peace treaty, and "an intermarriage agreement" (*Epigamia*), meaning either a dynastic marriage or an agreement for intermarriage between Indians and Greeks was a remarkable first feat in this campaign.

2.3.6.3. Megasthenes, first Greek ambassador

Megasthenes (350 – 290 BC) was a Greek ethnographer in the Hellenistic period, author of the work *Indica*. He was born in Asia Minor (modern day Turkey) and became an ambassador of Seleucus I to the court of Sandrocottus, who possibly was Chandragupta Maurya in Pataliputra (modern Patna in Bihar state), India. However the exact date of his embassy is uncertain. Scholars place it before 288 BC, the date of Chandragupta's death.

At the start of the *Indica*, Megasthenes talks about the older Indians who knew about the prehistoric arrival of Dionysus and Hercules in India. This story was quite popular amongst the Greeks during the Alexandrian period. He describes geographical features of India, such as the Himalayas and the island of Sri Lanka.

Especially important are his comments on the religions of the Indians. He mentions the devotees of Hercules (Shiva) and Dionysus (Krishna or Indra), but he does not write a word on Buddhists, something that gives ground to the theory that Buddhism was not widely spread in India before the reign of Asoka (269 BC to 232 BC).

Indica served as an important source to many later writers such as Strabo and Arrian. The 1st century BC Greek historian Apollodorus, quoted by Strabo, affirms that the Bactrian Greeks, led by Demetrius I and Menander, conquered India and occupied a larger territory than the Macedonians under Alexander the Great, going beyond the Hyphasis (modern Beas River) towards the Himalayas.